CAPITALISM AND CULTURE

To Erik Simon Jamieson

Capitalism and Culture

**A Comparative Analysis of British and
American Manufacturing Organisations**

IAN JAMIESON

Ealing College of Higher Education

Gower

British Library Cataloguing in Publication Data

Jamieson, Ian
  Capitalism and culture
  1   Industrial organisation—Great Britain
  2   Corporations, American—Great Britain
  I   Title
  658.1   HD70.G7

Published by

Gower Publishing Company Limited,
Gower House, Croft Road, Aldershot,
Hampshire GU11 3HR, England.

Reprinted 1982

ISBN 0 566 00356 2

Printed and bound in Great Britain by
Biddles Ltd, Guildford and King's Lynn

Contents

Preface

The origins of this work go back to the early 1970s, when Asher Tropp of the University of Surrey mentioned to me that he had always been puzzled about the reasons why American business appeared to be more efficient than British business. My own interests at this time were focused on the factors that persuaded people to enter business as a career in Britain, and I was familiar with the literature which suggested that British culture did not give high esteem to business or businessmen.The literature also made constant reference to the allegedly more favourable culture of American society and I could immediately see the possibility of combining my own concerns with Asher Tropp's 'problem'.

The framework of this study is provided by the discipline in which I was initially trained—sociology. What I have attempted to do is to combine the 'two halves' of sociology—the macro and the micro—in the analysis of a concrete problem, the examination of the workings of British and American manufacturing firms set in the context of the socio—cultural structures of the two societies. For too long the majority of sociologists have sat posturing on the sidelines of the economic world. Whilst they have been happy to talk about capitalism in abstract terms, too little work has been done on how the system actually works.When one examines the working of British and American firms one realises that the term capitalism covers a wide variety of different practices set within the same basic system. Very gradually there is beginning to emerge in Britain a sociology of economic life. Important work has already been done on inflation, corporatism, and the hidden economy,and my hope is that this study will make some small contribution towards this emerging area.

There were times when I wished that I had never embarked upon such a large project, which stretched over so many different fields of knowledge: sociology, economics, economic and business history and management, to name merely the major areas. I also quickly came to realise why it was that so many researchers in this area soon abandoned their methodological principles and ended up with unmatched or badly matched samples. The problems of access in business research in Britain are truly formidable and it requires the patience of Job and a great deal of hard work (not to mention stamps and telephone calls) to end up with an adequately matched set of firms. Through all these difficulties I received constant help and encouragement from Asher Tropp and

Keith MacDonald of the University of Surrey, to whom many thanks.

I would also like to thank two people who helped me through different stages of this project and who introduced me to the cultures of their own societies. First to Monika Markowska, who put up with the frustrations of the sample construction and the interviewing programme. Secondly, to Anne Pedersen, whose relentless analytical mind nearly drove me to despair, but who managed to improve the quality of the analysis and interpretation. Finally to friends and colleagues at Ealing College of Higher Education, who put up with me brooding over this work for some five years.

Ian Jamieson, January 1980

Introduction

The fascination with the way other societies organise their affairs has always been with us. This is perhaps particularly true when events at home are not entirely satisfactory, when for example there has been a crisis in the functioning of a particular institution or set of institutions. Of course in many spheres of social life there are difficulties in judging what counts as an efficient service, but this is far less true of the economic institutions of our society. Although few would wish to argue that an ability to make a profit or balance the books were the only criteria of successful functioning, the majority would probably agree that in a capitalist society these criteria are pre-eminent.

Until about 1850 Britain, as the first industrial nation, had some cause to be self-satisfied with her economic arrangements. That date marked the zenith of her economic performance however, and from then on she began to decline. The faster the decline the more earnestly Britain began to examine the economic arrangements of the other countries that overtook her in the economic race. In historical perspective it is the fascination with American practice that has dominated the popular literature,[1] although more recently there have been an increasing number of articles about West Germany, Japan and Scandinavia. A similar pattern can be found for America; whilst she maintained her position in the league table of economic growth external comparisons were no more than interesting, but as soon as her economic growth showed a marked decline, those comparative studies took on a new meaning and urgency. It is now very difficult to look through a journal like the *Harvard Business Review* for example, and *not* see an article on some aspect or other of the Japanese economy, the highest performing industrial economy.

The major problem in looking at another society's arrangements for ordering economic life is that they are not isolated entities; those arrangements are woven into the very fabric of the whole society. Thus in order to understand the working of a large Japanese business enterprise it is necessary to place it in the context of Japanese society as a whole. This raises a peculiar difficulty for 'modern' scholars because such analysis tends to cut across the academic division of labour. The study of political economy, which was pioneered by the founding fathers of social science, was used to coping with such complex problems, but more recently a division of labour has arisen which places the study of economic problems firmly within the province of economics, and the study of social structure and culture within the discipline of sociology. This distinction between economy and society has been strengthened by the type of economics that has been dominant in Britain for a generation, one that has placed a very high premium on deductive models that are capable of quantification. Sociologists have been dissuaded from breaking this line of demarcation, because it would have been difficult for their contribution to have been cast in suitable terms, i.e. the sorts of variables that sociologists could have concentrated on, like cultural constraints on economic behaviour, are ones that, by and large, defy meaningful calculation. The problems of the real world have a way of dissolving neat academic distinctions however, and certainly the relative failure of economics to come up with appropriate analyses of Britain's poor economic health, has encouraged a more multidisciplinary view of the economic dimension of social life. In a sense we have seen the rebirth of political economy and I would wish to place this study, which sets out to explain some aspects of the structure and behaviour of British as compared to American manufacturing firms, in that tradition.

An analysis of the growing literature on cross-cultural research on economic organisations reveals three major problems. First, there is the problem of finding an adequate conceptual framework to handle the major variables of culture and organisation, with the concept of culture clearly causing the greatest number of difficulties (Evan,1975; Glaser,1975). The second problem is the difficulties encountered in trying to link theoretically the macro context of a society with organisational variables, although there are signs of progress here (Etzioni,1968,1971; Evan 1977; Jamieson 1978). Finally there are the problems involved with developing an adequate methodology for testing hypotheses about culture and economic organisations, although the problems here would appear to be more practical than theoretical. (For a review of the literature and the methodological problems involved see Nath,1968; Jamieson,1980), I hope that this particular study makes a contribution to all three of these problems.

The origins of this work are to be found in a problem that has assumed increasing significance in British society. To phrase the question in the way it is usually encountered in the popular literature: why does Britain not perform as well as other countries in the economic league tables of performance? Or to rephrase the question at the micro level: why do British firms not perform as well as foreign firms? In order to make the research project a manageable one it was decided to concentrate the analysis at the level of the individual firm, whilst recognising the fact that the structure of the society, including of course the structure and management of the macro economy, would be intimately related to the structure and performance of individual firms inside the society. The second decision that was made was to limit the comparison to just one other country, and one other set of foreign firms. The choice was made to compare British and American manufacturing firms, and there were a number of reasons for that decision. First, as I will show in Chapter 2, America and American firms have been the traditional reference point for economic comparisons with Britain; this is particularly true at the level of the firm, where almost from the time of F.W.Taylor, American management methods have been looked up to as the 'market leader'. Secondly, there is a very large amount of secondary data about the general characteristics of British and American firms, which is easily available and which provided a useful source both of hypotheses and data checks. Thirdly, I wanted to make a study of the firms from the two societies by frequent visits to those firms and their managers, and time and money did not permit expensive trips abroad. The only solution to this problem was to select foreign companies operating inside the United Kingdom. Once this decision was made, the comparison with America rather than any other society began to look even more attractive because of the very large number of American companies operating in Britain.[2] I have enumerated all the advantages of comparing British firms with their American counterparts, but I am aware that there are some disadvantages—three are worthy of mention. In the first place it could be argued that if one wished to compare Britain and British firms with a really high performing economy, then one would not choose America, rather countries like Japan or Germany should be chosen. Secondly, it can be argued that America represents a poor comparison, because the non-social factors are obviously so poorly matched, e.g. natural resource endowment, geographical position, size. On these grounds also Japan or Germany might have been a better choice. Finally, as one of the focal points of this research was to be the effect of *cultural* factors upon economic performance, then arguably societies like Japan or Germany might have been better choices because, on the face of it, their cultures do appear to be distinctively different. Conversely, 'American culture' could be said to be largely in the Anglo-Saxon tradition. These arguments represent a powerful theoretical case for research into Japanese or German industry, but they were outweighed by the practical considerations of research. The problems of research access and language were felt to be overwhelmingly against choosing such societies.

Once the choice was made to investigate British and American organisations, one final decision was necessary about the *type* of organisation to be studied. It was decided to restrict the investigation to manufacturing companies for a number of reasons. First, the previous debate about the relative efficiency of British and American firms had largely been cast in terms of manufacturing industry and, furthermore, manufacturing industry occupied a dominant position in the economies

x

of the two societies.[3] Secondly, a very large number of studies of manufacturing firms existed in the literature which attempted to trace the relationship between external environmental variables and internal organisational variables, and it was felt that sufficient was known to allow theoretically adequate matching to take place. In other words, the study design could deliberately exclude the possible effect of contextual variables like size, product and ownership on the firms, and concentrate on the effects of socio—cultural variables on the structure and process, and hopefully the performance of the selected firms. It was felt that this would have been very difficult to do with organisations operating in the tertiary sector of the economy.

The methodology of the great mass of studies in the cross—cultural management area has been lamentable. If one wanted to compare the effect of cultural factors on business organisations from two different societies then the ideal methodology would be to match up the organisations for relevant variables like size, product, ownership etc., and to observe their operation in a third host country whose culture was distinct from the two 'parent' cultures. Only two studies in the entire literature approximate this ideal methodology: Richardson (1956), and Sim (1977).[4] The design of this particular study has led to a comparison of British and American manufacturing firms operating in England. I would argue that this is a more rigorous test of the effect of socio—cultural factors on business than the more usual comparison of indigenous firms operating in country *A* with indigenous firms operating in country *B*. In the first place the operating environment of the companies is held relatively constant. Secondly, if it can be shown that the American firms, despite operating in England and employing English nationals, still exhibited the effects of American culture on their structure and operation, then it can be safely assumed that cultural variables are relevant in the explanation of business behaviour. The study design does admit of the possibility, however, that any differences that are found between the British and American firms are a function not so much of culture, but of the fact that the American firms were *overseas subsidiaries*. Although this is a theoretical possibility the nature of the differences that were observed are such that it is very difficult to sustain the thesis that the major cause of the variation is a function of an 'overseas subsidiary effect'.

One consequence of the decision to match up rigorously the companies on a range of contextual variables, was that almost inevitably the size of the sample suffered: this study reports a comparison of five British manufacturing companies with six closely matched American manufacturing companies. The industries covered were pharmaceuticals, printing machinery, furniture, electronic instruments and consumer goods. It was felt that the study design was of far greater importance than sample size, indeed I believe that Richardson's (1956) study of just two organisations, one British and one American, teaches us far more about the effects of cultural variables on such organisations than all the other generally much larger but less well matched studies. In some areas I was able to supplement the data from my own study by some material obtained from the British Institute of Management. That organisation kindly made available to me two studies, one on selecting managers,[5] and one on fringe benefits,[6] that had been carried out on their member companies. I was able to reanalyse the data, and compare the results of American manufacturing firms included in their sample with those of British Manufacturing firms of a similar size.

Before I describe the content of each chapter, a note is needed on the terminology used in this study. I have generally used the terms United Kingdom and Great Britain/Britain interchangeably for stylistic variation; where the term England is used the reference is to that country only. The firms in the study are variously referred to as the British firms or the American firms, or occasionally 'the firms in the main sample'. Each firm has been given a realistic but fictitious name, and is always prefixed by the nationality of the owning group. The managers working for the British firms are referred to throughout as the 'British Managers'. The managers working for the American firms are referred to for convenience as the 'American' managers *despite the fact that they are not American.*

Chapter 1 examines the two frameworks that have been used to investigate the effect of cultural variables on business behaviour. The first framework is that of 'industrialism'; the analysis points to the logical and empirical weaknesses in the industrialism thesis and shows how industrialism has almost always been confused with capitalism. The advantage of viewing both societies and both groups of firms from the perspective of the capitalist mode of production is emphasised. The second half of the chapter turns to the analysis of the concept of culture. The importance given to cultural explanations of economic and business behaviour by 'practical' businessmen is contrasted with the relative neglect of this concept by academic writers at least until the 1950s. The interest in cultural explanations since the beginning of the 1960s is documented and explained along with an analysis of the conceptual problems of such studies. The chapter is concluded with the delineation of a strategy for undertaking socio—cultural explanations of economic behaviour.

Chapter 2 undertakes the important task of marrying together the concepts of capitalism and culture in an analysis of British and American society from about 1770 onwards. Very few studies that have attempted to investigate the importance of cultural factors on economic structures have made an adequate analysis of the culture of the society or of its historical origins and development; cultural values and themes are usually taken for granted. This chapter attempts to trace the growth of the capitalist economic order in the context of the pre-existing socio–cultural structure in both societies, and particular emphasis is placed on the interplay of culture and capitalism at the level of the business enterprise. The chapter concludes with an assessment of the extent to which the values of capitalism are imposing similar patterns on the two societies.

Chapter 3 begins the presentation of the empirical data on the main sample of firms. This chapter concentrates on the organisational structure and processes of the British and American companies and presents the results of the tests of a large number of hypothesised differences between the two groups of firms. Chapter 4 turns to the analysis of the characteristics and behaviour of the managers employed by the British and American manufacturing companies and reports on the differences that were found. Chapter 5 attempts to combine some of the data on the structure of the organisations with that on the characteristics of the managers, and presents data on the organisational climates of the two groups of firms. Finally, in Chapter 6 the findings of the whole study are discussed in terms of their effect on economic performance, both at the level of the society and the individual firm.

Notes

1 This is true for the majority of European countries, see Ferrari (1974).

2 Dunning (undated) estimates that in 1970 there were over 2,000 American affiliates operating in the UK.

3 It is of course true that the manufacturing sector has been shrinking in both societies.

4 Richardsons's study of British and American ships is particularly good because the ships are located in what amounts to a culture–free environment, the sea. Sim's study has two drawbacks. First, it does not provide adequate details of the matching procedure and so it is not clear just how well the firms were matched. Secondly, the setting of the study in Malaysia, an ex-British colony, was not ideal when one set of companies under investigation was British.

5 Kingston (1971).

6 British Institute of Management (1970).

1   Frameworks: economy and culture

One of the dominant perspectives in analysing British and American societies, and the dominant perspective in the analysis of the economic subsystems of the two societies has been that of industrialism. In the 1950s the industrialism thesis came to new prominence with the proponents of the logic of industrialism or convergence thesis.[1] There are several distinct versions of this particular theory,[2] but it would not be unfair to characterise the common elements of most of the varieties as follows: there is a central logic to industrialism that flows from the imperatives of machine technology and economic development. This logic manifests itself in every society utilising the new technology regardless of its historical background or current political orientation. The imperatives of industrialisation constrain societies towards a common institutional pattern. The implications of this analysis for a study comparing British and American manufacturing organisations are clear. One should expect to find few differences in the style and mode of operation of the companies under investigation. Economic and technological imperatives would *directly* impinge upon the operation of industrial organisations, and so one would expect to find fewer differences between the two societies in the economic sector than in any other.

It might be argued that even if the industrialism thesis was broadly accepted, one might still expect to find *certain* differences between Britain and America, even in the economic subsystem, and thus perhaps even at the level of the individual firm. The reason for this would be the different historical trajectories of the two societies. Proponents of the thesis often argue that societies begin to industrialise from very different starting points, and this can influence the rate and course of industrialisation in the *short run*. Kerr et al. (1960a) for example, argue that industrialisation is usually ushered in by an elite group, and the strategy can vary quite considerably with the character of the elite group (compare the strategy of the middle class in England with the revolutionary intellectuals in the Soviet Union). Kerr et al. also refer to the potentially distorting effects of the 'culture of a nation';[3] the 'special character of the basic resources and central industries' of a society (compare textiles and coal in England with oil in other societies), and finally, 'the demographic aspects of a nation' (compare 'empty' Australia with densely populated India). These important caveats lead

1

Dunning and Hopper (1966) to argue that 'one must be careful to take a long enough time span, and also be aware that societies change at different rates'.[4]

The idea that there exist stages of industrialism is an important one because it is often argued that the United States and, in particular, American firms are more 'advanced' than Britain or British firms. One way in which this claim could be understood would be to argue that American society was more industrialised, that is, has gone further along the developmental path of industrialisation. On this argument one could still maintain the crucial significance of the industrialism thesis, but expect to find significant differences between British and American firms, because the latter would be more highly developed. The 'first industrial nation' has been overtaken by the 'first new nation' and, so the thesis holds, it is America that now shows us the image of our own future, indeed the future of all industrial and industrialising nations. The industrialism thesis is above all a theory of development, a theory which sets out to expound the *logic* of industrial development; Kerr and his followers claim to have found, like so many before them, the key to societal development, or at least the key to the development of industrial societies. If industrialism is defined as the dominance of machinery and factory organisation in the productive capacity of the society, then the convergence theorists claim that the technology will, in the long run, constrain the economic, social and political arrangements of the society into a certain pattern. Armed with this theory of development it is then logically possible to talk of advanced and less advanced stages of industrialisation, and to claim that America represents a more advanced stage. A good example of this approach can be seen in Theodorson (1953) who uses Parson's pattern variables as check marks of industrial society. He writes,

> The reorganisation of society (from non-industrial to industrial) can be analysed in terms of four of Talcott Parsons' pattern variables. The thesis advanced here is that an increase in universalism, achievement, suppression of immediate emotional release (affective-neutrality) and specificity all accompany industrialisation in the long run.[5]

From here it is but a short step to giving these analytical categories empirical referents and thus comparing, in this example, British and American society. One would perhaps find that although both societies were heavily located towards the industrialised end of the continuum, i.e. the values of universalism, achievement etc. dominated over their opposites, even so American society could be shown to be more universalistic, more achievement—oriented etc. At the same time however, one could see just how far away from the present American position that Britain was. It is important to stress the *present* pattern, because several writers are now arguing that America is beginning to reach, if she has not already done so, the structural state known as post-industrialism, a society based not so much on the output of machinery and factory organisation, as upon 'knowledge'.[6]

There are a number of difficulties and confusions in the thesis which render it unacceptable as the framework of this study. It is very difficult to see why certain structural changes should *necessarily* occur in a society and its subsystems, because of the adoption of certain industrial technologies. In short the question must be asked: What, if anything, actually follows from industrialisation? Most social scientists, even those not wedded to the industrialism thesis in its extreme form, appear to think that a large number of social phenomena do necessarily follow industrialisation. The list generally includes urbanisation, changes in the occupational structure and consequently in the stratification system, as well as in rates of social mobility, changes in the role of the state etc. Exactly why must these changes occur under industrialisation?

A variety of arguments have been used by different writers to try and demonstrate a necessary connection between industrial manufacture and certain other features of social structure. First, one has the argument that the criterion of *techne* is efficiency, that is that in the technology of industrialism the ends and the means have become fused together such that the logic of efficiency dominates the whole society. One can see this argument most clearly in Bell (1974), but its origin can be traced back to Weber. Two questions are immediately raised by this claim: first, does industrialism *necessarily* have to display any more *zweckrational* than any other form of productive activity? Secondly, does the formal rationality that it is alleged is built into the industrial process, *necessarily* have to spread to other features of social structure? Both of the questions have to be answered in the negative. In the first case it is not clear why industrial production in a factory should necessarily be more oriented towards efficiency than say agricultural production; and in the second case, surely there is no necessary connection between the industrial sphere and the other institutions of society. The necessary truth of the industrialism thesis is deniable on essentially logical grounds. There is also empirical support for the view that is being advanced. First, Nash (1966) in his classic study of Cantel has shown how few changes necessarily occur when factory technology becomes the dominant method of production in a former peasant economy. He concludes his study by noting that 'Cantel teaches the general lesson that the upheavals in people's lives which often go along with industrialisation *are not built into the process itself*' (this author's emphasis).[7] In a more general review of such studies Blumer (1960) in

3

an earlier article concluded, 'I think the evidence points clearly to the conclusion that industrialisation, by its very make-up can have no definite social effect. It is neutral and indifferent to what follows socially in its wake'.[8]

It would be foolish to deny that there are great similarities to be found in the social structures of many industrialised societies, but this is not to admit that the reasons for this are the imperatives of industrialisation. Once Britain industrialised a model was created, every other country that later followed the path of industrialisation had British experience and techniques before them. This is not of course to argue that the British model was necessarily consciously copied, although the techniques certainly were, but merely to point out that once one country had industrialised, subsequent industrial revolutions could never be quite the same. What seems clear is that one society can serve as a pattern of industrialisation which other societies can, and clearly often do, imitate, or in some cases are persuaded to imitate by varieties of 'colonialisation', 'foreign aid' etc. The results, in social structural terms, would be consistent with the convergence thesis, but would not have been brought about by the economic system imposing certain organisational and institutional constraints on the social structure. This argument would appear to have particular salience in the case of America, which has, for a very large number of countries, long superseded Britain as the industrialising model.

The puzzling question is why should industrial technology be thought to cause convergence? If we examine some of the writings of the convergence theorists, it becomes clear why they think there is a causal mechanism. Take this quotation from Richman and Farmer (1965), which typifies the type of argument under examination: 'There are only a limited number of *rational* ways to make steel and a country does not get output in this sector by using prayer rugs, doctrinaire slogans, or wishful thinking'. (This author's emphasis)[9] Or again from Theodorson (1953):[10]

> Industrialisation means the introduction of machinery.....because machines are very expensive *they necessarily must be used economically.* In the early days of industrialisation labour is far less scarce than machinery. This means that there is a strong constraint on the part of those related to the industrial process to adjust labour to the machines. It is very difficult to tolerate *inefficient* use of the machines, in so far as this can be avoided. The necessity of teaching and enforcing these modes of adjustment demands a certain type of social organisation. This social organisation centred about the need to adjust to the machines in the factory system engenders certain unique social relations.(This author's emphasis)

4

It should be clear from these two quotations that whilst purporting to talk about the demands of industrialism, the writers in fact smuggle in an entirely different set of arguments and assumptions. Simply instead of talking about industrialism, they are talking about capitalism. There is no mechanism within industrialism that causes a strain towards 'efficiency', or 'rationality', and yet the model needs such a driving force to account for the hypothesised changes in the social structure which are deemed to be part of the logic of industrialism. The mechanism is to be found in the economic system of capitalism, the key features of which are that production is primarily oriented towards profit accruing to privately owned capital, and the whole process is organised in terms of a market in which all commodities are bought and sold according to the standards of monetary exchange. Almost all the debates about the logic of industrialism have managed to confuse industrialism with capitalism.

The crucial analytical difference between industrialism and capitalism is that capitalism as a system possesses a goal, profit, which gives the system a dynamic; this dynamic allows one to talk about the logic of capitalism. Industrialism lacks such a dynamic, there is no *inherent* goal in the system which would cause it to go in one direction rather than another. To emphasise this point return to the quotation from Richman and Farmer (1965). How one goes about the production of steel depends upon what one's objectives are. These objectives may include the desire to create jobs, or to make work socially satisfying and meaningful in itself, or to make the maximum amount of profit. Industrial manufacture *can* be consistent with any one of these objectives, and the resulting organisation of production would look very different whichever objective was pursued. Under capitalism however, the goal of profit is built into the very system, and the production of steel will tend to look very similar within the framework of such a system.

The economic framework of the analysis must be provided by the concept of capitalism not industrialism. Despite some arguments to the contrary, there seems little doubt that both Britain and America can be termed capitalist countries. To accept such a proposition as correct need not tell us very much, at least in the short run, about the structure of the society and the operation of the business enterprise within the society. In any particular case, capitalism does not automatically dictate the 'goals' of the society or the individual business enterprise. Even economists, who are after all the guardians, if not the inventors, of the concept of the 'trade-off', cannot pretend that the only choices open to political or business leaders are between purely economic objectives, so that one can ignore the possibility of wider trade-offs between economic and social objectives. It is this tension

5

between cultural or social objectives on the one hand, and the 'demands' of capitalism on the other, that will be used as the basic framework of this analysis. This framework is useful at the level of the total society, where the leaders can be seen to be confronted with a variety of social objectives as well as economic constraints, and where sometimes there is considerable tension between the two. It must be stressed that in a strict sense there never has been such a thing as a *laissez faire* capitalist economy, in which the mysterious 'hand' directed all the choices. The state has always performed various functions which have either 'aided' or 'hindered' the system. At the level of the individual firm the choices and constraints have probably been even more clear cut, as the organisation is more obviously dominated by economic forces. It is because there is no mechanical relationship between the demands of capitalism and the social structure of the society, or the organisational structure of the firm, at least in the short run, that it is fruitful to investigate to what extent Britain and America and, within these two societies, particular sorts of business organisations, have conformed to the economic demands of the capitalist mode of production. In particular attention is focused upon the strength of the cultural system in aiding or resisting such forces in the two societies and as the cultural system, like the capitalist mode of production, is the product of the *historical* process, it will be necessary to analyse the emergence of these two elements in British and American societies.

The tradition of noting cultural differences between the two societies and offering them as explanatory hypotheses of economic behaviour goes back at least as far as Tocqueville. Comparing America with Europe in the 1830s he noted of America:[11]

> The sole interest, which absorbs the attention of every
> mind, is trade. It's the national passion.....the American
> people is, I said, a merchant people. That is to say it is
> devoured by the thirst for riches which brings in its
> train many honourable passions, such as cupidity, fraud
> and bad faith. Thus they appear to have but one single
> thought here, but one single purpose, that of getting rich.

Even these observations were not entirely new. Crevecoeur as early as 1782 was attempting to probe the cultural distinctiveness of America with his famous question: 'What, then, is the American, this new man?'. These 'professional observers' were supplemented, by the 1850s, by a large number of Europeans specifically interested in industrial and economic matters. Their interest had been greatly stimulated by the American exhibits at the Great Exhibition of 1851. These exhibits were sufficiently distinctive to merit the title of 'the American system of manufacture', and were sufficiently competitive to send large numbers of worried European industrial commissioners across the Atlantic to report on the 'American system'. The British team, the British Ordinance Committee, reported back to the House of Commons in 1854, and they acknowledged the distinctive achievement of American manufacturing.[12]

Surveying the nineteenth century one is struck by the enormous consistency amongst the general travellers, official and other specialised reports of various industrial commissions, all supporting the cultural themes familiar from the classical accounts of Crevecoeur, Tocqueville and others. This continuity continues into the twentieth century; it is striking to contrast, for example, the reports of the sixty-six teams representing the Anglo-American Council on Productivity, who went to America after the 1939–45 war under the auspices of Marshall Aid, to see what could be learned and usefully applied in Britain, with the reports of the 1854 Commissioners. If anything, the later visitors put a greater stress upon cultural differences than did their predecessors almost a century before. Few of the reports, no matter how technical their starting points, fail to turn to social and cultural themes. Indeed Sawyer (1954) reports that, 'Socio–cultural categories of explanations are given a major place in two-thirds of the British reports and an absolutely crucial role in about half'.[13] These findings both reflected and encouraged the more popular literature on the importance of cultural differences between the two nations, for the analysis of economic behaviour.[14] The report of the Hudson Institute on Britain's economic situation in 1974, which again stressed the importance of socio–cultural factors, was merely the culmination of a very long line of similar reports. Yet if industrialists and popular journalists had always affirmed the importance of the cultural differences between the two societies for an explanation of economic behaviour, then social scientists have been more cautious. This point is amply borne out by Crozier (1964):[15]

> Intuitively, however, people have always assumed that bureaucratic structures and patterns of action differ in the different countries of the Western world and even more markedly between East and West. Men of action know it and never fail to take it into account. But contemporary social scientists.....have not been concerned with such comparisons.

The relative neglect of the effect of indigenous culture on economic behaviour is surprising in view of the part that this factor played in the work of writers like Marx and Weber. These writers were after all the intellectual precursors of much of that part of the social sciences that is interested in the social explanation of economic behaviour. Although Marx clearly operates within a general heuristic framework of historical development, he also pays scrupulous attention to the particular configurations of historical and cultural factors in the societies which he examines, and allows these factors to influence, although not to determine totally the societies' general development. Weber presents an even clearer case of a social theorist who took cognisance of the 'character structure' of each society, indeed most of his work can be viewed as an attempt to trace the genesis of the culture of various societies, and to analyse its relationship with capitalism. In particular he utilises the role that specific historical events have had in creating particular national systems of beliefs, and he operates with the concept of the ideal type, which attempts to link the general features of a situation with unique configurations. Thus he works in *The Protestant Ethic and the Spirit of Capitalism* not with a general concept of capitalism, but with a historically specific ideal-typical form of capitalism which he calls 'rational bourgeois capitalism'. The work of Marx and Weber highlights a major and continuing dilemma for the social scientist however, which can be presented by the traditional juxtaposition of the ideographic and nomothetic sciences. More specifically, the problem is whether historically anchored observations should be treated as specific to particular social systems or whether general theories, free of spatio-temporal parameters, can be developed and tested. Marx is often criticised for taking the nomothetic side and for being historicist, whilst Weber is often castigated, for example by Parsons, because it is argued that ideal types inhibit the formation of theoretical systems. This fundamental dilemma has proved to be a real stumbling block for the use of cultural configurations in the explanation of economic behaviour. In some senses this dilemma was 'solved' by the expansion of the division of labour in the academic world. Encyclopedic scholars like Marx and Weber, who took the whole field of political economy as their territory, declined in number, and the academic world of the social sciences gradually fragmented into separate disciplines. Some disciplines, like economics, largely turned their backs upon the problems of particular societies and worked on the basis of certain universal assumptions about human nature. It was left to disciplines like history, and certain schools of thought inside anthropology, to embrace the ideographic approach and concentrate upon the distinctiveness of particular societies. The different paths that these disciplines took goes a long way to explain the relative absence, at least until about the 1960s, of studies which emphasised the importance of cultural values in explaining economic behaviour.

In the studies of the anthropologists after the turn of the century one finds a strong emphasis upon cultural explanations of behaviour. Reacting against nineteenth-century unilinear evolutionism the anthropologists systematically went about challenging almost every generally accepted 'universal' concerning the psychological nature of man, and the basic elements of social, economic and political life. The cultural anthropologists in particular stressed the unique features of particular societies and operated with concepts like those of culture and national character. Early Anglo-Saxon sociology also found such concepts of interest. Sumner (1906) in America talked of the 'ethos' of nations, and in Britain Ginsberg (1961) attempted to utilise the concept of national character. In a rather different tradition one might even note Durkheim's concept of 'collective representations'. After the Second World War, and following these developments in the social sciences, historiography, particularly in America, attempted to utilise concepts like national character in explaining the course of historical events. David Potter (1954),for example, in his book *People of Plenty: Economic Abundance and American Character,* spends the first half of his monograph castigating his fellow historians for their superficial understanding of national character and praising through explication the contributions of the social scientists.[16] Of course cultural analysis can be traced back well beyond the turn of the century. If one includes the search for the spirit of an age, the genius of a civilisation, or for the *zeitgeist* as an effort by historians and social scientists to understand a culture as a patterned whole in terms of its leading ideas or ethos, then such analysis can be traced, through the *Kulturgeschicte* of the nineteenth century back to Voltaire.

Despite the long ancestry of culture and its allied concepts a number of conceptual and methodological problems remained. Tylor's original definition of culture in 1871, probably the first to be cast in anthropological terms, was enormously wide, doubtless reflecting the complexity of the reality it was attempting to mirror.[17] By 1962 Kroeber and Kluckholm were able to analyse 160 definitions that had appeared in English by anthropologists, sociologists, psychologists, psychiatrists and others, yet still the unwieldly complexity remained. How difficult it is to work with a concept which, according to Kingsley Davis's (1966) attempt to define it, 'includes art, music, architecture, literature, science, technology, philosophy, religion, and a million other things'.[18] Some attempts were made to systematise the enormous body of exhaustive descriptions that comprised the traditional method of ethnology. These attempts to create some sort of order out of the mass of cultural data resulted in the birth of the concept of national character of the 'culture—personality' concept. These studies can be dated from 1934 with the publication of Ruth Benedict's *Patterns of Culture,* which Gorer (1956) claims marks the birth of the 'scientific study of national character'. The influence of psychology on the writings of these cultural anthropologists was very strong, which has meant that the dominant interpretation of national character has been in terms of the concept of personality. Thus national character studies have used the individual personality concept as a model for the 'character' of a nation—seeking something connotatively comparable to the individual personality, but at the level of the nation state.

The dominant theory of personality used was the psychoanalytic one with the consequent stress being placed upon child-rearing practices as the ultimate explanation of national character. The psychometric tradition in psychology was also represented however, with Cattell (1950) attempting to run a factor analysis on cultural traits as a reflection of personality traits.

It was the unsatisfactory nature of these culture-personality writings, rather than the loose definition of culture, that ultimately brought this whole area of social science into disrepute. Many national character studies have certainly suffered from at least some of the faults enumerated by Smith (1966): 'Highly subjective modes of data collection and other "fuzzy" measurement techniques, small and non-representative samples, lack of systematic theory and specific articulation of concepts, simple analysis of tremendously complex phenomena, and little verification of results'.[19] To these could be added the problems of the researchers being influenced by the prevailing *zeitgeist*; compare for example the studies of England or America written in the heyday of Victorian optimism with those written in the depression. Finally, one should note the considerable problem of intercontamination between sources; very few studies of America fail to mention the pioneering work of Tocqueville, and it is a rare study of England that leaves out Bagehot. In summary then, one has a situation where nobody is questioning the existence of differences between cultures, but nobody has satisfactorily evolved a method for dealing with the potentially useful concepts of culture and national character.

Economics, that discipline principally concerned with economic behaviour and performance, must have found itself particularly reluctant to enter such conceptual confusion. By the 1930s the Anglo-American tradition of economics had largely ceased to be interested in the effects of cultural and institutional factors on economic activity. The great debates about method in economics, of historical induction versus deduction, individualising versus generalising, descriptive economics or an economics that searches for laws and patterns, raged in the 1880s, particularly in Germany, but were largely over by the end of the first quarter of the twentieth century. Although the institutionalist school, led by men like Veblen, still stressed the importance of institutional factors in economic analysis, the majority of professional economists had turned their back on these factors and stressed the benefits to be gained by ignoring such non-economic variables, at least for the purposes of analysis. The success of this approach compared with the performance of some of the other social sciences has been notable.

In particular Keynes showed how useful an analysis could be which based its reasoning upon very small amounts of primary data about human existence. The theoretical elimination of such cultural factors allowed a rigorous definition of purely economic concepts, and paved the way for the introduction of some very powerful mathematical techniques.

The argument above has been that economics did not for a variety of reasons find itself turning to socio–cultural explanations of economic behaviour. Instead, economics concentrated upon constructing theoretical models of a very high degree of generality. There were other areas of study interested in the analysis of business behaviour however; by 1900 management studies had more or less established itself as a field of knowledge at least in America. No one could of course accuse managerial theorists of constructing theoretical models of a high degree of generality, but there are some parallels to be found with economics. First one should note that classical management theory in the hands of men like Taylor and Fayol was conceived of having universal applicability. There was no thought that the management principles elaborated by these theorists were anything but universal truths that could be applied to all organisations irrespective of their purpose or social setting, notwithstanding Follett's 'law of the situation'. Classical management theory, like economics, was based on a simple and minimal view of human nature, that man seeks pleasure and avoids pain; indeed this view of man was drawn indirectly from the work of the English nineteenth-century economists and appropriately named, 'economic man'. The view of man in management theory that replaced this strange perversion of human nature was just as energetic in claiming universal applicability. The assumptions about human behaviour underpinning the human relations movement, pioneered by Elton Mayo and his colleagues in the 1930s, still left very little room for the intrusion of cultural or institutional variations. Although both the scientific management theories of Taylor, and the rather different gospel of human relations theory were developed in a particular American context, by 1950 there seemed little reason to doubt their general applicability. On a practical level, various international conferences, for example the conferences held under the auspices of the International Congress for Scientific Management, and the post-war productivity teams that had visited America, had successfully spread the theories and practices to many countries. More importantly, American business enterprise was overtly successful and was universally looked up to as the 'market leader', pointing the direction where others should follow. It is interesting to note that even today most literature surveys of European managerial practices or performance still take America as their measuring rod rather than other European countries. [20]

11

The apparent practical success of American management methods also found convincing theoretical backing in the shape of the logic of industrialism thesis. As early as 1941 James Burnham had suggested some universal tendencies in management in his influential treatise, *The Managerial Revolution.* Harbison and Myers (1958), co-authors of *Industrialism and Industrial Man* in 1960 had, six years previously, laid the foundations for such a view in their study of management in the international context. After surveying management practices in twenty-three countries they came to the conclusion, 'Organisation building has its logic.....which rests upon the development of management.....and..... there is a general logic of management development which has applicability both to advanced and industrialising countries in the modern world'. [21] A diverse range of other studies ranging from Inkeles' (1960) apparent finding that the institutions of industrial society, notably the factory system, produced a relatively homogeneous 'industrial man', [22] to the much quoted study by Haire, Ghiselli and Porter (1966), which attempted to answer the question, 'When managers think about managing, are their ideas all pretty much the same, or does managerial thinking differ from country to country?', [23] all led in the same direction, and supported the view that the logic of industrialism was indeed a fact, and a fact which legitimated the development of a universal management theory.

Until about the 1950s there had not been a great deal of interest in using socio—cultural factors in the academic explanation of business behaviour. The potentially useful concepts of culture and national character had largely fallen into confusion and disrepute at the hands of the cultural anthropologists. Economics as a discipline had found that enormous progress could be made by adopting a highly rigorous and positivistic methodology that left no room for the relatively 'soft' measures of socio—cultural factors. Finally management theory believed that all the evidence pointed in the direction not of cultural diversity but of a convergence—the basic principles of management were universal. By the 1950s the universalist stance in economics and management theory began to come under sustained attack. [24] There were a number of reasons for this. First, one should note that the Second World War had seen the necessity for some social scientists engaged in war duty to concentrate their attention upon the culture of the enemy societies in order to try and make strategic predictions. These studies, which became known as 'the study of culture at a distance', were not without their successes, [25] and thereby encouraged the view that socio—cultural explanations of behaviour did have some validity. The aftermath of war brought with it a large number of American-backed agencies to help with the process of reconstruction and although in many ways they could be said to be successful by their own standards, they were not without their problems. Many of those problems arose because the assumptions about behaviour that were common in American society were not found to hold so easily in every other country. Economists who found themselves involved in aid programmes to the so-called underdeveloped countries, soon found that their stock of economic knowledge, which they had taken to be culture free, turned out to be largely restricted to the competitive phase of modern capitalism. [26]

During this period there was also increased interest in international league tables of economic performance and by the mid 1950s Japan, which apparently had a very different cultural system which was in turn reflected in her economic organisations, was managing to out-perform most of her European and American competitors. The performance of this country thus served to increase interest in the role of cultural factors in economic performance. By the late 1950s large numbers of American multinational companies were beginning to operate systematic comparisons of the performance of their various plants. This exercise revealed a variety of difficulties that were being encountered in introducing and applying American managerial techniques and philosophies. For example, a large study undertaken by the American National Industrial Conference Board reported that the most common problem in American companies operating abroad was that local national managers were unfamiliar with American business methods and philosophy. [27] Finally, there began to appear in the managerial literature a series of careful studies, of which Richardson's (1956) study of organisational contrasts on British and American ships is probably the best known, which seemed to show beyond all doubt that cultural factors could, and indeed did, influence economic organisations.

It has already been argued that economics, of necessity a major contributor to any debate about comparative economic performance, had not shown any great interest in the role of cultural variables in business performance. Yet the changes described above that were occurring by the 1950s did provoke some interest in cultural factors, broadly understood, within the discipline. Of primary significance was the setting up in the late 1940s of the research centre in entrepreneurial history at Harvard. The inspiration for this centre, and for many years its mentor, was Joseph Schumpeter, one of the few economists who still believed in the usefulness of the notion of political economy. Schumpeter of course had always laid considerable stress on the role of the entrepreneur in economic analysis, and to talk of entrepreneurs is necessarily to widen the discussion and to admit the contribution of non-economic factors to economic analysis. This was not an easy task for economists schooled in the paradigm of positive economics. Even members of the Harvard centre felt uneasy with cultural factors. Aitken (1965) for example, recalling the early days of the centre, noted how strange it was to be dealing, 'with values, with perceptions, with social sanctions and social definitions.....with all sorts of seemingly "soft" and "subjective" variables'.[28] Despite these difficulties this group of scholars went on to produce some outstanding pieces of research, which stressed the crucial role of socio–cultural factors in economic analysis. In particular one should note the work of David Landes (1965) and his analysis of French business, where he attempted to account for the slow growth of the French economy up to the time of the Second World War by reference to largely non-economic factors.[29] Similar developments to those at Harvard took place at the University of Chicago. At this centre economists like Bert Hoselitz and W.E.Moore also concentrated upon the non-economic barriers to economic development and, like their colleagues at Harvard, founded a journal, *Economic Development and Cultural Change,* to further their analyses.

It would be wrong to give the impression, however, that this style of analysis became dominant even in economic history. For example both Habakkuk (1968) and Gerschenkron (1962), two leading economic historians both argued, in their different ways, that economic progress in various countries could largely be accounted for by reference to such factors as population, capital, technology and market characteristics. They both seemed to have enormous difficulty in knowing exactly how to handle socio–cultural factors within the normal paradigm of econometric history. Habakkuk (1968), for example, writes: [30]

> It is often argued that some countries had more venturesome entrepreneurs for such reasons as national character, cultural background and institutions, political and social attitudes, i.e. for non-economic reasons..... it is extraordinarily difficult to know how much weight to attach to this factor since it is impossible to test entrepreneurial ability except by achievement and this begs the question.

The methodological scepticism of this school of thought was further encouraged by the fact that no sooner had Landes 'explained' the long standing socio–cultural reasons for French backwardness, when the French economy began to revive. Not only did it revive, but as Landes ruefully admitted in a later paper, the economy went through, 'what may be the most rapid growth France has ever known, almost as rapid as the German "miracle" and possibly more sustained'. [31] Although Landes attempted to explain this growth rate in terms of his major explanatory variables, Gerschenkron in particular took these failed predictions as prima facie evidence of the poverty of this explanatory approach.

Despite the problems of an analysis which focuses upon socio–cultural factors as contributory causes of economic performance, it seems that there is a growing recognition inside economic science of the value of such an analysis. [32] Such a recognition has been spurred on by the gradual realisation that when the data of national accounts, fitted to various production functions, are used to attempt to account for economic growth, only a fraction of the resulting growth can be explained in this way. Even the so-called 'heavy' economic factors like population, capital and technology are after all ultimately determined to a large extent by forces generally considered to be outside the realm of economics.

Just as more economists and economic historians began to include socio-cultural variables in their analyses, so too with management theorists. Management theory, in the hands of Taylor or Mayo, had largely believed that organisational efficiency lay in manipulating variables *inside* the organisation, like the formal structure or the style of supervision. By the 1960s the experience of American firms abroad was beginning to supply evidence that was to cast doubts about the universal applicability of such findings. These doubts were supported by the more rigorous testing of these propositions by the academic world. As early as 1947 Simon had cast considerable doubts on the value of the 'management principles', and by the 1960s evidence was beginning to emerge that suggested that the principles of the human relations school probably did not apply even throughout the United States. [33] In 1960 French, Israel and As attempted to replicate the famous Coch and French (1948) participation experiment in a Norwegian factory, and found that the participative approach did not elicit the same responses that had been found in the American experiment. From the 1960s onwards a great flood of work within the general framework of management studies testified, with varying degrees of certainty, to the culture bound nature of management theory. The general dilemma was summed up in the title of an article by Negandhi and Estafen published in 1965, 'A Research Model to Determine the Applicability of American Management Know-How in Differing Cultures and/or Environments'. The problem was indeed to find out whether the principles of management, largely developed in the United States, were generally applicable, and to devise a methodology that would permit reasonable hypothesis testing. An acceptable methodology was crucial because, as Nath (1968) had shown in his methodological review of cross-cultural management research, the methodological quality of many of the studies left a lot to be desired. The majority of management researchers in this area gave up the problem almost before they started. Ajiferuke and Boddewyn (1970) in a review of 22 studies of comparative management that invoked culture as an explanation observed that only two authors ventured a definition of the concept. The most common type of study reported by Nath was that of the operation of American companies operating abroad. These studies testified to the problems that American companies faced in getting local managers and workmen to adapt to American methods. [34] Alternatively, there was the investigation in depth of one culture, through a long-term stay in the country by the researcher, who then compared it with his native culture. [35] Three basic problems stood out; first, researchers had difficulty in getting adequate samples of managers, workers, or organisations in the foreign culture to compare with their own culture. Too many studies did not even bother with the niceties of sampling and were quite happy to 'gain an impression' of the foreign culture and its business organisations, just as they had 'gained an impression' of their own country. The second problem was one of knowing exactly what factors to control for and treat as dependent variables. For example, did one control for organisational structure on the grounds that it was culture free, or did one treat it as a dependent variable on the grounds that it must be influenced by cultural variables? Thirdly, there was what is known in anthropology as Galton's problem, that is the problem of diffusion. When similarities are observed in two distinct societies in the area of, say, business organisational structure, are these to be explained in terms of similar structural constraints, as the contingency theorists argue, or could they be the result of the process of diffusion of managerial methods? The diffusionist argument which is rarely ever mentioned by the contingency theorists, is a very powerful one in the area of management theory, because management theory is largely an American artifact and has been heavily exported throughout the world by management consultants, American-run or inspired management education institutes and most powerfully of all by successful American companies. Finally, there was the still unresolved problem of how to handle the multidimensional phenomenon of culture, and of determining what features of the business it effected and how it effected them.

An influential attempt to try to determine what the most relevant features of the external socio–cultural environment of a firm were was devised by Farmer and Richman (1966). They largely appeared to concede that managerial efficiency did not reside in adherence to universal management principles or in individual efforts. They stressed instead the importance of external factors constraining managerial endeavour, and concluded that management theory needed instead to concentrate upon those crucial environmental variables, rather than on what went on inside the managerial 'black box'. The environment was conceptualised as consisting of economic, legal-political, sociological and educational constraints, and an attempt was even made to assign a mathematical weight to each variable and then by empirical investigation assign each variable a score in any particular country under investigation. Despite this interesting attempt to come to grips with the socio—cultural environment in cross-cultural management research, a fundamental problem remained which Richman (1965) acknowledged. Thus he noted: 'In undertaking cross-cultural research of this type, one must have a common denomination or classification scheme which can be used for comparing the management process in different countries'. [36] It was for failure to solve this particular problem that culture became a very difficult and unattractive concept with which to work. One can see the desperate need for some organising principle in some of the national character writings. Daniel Bell (1965), for example, commenting upon the attempts of Max Lerner to capture the spirit of American character in his book *America as a Civilisation,* writes: [37]

> Like all of us Lerner is trapped by sheer inability to capture a definition which will not fall apart on close analysis. One can see him, year after year, desperately mulling over the questions, reading all the previous answers, spotlighting their deficiencies; yet, in the end, like a mountain climber unable to gain a foothold on the slippery rock face, he suddenly lets go, and says: 'There is no single talisman to the secret of American civilisation, there is no single organising principle'.

This is not to argue however, that organising principles were totally lacking in the national character literature. Clearly those that were organised around some psychological theory possessed organising principles, and as early as 1934 Ruth Benedict attempted a rudimentary form of categorisation of cultures, albeit in the form of metaphor, when she wrote of the Apollonian and the Dionysian cultures. Yet this and other similar attempts at comparative work, carried out in literary-metaphorical terms, were hardly the comparative scheme that were required. The ideal type was also seen as of little value in empirical work; as a method Heydebrand (1973) claimed that it 'remains essentially as a device for "intellectual comparisons", for conceptual rather than empirical testing, and for the establishment of comparative histories and etiologies'. [38]

One view of the major problem facing researchers interested in the effect of culture on business enterprises was the need to develop culture-free classification systems for the analysis of both societies and economic organisations. In one of the most stringent formulations Sjoberg (1970) argued that genuine comparison was possible only if non-culture bound units had been isolated. He argued, 'Certain invariant points of reference or universal categories are required which are not merely reflections of the cultural values of a particular social system'.[39] The goal then is to substitute names of variables for the names of social systems, in other words, a metalanguage is required which will allow the researcher to refer not to country *A* or country *B* or to organisation *X* or organisation *Y,* but to certain patterns or combinations of variables that can preferably be measured.

At the level of the organisation it is clear that the Aston school of contingency theorists clearly believe that their studies have isolated culture-free units of analysis. Heydebrand (1973), in his review of comparative organisational research, commenting on the Aston studies, writes, 'It is studies of this kind that constitute the most significant advance over organisational case studies of the 1950s and promise to contribute to a *general theory of organisation'* (this author's emphasis).[40] There are a number of problems with this claim. First, one should note that much of their work is at considerable variance with the findings of other authors. For example, researchers have shown that the same relationships between organisational structure and context hold for organisations in Britain, the United States, Canada, Sweden and Japan.[41] If one singles out Japan from the rest one is clearly faced with a problem, because there is clear evidence from researchers like Abegglen (1958) and Dore (1973) that Japanese business is in fact run on very different lines from that in, say, Britain or America. It is notable that these latter studies, particularly the one by Dore, are based upon more 'anthropo-logical' methods and considerable account is taken of the meaning of particular organisational forms, placed in the context of historical and socio-economic position of Japanese society.[42] This focus on meaning is important because a major charge laid at the door of the Aston school is that of 'abstracted empiricism'. In other words it is claimed that the phenomena which are being measured and correlated with such care by the Aston researchers are not clearly deduced from any theory. It is arguable, however, that there is an implicit theory in the Aston research; it is a theory which entails a concentration on the features of *one* economic system. Simply, the contingency theory of the Aston school is based on ideas about organisational performance, set in the context of the capitalist economic order. Only by making certain assumptions about company goals in terms of profitability, can one understand why the company structure is likely, in their view, to adapt to the environment in certain ways. The fact that the contingency theorists seem to have difficulty in accurately predicting structure from contextual factors, and their general failure to clearly link performance with organisational structure does show that the operation of market forces is always constrained by cultural and political forces, both at the level of society and the individual firm.[43]

At the societal level the difficulties of developing universal categories of analysis have been just as great; the old classical generalised distinctions of mechanical-organic, gemeinschaft-gesellschaft, sacred-secular, folk-urban, still seem to be used despite their obvious deficiencies. The sociologist who has given this matter most attention is Talcott Parsons and, in particular, he has been interested in developing universal categories for the analysis of culture. It must be remembered that Parsons began his academic career by studying the theories of Sombart and Weber on the emergence of capitalism. Both Sombart and Weber, in contradistinction to the works of Marx, gave a greater amount of autonomy to the role of *values* in social action, and in his *The Structure of Social Action* (1937), Parsons saw this emphasis as the distinctive focus of social theory in the late nineteenth century. Parsons himself adopts the view that a crucial element in the explanation of social action must be the value system to which individuals refer when making choices in social life. As Parsons (1960a) puts it:[44]

> (that).....a system of value-orientations held in common by the members of a social system can serve as the main point of reference for analysing structure and process in the social system itself may be regarded as a major tenet of modern sociological theory. Values in this sense are the commitments of individual persons to pursue and support certain directions or types of action for the collectivity as a system and hence derivatively for their own roles in the collectivity. Values are, for sociological purposes, deliberately defined at a level of generality higher than that of goals—they are *directions* of action rather than specific objectives, the latter depending on a particular character of the situation in which the system is placed as well as its values and its structure as a system.

It is important to note two points of difference from Weber's position. First, in Weber social relations are ultimately reducible to inter-subjective relations, but it is not clear that this is true for Parsons. In *Towards a General Theory of Action* Parsons goes to considerable lengths to explain the ontological position of culture and stresses that it is not an empirical system. He writes: [45]

> A cultural system is a system which has the following characteristics: (a) the system is constituted neither by the organisation of interactions nor by the organisation of the actions of a single actor (as such), but rather by the organisational of values, norms and symbols which guide the choice made by actors and which limit the types of action which may occur among actors. (b) Thus a cultural system is not an empirical system in the same sense as a personality or a social system, because it

19

represents a special kind of abstraction of elements from these systems.

Despite this lengthy elucidation and other similar ones, [46] it is still not clear what is the logical status of culture. At times it appears to be more like the agelecism of Durkheim's 'collective conscience', and Parsons's liking for the elaborate metaphor in exposition does not always aid clarity. [47] The second way in which Parsons differs from Weber, in terms of his analysis of the place of values in social explanation, is that Parsons is critical of Weber's ideal type methodology. In Weber there can be as many types as there are appropriate value positions to produce 'one-sided accentuations of reality'. These types exist independently of one another and do not permit the formulation of a general theoretical system. Parsons is manifestly interested in this latter task, at least in the sense that he is anxious to build a complete set of concepts that will permit the analysis of all social action, all societies and all social systems. These interests have led to what Gouldner (1970) has rather disparagingly called his 'taxonomic zeal'.

One can see this 'taxonomic zeal' at work when Parsons attempts to classify the values which guide men's choice of action. Man, explains Parsons, is always faced with 'dilemmas of choice' in social situations. These choices are divided by Parsons into five fundamental alternatives and they constitute the pattern variables: affectivity/affective-neutrality; diffuseness/specificity; particularism/universalism; ascription/achievement; collective orientation/self-orientation. Although the pattern variables apparently use the unit act as their building block, Parsons is not much interested in this level of analysis, for him the important point is that practically all action occurs in systems. The pattern variables should permit analysis of the culture of a society in terms of a certain pattern of value choices, although Parsons does also stress that as the society becomes more complex and structurally differentiated, different subsystems within the society emerge to deal with different functional tasks. Thus, while it is possible to talk of the general pattern of values at the societal level, there may well be subpatterns in the different subsystems of the society. Parsons argues, for example, that the family system will stress a different pattern of choices from the business system. It is for this reason that when various researchers have used Parsons' pattern variables they have not necessarily used all of them. Burrage (1969) for example, in his comparative analysis of British and American business practices, only uses the variables of achievement/ascription, universalism/particularism and diffuseness/specificity. Although Burrage does not explain why he neglects the other two patterns, it is presumably because he does not think that they are relevant for the analysis of the business world.

There are several problems with such an analysis which are relevant for those interested in using such categories in 'cultural analysis'. Are the pattern variables meant to be *causal* factors, i.e. is it enough to assert that a stress on certain value patterns is itself a cause of certain types of economic behaviour? It is not really clear whether Parsons is interested in explaining social action with the pattern variables, or whether he is only interested in creating a taxonomy. Max Black (1961) and Gouldner (1970) for example, both accuse him of analysing only social statics, or of mere formalism. On the other hand, it could be argued that even his static equilibrium model does assume that the cultural values are holding relations in place inside the system,[48] and furthermore, in his work *Societies* (1966) a much more dynamic role is spelled out for culture in social relations. Here Parsons even admits that, at the level of general social development, '.....I am a cultural determinist, rather than a social determinist'.[49] If culture influences action, how does it do it, and how are we to verify its influence? It is tautologous to observe human conduct, deduce value structures from this, and then go on to use these cultural variables to explain human conduct. Aspects of the social structure cannot be used as an index of cultural values in the Parsonian system, because Parsons specifically separates the social structure as an individual element. Neither can one argue, within the Parsonian framework, that culture is that which is internalised in the individual, because again Parsons has a separate category for this in the personality system. Thus culture affects the social structure and the personality system and yet it is ontologically separate from both of these. How does Parsons explain the particular pattern of values in a subsystem of society or a society in general? His answer is a typically functionalist one, thus the normative pattern arrived at is one that is relevant for the effective functioning of the system or subsystem. This is why the normative pattern is different in the family compared to the economic sector in society.

Perhaps the major problem with Parsons' attempt at developing universal categories for the analysis of societal values is the one that has flawed the Aston researchers' claim to have developed universal measures for the analysis of organisational structure. The main stumbling block is the claim to universalism, the implicit claim to have refuted Wittgenstein's dictum that 'there is no way of getting outside the concepts in terms of which we think of the world'. It is surely the case that each of us is located in a particular socio–cultural context, and that both organisations and societies are socially constructed and, what is more, that our only way of analysing and describing these entities is via the medium of language, itself a reflection of our social constructions. The only way round this conclusion, as Sjoberg (1970) and Dixon (1977) have shown, is to attempt to show that human action presupposes a universal picture of rationality, presumably one based round the concept of human needs. For a study which is interested in comparing two societies of the same economic type however, it is not necessary to determine *universal* categories of analysis. Capitalist societies possess a certain rationality or logic such that the demands of the economic system set up certain pressures for the social system to move in one direction rather than another. Under ideal-typical capitalism it is indeed necessary to relate to people on the basis of their achievements rather than on their ascribed qualities. Furthermore, decisions cannot be made on the basis of emotional considerations (affectivity), but rather on the basis of rational calculation (affective-neutrality). Relations inside the ideal-typical capitalist economy are dominated not by ill defined obligations to people (diffuseness), but on the basis of the specific roles they play in the division of labour (specificity), and a response is made to people on the basis of their membership of specific categories (universalism), like employee or consumer. Finally, the ideal-typical model stresses self-orientation for its harmonious working.

The pattern variables do not constitute Sjoberg's culture-free universal categories. On the contrary one can see their origin in the specific historical structures which saw the rise of capitalism. [50] This fact does not inhibit their use for the analysis of capitalist societies. Furthermore, the pattern variables are sufficiently general to allow them to be applied both at the level of the society and, within the economic subsystem, at the level of the firm. [51] For empirical work it is necessary to treat the value patterns as continua rather than dichotomies, in other words it is necessary to hold the view that there can be degrees of commitment to the values of universalism, achievement etc.[52] In addition the ontological position of socio—cultural values needs to be made clear. In this work cultural values are conceived as being manifest in the social structure, particularly in the institutions of society, e.g. the education system, as well as potentially in the personality system of members of a society. Thus it is arguable that to say that a society or firm has a commitment to a particular normative pattern must be to argue that it is manifested in the structure and organisation of that society or firm.

The historical analysis of the growth of the capitalist economic order in Britain and America, which follows in the next chapter, will attempt to show that in Britain the social structure has tended to constrain the economic system to a greater degree than has been the case in the United States. This formulation might lead one to think that primacy is being given to social structural forces, but this is not in fact the case. Even Parsons does in places recognise the primacy of the economic subsystem. For example, in spelling out the normative pattern of the economic system in what he calls modern societies, as revealing a stress upon affective-neutrality, universalism, achievement and specificity, he also concedes that this is also the pattern for modern societies in general. In other words, the dominance of the economic system in societal analysis is recognised at least covertly. The general view being advanced here is of a determining economic base and a determined superstructure, to put it in the more familiar terms of Marxist theory. Yet the analysis of historical material is never as simplistic as this formula might imply, and indeed Marxist theory, stripped of its vulgarisations, does not embrace such a simplistic view. Although Marxism unquestionably does contain within its labyrynth the view of a determining base, it is also the home of the view that the origin of determination lies in men's own activities. Raymond Williams (1973) has lucidly argued the qualifications and amendments to the three key concepts in the Marxist theory of the superstructure. He argues that the idea of an economic base must be seen not as a fixed economic or technological abstraction, but as the '.....specific activities of men in real social and economic relationships, containing fundamental contradictions and variations and therefore always in a state of dynamic process'. [53] Similarly the superstructure is to be seen not merely as a set of structures and values which are a total reflection of, and dependent upon, the economic infrastructure. Finally, the idea of determination must be revalued away from the mechanical process that it has become at the hands of the vulgar Marxists. Williams correctly notes that it is '.....one of the central propositions of Marx's sense of history that there are deep contradictions in the relationships of production and in the consequent social relationships. There is therefore the continued possibility of the dynamic variation of these forces'. [54] These complex formulations recognise the complexity of the real historical situation, and it is perhaps reasonable to point out that Marxist cultural theory is much more at home in distinguishing the large features of different epochs of society than in dealing with the complexities of any particular historical process, like the capitalist period. It must be recognised that the hegemony of a particular class, like the landed aristocracy in Britain, is not swept away over night to be replaced by a social structure that reflects the interests of the new capitalist class. The process is complex and subtle and at any particular moment in time is reflected in considerable contradictions in both the infrastructure and the superstructure. The next chapter will attempt to chart the emergence of capitalism in Britain and America, and to show how the economy and the social structure interacted together to produce two distinctive socio-economic systems .

Notes

1   There are many exponents of this thesis. The fullest and clearest statement is made by Clark Kerr and his associates, to whom reference will largely be made: Kerr, Dunlop, Harbison and Myers (1960a, 1960b, 1971).

2   The different versions of the industrialism thesis are brought about because of different views about the concept of industrialism. Nettl and Robertson (1966) for example, have described the concept as 'something resembling a Portugese Man-of-War; a small, fairly easily distinguishable body trailing a series of highly colourful and "dangerous" strands behind it' (p.280).

3   Kerr et al . note in their 'Postscript to Industrial Man' (1971) that, 'The forces of industrialism have appeared in many countries to be stronger, and cultural factors somewhat less of a force, than we thought in 1960' (p.520).

4   Dunning and Hopper, 1966, pp. 167–8.

5   Theodorson, 1953, p. 481.

6   Cf. Bell, 1974.

7   Nash, 1966, p. 118.

8   Blumer, 1960, p. 9.

9   Richman and Farmer, 1965, p.41.

10   Theodorson, 1953, p.481.

11   Pierson, 1959, p.45.

12   Parliamentary Papers, House of Commons, Accounts and Papers (21). 1854–1855. Quoted in Sawyer, 1954, p.372.

13   Sawyer, 1954, p.372.

14   A certain amount of care must be taken in reading these reports. First, although there is a great emphasis upon cultural, social and psychological factors in the reports, it is notable that not one of the members of the 66 teams was a social scientist. Secondly, some of the reports were openly polemical. The Brassfounding report, for example, quoted Jefferson's declaration that 'All men are created equal' and then went on to ask, given this statement, 'How could labour relations be other than excellent?' Finally, one should note the inherent problems in any 'official' visit, the firms on show tended to be exemplary examples of their industry and it is doubtful whether the teams got a realistic picture of the great mass of American industry. For a further elaboration of these points see Balfour (1953).

15   Crozier, 1964, p.210.

16   Berkhofer (1973) has noted that this stress upon cultural explanations, which stressed the ideas and values common to all Americans throughout the course of their history, served important

ideological purposes during the cold war period after the Second World War.

17   Tylor's definition was, 'Culture.....taken in its wide ethnographic sense,is that complex whole which includes knowledge, belief, art, morals, law, custom, and any other capabilities and habits acquired by man as a member of society'. Tylor 1871, p.l.

18   Davis, 1966, p.4.

19   Smith, 1966, p.526.

20   This fact is noted for the case of Britain by Lewis and Stewart (1958), and for France, Italy and Spain by Ferrari (1974).

21   Harbison and Myers, 1958, p.117.

22   This study by Inkeles needs to be treated with considerable caution. The questions asked were rarely in the same form from country to country, and included questions about beliefs in the possibility of peace, estimates of the long-run effects of atomic energy, estimates of how 'happy' people were etc. It is not at all clear what the responses to such questions would mean. Finally, one should note that the Soviet sample was drawn exclusively from Soviet refugees living in the United States.

23   The study by Haire, Ghiselli and Porter is usually quoted as evidence in favour of the universality of managerial thinking in that they note that only 25 per cent of the observed differences were associated with national, i.e. cultural, differences. Even if one ignores the sampling problems involved in this study (they admit that the sample was drawn 'impressionistically and sometimes opportunistically', and that the majority of managers were attending management training courses, pp.6–7) it is not at all clear that it is permissible to draw the above conclusions. For example, they found that management from Spain and Italy tended to agree more in their attitudes towards management, despite their dissimilarity in degree of industrialisation, than did, for example, managers from Italy and Denmark, whose degrees of industrialisation are more similar.

24   It is always difficult to pick precise dates for matters of this complexity, and of course there had always been individuals who had argued for the role of culture in social analysis, but by the end of the 1950s these individuals had grown into significant groups.

25   Mead and Metraux, 1953.

26   For an excellent summary of the problems of economics in non-Western societies see Firth, 1971.

27   Duerr and Greene, 1968.

28   Aitken, 1965, p.l2.

29   Interest in the role of the entrepreneur in economic growth also came from another quarter. The work of the psychologists Hagen (1962) and McClelland (1961) attempted to elaborate the psychological

mechanisms whereby certain individuals became motivated to put all their energies into economic activity. McClelland's studies in particular, of the relationship between 'need achievement' and economic activity, have revealed some surprisingly high correlations (of the order of 0.4 - 0.5 depending on the study in question) and the relationship appears to pre-date the rise in economic activity by about the right time interval. Hagen and McClelland both stress the crucial role of child rearing practices in their analysis, although neither of them offer very satisfactory explanations of what causes the child rearing practices. Several writers have suggested that perhaps this work explains in more detail the mechanism which connected the Protestant Ethic to the Spirit of Capitalism in Weber's classic work (e.g. Argyle (1972), Turner (1975)). Overall however, there must be some doubt as to the validity of these studies. Laboratory experiments have not found a very consistent relationship between projective methods of achievement and achievement-orientated behaviour (Argyle 1967), and whilst it may be true in some countries that high achievement motivation may lead to money making and business expansion, clearly in different cultures it may seek different outlets. Finally, both Hagen and McClelland pay scant attention to the political, social and economic structures that would have to be of a certain form for high N.Ach scores to make any difference to economic growth.

30   Habakkuk, 1968, p.37.
31   Landes, 1963.
32   It is worth noting here that even Gerschenkron and Habakkuk, for all their protestations about the problems of using socio–cultural variables in economic explanation, do themselves resort to them from time to time. For example, in examing the case of Russia in the second half of the nineteenth century, Gerschenkron (1962) admits that there is, 'some plausibility in the argument that the existence of widespread social attitudes in Russia which were so patently unfavourable to entrepreneurship greatly reduced the number of potential entrepreneurs and thereby reduced the rate of economic development in the country' (p.62). Similarly Habakkuk (1967) in his work on American and British technology in the nineteenth century does concede some role for what he calls 'sociological' influences (ch.6).
33   See, for example, the review of studies in Vroom, 1959.
34   This material is voluminous, many studies being reported in journals like the *Harvard Business Review* and *Business Week.* Some notable examples are: Lee (1966), Newman (1970) Fayerweather (1957), Fayerweather (1969).
35   Nath (1968) provides a good bibliography of these studies. Some of the best known are Abegglen (1958), Gonzalez and McMillan (1961), Oberg (1963).

36   Richman, 1965, p.295.
37   Bell, 1965, p.90.
38   Heydebrand, 1973, p.58.
39   Sjoberg, 1970, p.25.
40   Heydebrand, 1973, p.58.
41   Hickson, 1974.
42   There are three possible conclusions to be drawn from these
conflicting findings:
(a)   It is possible that the results could be accounted for by sampling
variations. Although both Abegglen's and Dore's sampling can be
criticised, this seems an unlikely interpretation.
(b)   One of the findings is mistaken.
(c)   The studies are looking at different phenomena — this seems much
the most likely explanation. The Aston studies concentrated upon some
limited aspects of the formal structure, whilst the other studies were
more concerned with the total working of the organisation. It remains
to be seen how useful the former studies are.
43   An important critique of contingency theory along these lines
is included in Child (1972).
44   Parsons, 1960a, p.172.
45   Parsons and Shils (eds.,) 1962, p.55.
46   Parsons makes the same point a little further on in the text:
'Analysis of the third kind of system (culture) is essential to the theory
of action systems because systems of value standards.....when
institutionalised in social systems and *internalised* in personality systems,
guide the actor with respect to both the *orientation to ends* and the
normative regulation of means and of expressive activities whenever
the need-dispositions of the actor allow choices in these matters;
Parsons and Shils, op. cit., p.56.
47   At one point Parsons tries to explain the place of culture in his
analysis by reference to a cybernetic model. He writes, 'By virtue of this
mode of thinking it could be respectable for biologists, for example,
to treat the genetic constitution of organisms as a set of information
bearing mechanisms which did not constitute the primary energy system
of the particular organism or species, but yet could be the primary
determinant of pattern and form. The parallel for the human sciences
dealing with cultural matters could not for very long be missed,
especially with the grand-scale application of cybernetics and information
theory in computer technology' (1973), p.45.
48   See his argument along these lines in Parsons, 1960b, p.481.
49   Parsons, 1966, p.113.
50   Habermas (1972) puts the matter succinctly: 'Parsons claims that
his list systematically represents the decisions between alternative
value-orientations that must be made by the subject of any action

whatsoever, regardless of the particular or historical context. But if one examines the list, one can scarcely overlook the historical situation of the inquiry on which it is based. The four pairs of alternative value-orientations.....which are supposed to take into account *all* possible fundamental decisions, are tailored to an analysis of *one* historical process' 1972, p.353.

51   See their use by Burrage (1969).

52   This view seems to be accepted by a number of writers, e.g. Lipset (1963), Pugh (1964). Pugh argues that Parsons himself latterly adopted such a position.

53   Williams, 1973, p.6.

54   Ibid., p.7.

2 Capitalism and culture: an historical analysis of the emergence of capitalism in Britain and America

It has been argued that the demands of the economic system are always mediated through the cultural fabric of the society. As Schumpeter (1947) persuasively put it: [1]

> Social structures, types and attitudes are coins that do not readily melt: once they are formed they persist, possibly for centuries; and since different structures and types display different degrees of ability to survive, we almost always find that actual group or national behaviour more or less departs from what we should expect it to be if we tried to infer it from the dominant forms of the production process.

In other words, although it is analytically possible to talk about the 'logic of capitalism' as in Chapter 1, the 'rational imperatives' of this system are never unreservedly met. [2] The history of each society deposits a residue of institutions, conventions and assumptions, and the political elite, at least in Britain and America, has had to work within the respective historical frameworks of the two societies. This chapter will attempt to show how the rulers of these two societies adapted to the demands of the capitalist economic system in different ways, because of the different socio–cultural frameworks within which they worked.

There are several problems in embarking on an historical analysis of Britain and America to demonstrate the key role that historical factors have played in setting the socio–cultural framework within which capitalist economic enterprise has had to work. First, there is the vexed question of where in historical time to begin the analysis. History is indeed a Heraclitean flux, the historian interrupts the flow by the imposition of 'periods' and 'stages' merely for his own convenience: the historical process does not divide itself in this way. Yet if one is to make use of historical material for the purpose of understanding a particular phenomenon, then one must do a certain amount of violence to the continuity of the historical process and break the flow. The historical analysis of Britain and America will begin at the time when America began to exist as a separate entity, 1776, although some brief reference will be made to the preceding period under English rule. This date approximately marks the beginning of the period of *industrial* capitalism in English society and thus would appear to be a suitable starting point for the analysis of both societies.

Just as the unending flow of events and processes in historical time presents the researcher with problems in knowing quite where to begin, it also presents a more general problem of analysis in attempting to assess such a general proposition as the effect of socio—cultural factors upon the development of the capitalist mode of production. The procedure adopted follows directly from the conceptual analysis of the concept of culture in Chapter 1. The historical process in both societies will be analysed in terms of the pattern variables. The extent to which the socio—cultural structure can be shown to stress the values of achievement, affective-neutrality, specificity, universalism and self-orientation rather than their opposites will be taken as evidence that the society is more attuned to the needs of the capitalist economic system.[3]

The final problem that has to be contended with in an historical analysis of Britain and America is one of methodology. When one is dealing with such complex relationships between variables like social class, the development of particular institutions, entrepreneurial recruitment, the value system of a society, and attempting to relate all these to the economic system, then the best that one can do is to present as much validating evidence as possible in support of the view that the socio—cultural structure, so conceived, either on balance supports the economic system or detracts from its efficient working. Whatever the merits of Popper's view, that the scientific method essentially proceeds via falsification, this strategy is not possible in a project such as this.

Before the relationship between particular aspects of the socio—cultural structure and the economic order can be investigated there is a prior task. The task is to observe the manner in which the capitalist economic order emerged in the two societies. To begin the analysis with Britain, the most important general historical fact to take into account when considering the structure of British society towards the end of the eighteenth century was the fact that Britain was emerging from a feudal past. The central features of feudal society, from the point of view of this analysis, were in marked contrast to those of the new order of capitalism that was gradually to follow.[4] Inside the feudal structure there was a tendency for actions to be adjudged according to their contribution to the 'health' of society, production was for use not profit. The feudal system controlled social relationships as well as economic ones, all members of the society, from the nobility at the top to the humble serf at the bottom, were bound to each other in mutual obligation.[5] The hierarchical feudal structure was still reasonably intact in England by the beginning of the fourteenth century, yet during that century the first signs of decay were to be seen. First in the towns and then in the countryside production for personal gain rather than use began to emerge. By the sixteenth century the Crown, for a variety of reasons, found itself in opposition to the commercial interests in both the countryside and towns. The greatest conflict was generated by the fact that the commercial interests represented, in embryonic form at least, the rights of individual property, against the multiplicity of rights and obligations claimed by the Crown.

The seventeenth century saw the continuing rise of the power of the landed aristocracy with their symbolic victory in the Civil War. By the eighteenth century historians were writing about the consolidation of that power and, as Barrington Moore notes: 'The strong commercial tone in the life of the landed upper classes, both gentry and titled nobility, also meant that there was no very solid phalanx of aristocratic opposition to the advance of industry itself. .....the most influential sector of the landed upper classes acted as a political advance guard for commercial and industrial capitalism'. [6] By 1750 then in no sense could English society be described as feudal in either an economic or a social sense, yet neither would it be satisfactory to describe the society as firmly capitalist. From a purely economic point of view, the mode of production was predominantly capitalist, yet in terms of social relations, the society lay half way between the stress upon ascription, affectivity, diffuseness, particularism,collective orientation and their opposites. The society was an aristocracy, a hierarchical society in which men took their places in an accepted order of precedence, and yet it was also a society in which there was a good deal of social mobility: it was not yet a society marked by social classes. This society, perched between ideal-typical feudalism on the one hand, and ideal-typical capitalism on the other, was based firmly on the twin principles of property and patronage. One's place in that society was wholly determined by the amount and kind of one's own property. After property, and emanating from it, the most important factor in determining status was patronage. As Perkin (1969) notes: 'At all levels, patronage, the system of personal selection from amongst one's kinsmen and connections, was the instrument by which property influenced recruitment to those positions in society which were not determined by property alone'. [7] The system represented a half-way house between the formal and inescapable structure of feudal homage, and the contractual relationships of the wage system of capitalism—a society based as much on the values of ascription and particularism as upon achievement and universalism.

The triumphant landed aristocracy that emerged from the struggle with the Crown also created, albeit unwittingly, the doctrine of *laissez-faire,* which became such an important condition, in the English context, for the development of industrial capitalism. It should be stressed that the new landed rulers of England did not deliberately choose such a policy. On the contrary, they continued to hold the view, common to all their European contemporaries, that it was the duty of a nation's rulers to take positive action to increase its wealth and power relative to its neighbours. [8] The paradox is to be explained in the fact that although the landowners had defeated the old monarchy and replaced it by one more to their liking, they still had no wish to rule in its place. The effect of their opposition to effective governmental interference with themselves led to the system of *laissez-faire* and certainly promoted the initial development of industrial capitalism.

As one can see, it would be quite wrong to argue that the landed aristocracy, as a class, stood implacably opposed to the increasing power of the industrial owners of capital. What they largely did stand opposed to however, was the acceptance of the full social and political consequences of the capitalist economic order. Their reaction to the French Revolution, which in some respects at least was a symbolic affirmation of that pattern of values which it has been argued are the natural concomitants of ideal-typical capitalism, was significant. They closed ranks against the threat that such a value system would have had on their system of privilege. They still held very tightly to the levers of political power as well. Until about 1815 the distribution of political power between various interest groups was hardly an issue, only very gradually was the political power of the landowners challenged by the rising bourgeoisie. One of the most distinctive features of English history has been the way that the ruling class has always accommodated the claims of the rising group rather than risk outright confrontation. The passing of the Reform Bill in 1832, which effectively gave the industrial capitalist the vote, and the striking down of the Corn Laws in 1846 showed that the landed aristocracy was prepared to give way when it mattered.

The manner in which the owners of land gradually left the centre of the political and social arena is itself of quite crucial significance. There was no sudden handover of power, no symbolic incident which heralded the dominance of the bourgeoisie, rather the process was one of a gradual transformation. [9] In that transformation it was as much a change on the part of the urban business class as it was on the part of the rural landed class. Although there was a downward movement from the ranks of the aristocracy to the world of business via the sons of the former, of much greater significance was the movement from business and trade into the ranks of the aristocracy. The English landed aristocracy in the nineteenth century was above all an 'open aristocracy'. Their ranks were open 'to all who could acquire the one necessary qualification, the purchase price of an estate'. [10] Initially this was probably done with a certain amount of distaste, [11] but not only did it ensure the survival for almost a whole century of the political power of the landed aristocracy as a class, much more importantly it meant that the *values* of the landed aristocracy were substantially maintained for an even longer period of time. They accommodated the demands of the rising bourgeoisie by allowing them entry to their group and converting them, more or less, to landed aristocrats. Thus the commercial and industrial elites in Britain, rather than developing their own distinctive culture, accepted and adopted those of the old governing class. As Barrington Moore (1973) argues: 'All accounts of England prior to 1914, and to some extent even beyond that date, give the strong impression that rolling green acres and a country house were indispensable to political and social eminence'. [12] Of course there were some, like the brewer Bass, who preferred to be, 'First in the beerage rather than last in the peerage', but the central point is that the values of the 'old world' were not quickly swamped by the values of the new entrepreneurs, who by the end of the nineteenth century were clearly the new governing class. Because of the accommodating tactics of the landed aristocrats, the value structure that should have been reflected by the economic base, still bore the strong marks of the past era.

Why were there no strong pressures emanating from the capitalist infrastructure to work upon the institutions and values of the society pushing them in the appropriate direction? The answer to this question is to be found in the economic position of British society until at least the end of the nineteenth century. As the first country to industrialise, Britain naturally reaped all the advantages of being the world's first 'industrial workshop'. This temporal advantage clearly wore off as other countries industrialised, and indeed became something of a handicap as Gershenkron (1962) and others have argued. [13] Yet Britain was cushioned from many of the later economic effects of being first in the field by her colonies. The colonies, by initially supplying cheap raw materials, and later providing a protected market for British manufactured goods, allowed British business to operate within a social and cultural milieu which was by no means entirely favourable to business success. Only when the cushioning effect of the colonies was removed, coupled with the effects of the Second World War, did Britain finally pass from being a creditor to a debtor nation. Once this happened, as will be shown later, the demands of the economic system bit deep into the incongruent superstructure, and put enormous pressure upon the ruling group to effect superstructural changes. Yet given the socio—cultural structure of British society which has been described, it does require sustained pressure from the economic sphere to promote such changes, indeed it very often requires something of the order of a crisis to promote radical change. To choose an example from the nineteenth century to illustrate this point: it took the crisis of the Crimean War to expose the crass inefficiency that the system of patronage and the purchase of commissions had bequeathed to the armed forces. After this was exposed army reforms, based largely on the values of achievement rather than ascription, and universalism rather than particularism, were not long in coming. The Crimean debacle had a similar effect upon the principles of recruitment and adminstration inside the Civil Service and hastened the implementation of the Northcote-Trevelyan Report.

In order to understand the structure of British society at the end of the eighteenth century it is necessary to take cognisance of the fact that she was emerging from a feudal structure. If one turns to America at the same period of time, perhaps the single most important point to note is that the country possessed no feudal past—at least not in anything like the fully developed form that had existed in England. Certainly one can find evidence in parts of New England in the seventeenth century, that the combined power of the English aristocracy and the Puritan clergy did utilise the medieval doctrine of *justum pretium* to regulate commerce.[14] But by the middle of that century these regulations had been successfully opposed by the Boston merchant class, and the influx of immigrants had begun to kick over the remaining traces of feudalism. Perhaps the major impediment to the development of business in America at this time was the colonial power of Great Britain. British trading and manufacturing interests opposed many developments in the colonies simply because they were not in their interests. The reaction to colonial rule on the part of the American merchants is well known. Goaded in particular by British taxes, they began to devise substitutes for British trade and credit, signed no importation agreements and planned strategies for the defence of their own trading position. When it finally came the revolution was in essence a contest between the commercial interests of Britain and America, although other issues did play their part. There is some dispute among the historians of the American past about whether the resulting American Constitution and new administration represented directly or not the interests of the business class. It is certainly possible to see the leaders of the revolution as split into two groups, northern capitalists and southern plantation owners, and the resulting constitution represented not a victory of one over the other, but a compromise between them. In one sense, whichever side one takes in the debate over the Constitution is not of great significance here. Even the values enshrined in what Lipset (1963) calls the 'anti-urban agrarian utopia of the Jeffersonians', embraced a set of values which were clearly supportive of the capitalist system, either in its urban or agrarian form. These values derided unearned privileges, stressed the equality of all to get on in the market place, praised the values of frugality and hard work, and above all elevated the material rewards that were the prizes for the successful. So powerful were these values, at least in the North and West, so readily do they reflect the stress on achievement, affective-neutrality, specificity, universalism and self-orientation, that many of the old aristocracy fled to the privileged shelter of Canada, where the values of the Old World were still largely preserved. In America the true ground work was laid for a society based on the idea of contract, the essence of capitalism.

One of the factors which helped bring about the revolution was the increasing number of immigrants who were coming to the New World. Although it was certainly true that many of these people had been 'pushed' from the Old World as the result of persecution or discrimination of one sort or another, it is equally true that many were also pulled by the attraction of America. These immigrants, drawn preponderantly from the poorer classes, shut out from wealth and privilege in their own societies, savoured the chance to get on in a society that, by contrast, placed few restrictions upon a man willing to work hard for his own profit. These people, sufficiently brave and adventurous to make the Atlantic crossing, who had given up their stake in European society, were naturally not to be easily frustrated in their labours by the hand of Europe that stretched out across the Atlantic from the shores of the British Isles. British colonial rule represented the decadent, oppressive and restrictive society which many of them had left.

If a prime attraction for the immigrant was the desire to achieve the economic success that was largely denied them because of the structure of their own societies,[15] then it has also to be argued that, at the very least, the experience of America provided a very fertile soil on which this value system could develop. The individualism that is to be found in the Constitution was clearly fostered not only by the selective effects of migration from the Old World, but also by the conditions of life in what was to be known as the 'Frontier'. The Frontier, it is often argued, must have further heightened the exercise of individual resourcefulness, for the conditions there constantly confronted the settler with circumstances in which he could rely upon no one but himself, and where the capacity to improvise a solution for a problem was not infrequently necessary to survival.[16] Such conditions also stimulated the values of hard work and those of practical ingenuity. As Schlesinger (1970) puts it:[17]

> The complicated nature of the farmer's job, especially during the first two and a half centuries, afforded an unexcelled training in mechanical ingenuity. These ex-Europeans and their descendants became a race of whittlers and tinkers, daily engaged in devising, improving and repairing tools and other

utensils until, as Emerson said, they had 'the power and habit of invention their brain'.

The Frontier was also a moving frontier; rates of geographical mobility were spectacularly high in nineteenth century America as the new immigrants pursued their fortunes in new jobs, new settlements, new farms. Failure in a particular venture or place did not necessarily mean a permanent failure, the inherent optimism of the immigrants at least ensured that most would try again, probably in another location. [18] The effect of this constant movement can be related to the importance of money in the American value system. On a journey, or in a new community, money was one of the few things that could be easily transported. More than that, money also demonstrated, in the context of American society, the presence of admirable qualities in the man who attained it. Cash took the place of pedigree in the new society. Thus, as early as 1836, Washington Irving coined his classic phrase concerning 'The almighty dollar, that great subject of universal devotion throughout the land'. In summary, as Thistlethwaite (1955) argues: 'The westerner, whatever his occupation, was fundamentally concerned to make money, and where so much around him was uncertain, so much awaited exploitation and men felt free of the restraining hand of custom the cash nexus increasingly governed his social transactions and capitalism found a uniquely fair field to grow in'. [19]

Few men desire money for its own sake of course, eventually some invest in some form of property. The private ownership of property became an important value in the American state from its inception. It was Jefferson, following Locke, who enunciated the principle that: 'Who would govern himself must own his own soul. To own his own soul he must own property, the means of economic security'. Jefferson's view of the optimum society for the fulfilment of the American ideals was a society composed of independent farmers, and to some extent this form of society was probably attained in the West during the first half of the nineteenth century. These Jeffersonian ideals and their practice provided a wholly appropriate set of values for the later emergence of the industrial market society. After all, if one imagines a subsistence farming community, in which each family receives each year exactly what it produces, and each family is thereby perfectly free to make its own choices concerning the 'trade off' between goods and leisure, then these are the classic conditions of the market society expounded by Adam Smith.

Finally, one might note how the different conditions of the New World led to a greater stress upon the value of achievement rather than that of ascription. One can illustrate this point by considering the role of women in American society. In the migrating stream, whether from Europe or from the eastern seaboard, young and unmarried men predominated. [20] Women had scarcity value, but this scarcity value was not just as wives or sweethearts but also as workers. In the West, where the demands for labour were greatest, the Old World attitudes were ground away by the forces of economic necessity, as women laboured alongside the men, albeit often doing different tasks. This new position in the society, particularly in the Western states, allowed women to become independent and self confident, and this eventually led to them demanding, at a very early period, formal rights for their sex.

Turning to the role of the state in early American society, it is suggested that the popular view of the state's role in economic life in America up to say, 1850, was one of the vigorous pursuit of a *laissez-faire* policy. Many commentators have in fact argued this particular proposition. The origins of the policy, it is argued, can be traced back to the hostility felt by the colonists for the regulations imposed by the mother country. Bendix (1964) notes, that 'among the complaints of the colonies against the "repeated injuries and usurpations" of the King of Great Britain is the declaration that "he has created a multitude of new offices, and sent hither swarms of officers to harrass our people and out their substance" '. [21] This hostility to government, it is argued, was perpetuated beyond the Alleghanies. The enormous resources of empty land, with accompanying minerals and other materials, demanded a minimum of social discipline. Instead, authority rested on the isolated individual who, owing no obligations to any wider corporate unity, carried so much of the responsibility for ordering his life. This account, which is put forward by a large number of writers, [22] fits in well with the dominant cultural values in American society, which have been expounded in the previous pages. Yet despite this 'goodness of fit', the thesis is, in some ways, a mistaken one. Shonfield (1965), is one of the few writers who correctly notes that: 'Historically, American capitalism in its formative period was much readier to accept intervention by public authority than British capitalism'. [23] One of the major reasons for this is that an interventionist policy was vastly beneficial to the needs of the embryo capitalist economy at that time. In particular, the state had a considerable role to play in providing the essential services of the economy, like those of transport (canals and railways) and banks, which were largely beyond the means of private enterprise as it then existed. Clear evidence of the role of the state governments during this period is provided in Hartz's (1948) study of the development of economic policy in Pennsylvania. Hartz finds a total of over 150 'mixed corporations', in which state government and private enterprise were partners, in the records of the year 1844. [24] Why have so many historians apparently been mistaken? The problem can be solved by clearly distinguishing between the powers of individual state legislatures and Federal power. The opposition to government interference in the economy which so many writers have, quite correctly, picked up as a distinguishing feature of the American value system, is an opposition to *Federal* power. The opposition was not to the use of public power in the economic system where this was thought to be beneficial to the development of private enterprise, but only to any reinforcement of central power wielded through the Federal authority. As Shonfield (1965) writes: 'The fear was only of the potential Leviathan in Washington'. [25] It should be noted however, that once private enterprise had grown in power and size by the last quarter of the nineteenth century, public enterprise, even at the level of the state, was deemed to be interference with the natural operation of the private enterprise system.

In attempting to show the historical origins of the American cultural system, the ways have been stressed in which the pattern of the values was largely congruent with the needs of the capitalist economic order. What has been described however, although largely true of the North and West, was not true of the South. Certainly the southern economy was capitalist in the sense that it was production for private profit, yet it was not bourgeois; the capitalist economic order existed inside a social structure which reflected the value structure of the Old World. It reflected the values of ascription over achievement, of affectivity over affective-neutrality, of diffuseness over specificity and of particularism over universalism. It is doubtful whether it can be argued that the southern economy was dying out for internal reasons, or that it was an economic fetter upon industrial capitalism in the North. [26] The real divide between the South and the North was the symbolic one of culture. In the North and West were to be found the development of essentially bourgeois values, and these values were strengthened as industrial capitalism gained more of a hold in the North. In the South, if anything the landed wealthy inhabitants appeared to look around to discover and emphasise whatever aristocratic and pre-industrial traits they could find in their own society to distinguish them from the men of money in the North. The clash was essentially over the issue of what type of society America was to be, as Barrington Moore (1973) notes: 'Labour-repressive agricultural systems, and plantation slavery in particular, are political obstacles to a *particular kind* of capitalism, at a specific historical stage'. [27] Striking down slavery therefore was an important symbolic step, it represented the end of the uneasy compromise that had lasted since 1776, and a victory for bourgeois capitalism. The victory of the North meant that the southern whites would have to conform to the value system of industrial capitalism.

The victory that came in 1865 was not a total victory for that side of the pattern variables that have been designated capitalist or bourgeois. This should hardly be surprising because the complete acceptance of such a set of values would be a partial contradiction of the relations of production inherent in such a society. For example, although there was a movement inside northern capitalism, the Radical Republicans, who wanted to totally revolutionise the South, even to the extent of confiscating all plantation estates over 200 acres in size and giving each negro household '40 acres and a mule', they were not successful. Ultimately, northern capitalism was in no mood to tolerate an outright attack on property, even the property of the plantation owners. To have done so would have been to have symbolically attacked one of the fundamental principles of the capitalist economic order itself, the protection of private property.

The preceeding historical analysis of the emergence of bourgeois society in Britain and America, although of necessity hastily drawn, should provide a sufficient background for the analysis of those elements of social structure that can be directly related to the operation of business enterprise in the two societies under discussion. It is the intention to consider those aspects of the social structure of society, like the polity, the system of social stratification, the education system and the system of public administration, which provide the social setting within which business operates. This will be followed by a comparative analysis of the way in which these factors have affected the structure and operation of business organisations in Britain and America.

The relationship between the owners of the means of production and the political rulers is a complex one in both societies, but the capitalist class has had greater power in America than Britain. Britain saw the very gradual rise to power of the capitalist class and not without some opposition from the class it dispossessed of power, the landed aristocracy. The two groups confronted each other on every issue in the nineteenth century. In politics the capitalists demanded the abolition of protection as symbolised by the Corn Laws and the completion of the system of free trade. In industrial relations they mostly demanded the abolition of all state interference between employers and employees (except for children), and the substitution of the contractual relations of employer and employed for the paternal relations of master and servant. All this and more was conceded despite the fact that the landed aristocracy held on to the formal positions of power until around the turn of the twentieth century.

Many of these 'victories' on the part of the bourgeoisie were somewhat less than complete: for example, the education system that eventually developed in the nineteenth century was not one that was directly geared to the needs of industrial capitalism, rather a system at least as much in keeping with the ideas and values of the landed aristocracy was instituted. There are several reasons for this phenomenon, but by far the most important was the fact that the English aristocracy possessed an acute sense of history. They recognised an irresistable force when they met one, and so rather than provoke an open confrontation with the rising bourgeoisie, they accommodated to their demands and in so doing they managed to preserve many of their old values, as well as their hold on many of the institutions of English society. By accommodating they managed to retain their values and style of life to an extent that the rising bourgeoisie at worst felt ambivalent towards them, and at best wished to emulate them.

In Britain capitalism has always competed with other ideals, the aristocratic ideal and the socialist ideal to name but two. In the United States, although this competition has not been entirely absent, it has never reached the level of a full confrontation. The promises which capitalism offered have never been seriously challenged. [28] In one sense it could be argued that the political elite in American society has been a rather less important group than its counterpart in British society. The American Constitution was drafted with a vivid sense of the dangers of strong government. This has resulted firstly, in a Federal structure, with less power concentrated in a centralised political elite. Secondly it has meant, as already noted, a comparative lack of government compared with Britain. In other words, it has influenced both the type and quantity of government in the United States. This peculiar American heritage, of government viewed merely as a service agency with certain limited regulatory functions, made it easy for powerful groups in American society to see themselves as the real locus of power. Business capitalism, as such an interest, had few rivals in this society. The absence of an established church, the lack of an hereditary aristocracy of landowners, or of competing careers in the civil service or the army, made it easy for business to become the dominant ethos and thus the dominant political group.

Business men have certainly been important in the Federal government itself, even Mills (1956), who believed that there was a separation of the business and political domains, noted that up to his time 60 per cent of the members of American cabinets had 'business backgrounds'. Even Lasswell (1952), a political scientist of very different persuasions from Mills, claims that businessmen were the largest single occupational group in cabinet between 1889 and 1949. This is in considerable contrast to the position in Britain, where for roughly the same period of time rather less than 30 per cent were businessmen. [29] The evidence from 1949 is just as strong. Schecter (1968) reports that in the eighteen years of government from 1949 to 1967 businessmen accepted almost 180 appointments at the level of assistant secretary or higher. If one concentrates on just four areas of government, defence and military services, the Treasury, the Commerce Department and the Post Office then one finds that under Truman one-third of the total number of appointments went to businessmen, under Eisenhower two-thirds, and under Kennedy and Johnson about one-quarter. Yet in the American political system, because of the constitutional separation of powers and the loose structure of the two major political parties, pressure groups are of fundamental significance. Some commentators have even gone so far as to refer to them as the 'fourth branch of government'.[30] It is at this political level that business is really powerful in the United States.[31]

One can note the same differences between Britain and America even at the local political level. In an interesting study in the 'sociology of leadership' tradition, Miller (1958) investigated the community power structure in two American and one British city, all matched for size, economic, demographic and educational characteristics. His results, he claims, show 'a striking difference between G B and U S A ..... Businessmen do exert a predominant influence in community decision making in Pacific City and Southern City' (U S A). 'However, in English City the hypothesis is rejected. The key influentials come from a broad representation of the institutional sectors of community life'.[32] He also notes that business pressure groups are active even in community politics in America, whilst such organised lobbying is condemned in Britain.

The differences that have been described in the character of the political elites in Britain and America are crucial, because of the potential power of such groups to determine the structure of their societies. One fundamental feature of social structure, which can have marked effects on the running of business, is the stratification system. Some writers appear to take the view that the broad dimensions of the stratification system are determined by the needs of the economic structure itself, without any reference to the character of the political elites.[33] This view is here taken to be untenable. The real issue is the nature of the interplay between economic/occupational forces and the political superstructure in determining the nature of the stratification system. Given that there are differences in the nature of the political elites in the two societies, it follows that one should expect to find differences in their stratification systems.

In broad terms it has been argued that America has placed greater emphasis upon the pattern variables that have been associated with capitalism, than Britain. The stress on the value of achievement rather than ascription in particular, should be reflected in the stratification system, other things being equal.[34] Certainly it can be argued that, *subjectively,*[35] class and status distinctions have been less important in the United States than in Britain. Probably the majority of the immigrants who moved across the Atlantic in the nineteenth century welcomed the move into a society which was more 'open', and where achieved wealth was much more important than ascribed rank. The relative lack of status distinctions inside the American population had profound effects upon the structure of the population as a consumer market. Observers from De Tocqueville to the present day have found American consumers less distinguished as individualistic judges of quality than as anxious conformists to remarkably uniform and standardised patterns. There are a number of reasons why this should be the case. First, the consuming public in America was more homogeneous in terms of income distribution than Britain. Secondly, since consumption patterns reflect social status distinctions, in a society where those distinctions are fewer and less important, the market is more likely to accept relatively standardised products. In Britain on the other hand, the consuming public was more heavily stratified and, because of less geographical mobility, more localised. In brief the stratification system was itself partly a cause of the fact that America was much further advanced in *mass* production techniques than was Britain. In the latter, the small firm, which existed to supply products with *individual* character, reflecting highly differentiated status distinctions, occupied a much more important place in the British economy than in its American counterpart. Although these differences have probably narrowed, there is plenty of evidence to suggest that there is still a difference which materially effects the business environment of firms operating in the two economies. [36]

Whilst it has been argued above that the nature of the stratification system, as it affected the structure of the *consumer* market, undoubtedly affected the operation of business in the two societies, it is also necessary to examine the effect that the nature of stratification had upon *inputs* to the business firm as well as outputs. Considerable evidence has been accumulated which suggests that the existence of large numbers of unskilled immigrants in America in the nineteenth century also encouraged the early development of mass production techniques. The existence of liberal land policies, westward expansion, and the demand for such men in transport and construction, kept this type of labour relatively scarce in the manufacturing sector. There was thus an economic incentive to replace such labour by more capital intensive methods of production, and this economic reasoning was encouraged by the fact that the work performed by the unskilled was relatively easy to adapt to machinery. [37] It has also been argued that the relative absence of *skilled* craftsmen in the United States also led to a general tendency to mechanise industrial processes wherever possible. The structural conditions influencing the manufacturing process in nineteenth century Britain and America are probably no longer operable, but much popular literature still testifies to similar important differences in the manufacturing sectors of the two economies that undoubtedly have their origins in these antecedent historical conditions.

The full institutionalisation of a value system that stresses affective-neutrality, specificity, universalism, achievement, and self-orientation would set up considerable social strains. The potentially fragmenting effects of a *gesellschaft* society have been noted as far back as the eighteenth century, and of the founding fathers of sociology, Durkheim devoted much of his attention to the potential anomic nature of such societies. American social structure, although firmly committed to this potentially anomic value set, appears to have developed a coping mechanism. It is a fact that status differences appear to be far less important in the United States; *personal* relations, for example, are not so much affected by status reference. [38] Sutton et al. (1962)phrase the point nicely: 'If "capitalism" is still respectable in the United States, the fluidity of "informal" social relations has greatly contributed'. [39] In Britain the problem has been partially surmounted by the fact that the potentially anomic value set has not been so firmly grasped, vestiges of the value system of the aristocracy, of paternalism and deference, still have *some* hold on British society. That such differences between America and Britain are still manifest is testified by numerous writers including Lipset (1963). [40] These differences in the stratification of the two societies will almost certainly be reflected in the economic system, a more informal business style is likely in American business organisations. [41]

The widespread belief in the possibilities of upward social mobility, the 'log cabin to White House' ideology, is a potent reason for the relative lack of a well developed system of status consciousness in the United States. To what extent there actually has been a greater degree of vertical mobility [42] in the United States than Britain is a difficult question to determine. Certainly the 'popular' view of the contrast between America and Britain in this area seems to support the idea that America, particularly in the nineteenth century, was a land where anybody with talent could make their way right to the top. In contrast, Britain has been viewed as a more 'traditional' society, where social mobility rates have been held back. This view would fit in well with the general thesis that is being advanced. The full thrust of capitalism should encourage the movement of labour in defiance of inherited privilege and handicap, and ideally opportunity and corresponding risk should be renewed, as it were, in each new generation. Such a situation would be impossible in a capitalist society of course, because wealth and power accumulated in one generation, in the form of private property, would inevitably be transmitted to the next generation, who would then start the race with considerable advantages. Despite this contradiction, embedded in the very nature of capitalism, it is not unreasonable to hypothesise that a society with a value system more in keeping with the needs of capitalism should have higher rates of mobility than a society with a value system less committed. Social mobility data are so fraught with methodological problems, particularly when one wants to make historical comparisons, that no easy test of the hypothesis is possible. Official records, for example, rarely contain the information from which social mobility in the population at large could be reconstructed, and so one has to rely on specialist studies which are almost solely the province of the twentieth century. If one considers more localised studies of the nineteenth century in particular areas of Britain and America, the conclusion that America had markedly higher rates of mobility than Britain is not upheld. Thernstrom's (1964) impressive study of social mobility in Newburyport does not support the view of America being a highly socially mobile society in the nineteenth century. On the other hand, British studies tend to refute the view that there was relatively little social mobility in nineteenth-century Britain. [43] To come up to date, although there is considerable controversy surrounding the interpretation of comparative mobility data made by Lipset and Zetterberg (1956), even such a critic as Miller (1960) concludes that the data show that probably Britain had rather more inter-generational mobility across the manual/non-manual line than the United States. The most recent studies of mobility in Britain, e.g. Goldthorpe and Llewellyn (1977) and Payne et al. (1977), reject the view of Britain's low rate of social mobility. Even the thesis that recruitment to the small elite at the top was tighter in Britain now seems less safe than it was. On the face of it, the hypothesis that a society with a value system more in keeping with the needs of the capitalist infrastructure should have higher rates of social mobility would appear to be refuted. It is difficult however, to know just how much reliance can be placed upon such a conclusion. First, it is known that a lot of other factors, not directly related to the value system of a society, can affect mobility rates.[44] Secondly, it is admitted that the national mobility studies themselves are not *directly* comparable. Thirdly, the data for the United States naturally enough include the black population, whose existence, as a sort of 'underclass' in America unquestionably has an influence upon the data. It should also be noted that the data refer only to the *male* population, while there is good reason to believe that the opportunities for the mobility of women are comparatively higher in the United States. Finally, an interesting comparative study by Marsh (1963) concludes with the timely warning that 'universalistic-achievement values, while professed by some industrial societies, may not be strongly institutionalised in mobility channels, and without effective institutionalisation these values cannot affect mobility any more in societies that profess them than in societies that do not'.[45]

If the general comparative social mobility data for Britain and the United States remain somewhat inconclusive, the more specialised data for recruitment into business in the two societies is more certain. In the United States the general picture is that business and industry have always been relatively high-status occupations, which have attracted people from all ranks of life. Habakkuk (1962) notes that the general belief in an open avenue to wealth was one of the main reasons for the amount of ability devoted to business enterprise in that country. He also argues that in the United States, 'there were few competitors to business success as a source of social prestige. There was no large and powerful bureaucracy, no hereditary aristocracy. There was no professional military class and soldiers were not held in high esteem'.[46] Not only did the relatively high prestige of business encourage recruitment into its ranks in America, once there, successful men were encouraged to stay. Unlike many of their English counterparts, whose ambition was to rise in the social scale by acquiring landed estates, marrying their daughter into county families or sending their sons into Parliament or the professions after they had been through public school, successful American businessmen largely stayed with their business and encouraged their sons to follow them.

In spite of the widespread evidence that America was a 'business society' and businessmen were, as a consequence, high prestige members of that society, high esteem did not totally flow in their direction. The business journalist John Chamberlain complained in *Fortune* that American novelists have consistently done rank injustice to American businessmen.[47] This view is supported by Sutton et al. (1962), and Hobsbawn (1975) provides examples of American communities failing to support businessmen in particular situations. All this is a useful antidote to the belief in the total dominance of business values in American society. It should also be realised that, for the majority of Americans, business is valued not so much as an end in itself, but as one of the broadest and shortest avenues to an enormously important goal in American society, money. Once this is comprehended one can readily understand why the heroes of American business tend not to be those who have behaved most graciously and scrupulously in terms of 'traditional' standards, but those who have shown initiative and been materially successful. It is this fact which would appear to explain the widespread finding that Americans revere business leaders, but do not trust them.

The high relative prestige of business and businessmen in America stands in marked contrast to the situation prevailing in England. This was probably not always the case. Wilson (1965) argues that 'for nearly a century after the inauguration of the industrial revolution, industry and trade floated on a tide of social, even intellectual approval. It reached its peak round about the mid-century and the Crystal Palace Exhibition'.[48] In that early period, as has been argued, even the aristocracy became interested in the novelty of invention or the glamour of a great adventuring or plantation company. The structure of English society was also one where the counter-tradition to business ran deep, and by mid-century there was a formidable body of opponents to challenge industrial capitalism. The opponents were drawn from many traditions; from literature Dickens, Carlyle, Ruskin and Scott mercilessly attacked the philistinism of business and the apalling social consequences of the system of industrial capitalism. The Christian socialists, led by men like Kingsley, accused them of being ungodly; the conservationists accused them of destroying the countryside. Finally, romantics like Blake and Morris pointed to the type of society that could have been. This great counterblast was joined at the end of the century by the Fabian intellectuals, who by the 1920s, so it is claimed, 'had turned the sacred word of *profits* into an obscenity'.[49]

This opposition to industrial capitalism had very severely dented the prestige of the entrepreneur by the 1870s. Yet this was by no means the only reason for waning prestige. As already indicated, in Britain many took the path to business merely to gain enough money to enter the 'leisured classes', or at very least the professions. The literature readily testifies to the fate of the third generation who looked for a calling outside the world of trade and industry.[50] Alternatively, the business itself could be run along lines that would gain the approval of the aristocracy. Numerous commentators claim that the City has long been marked by these features,[51] and Coleman (1973) produces some very interesting evidence which suggests that some large British companies are almost run like 'gentlemen's clubs'.[52]

It is impossible to discuss, in a meaningful way, the difference in the prestige and recruitment patterns of particular occupations without reference to the educational system of the society in question. As the majority of studies of occupational choice have shown, the educational system is intimately connected to the occupational structure. Certainly the differences in the prestige of business as an occupation between Britain and America cannot be readily understood without an examination of the education systems of the two societies. Education in the early days of the newly independent state of America bore the strong mark of the former British presence. Initially, the educational ideal of the gentleman, so strong in the English background, was cultivated, particularly in New England and the antebellum South. This, after all, was the type of education that the majority of the early political leaders in America had received. This elitist form of education was more a reflection of the Old World rather than the New however, and although it has never disappeared from the American educational scene, in many ways it can be considered as 'uncharacteristic'.[53] The elitist features of the system of education, bequeathed to America by the British colonialists, could not long survive the influx of immigrants with their very different ideals. For these early Americans education was their religion, and Hofstadter (1964) notes that the Americans were the first other people in modern history to follow the Prussian example in establishing free common-school systems. Among their earliest statutes were land ordinances setting aside a portion of the public domain to support school systems. The American educational system is more marked by what Turner (1960b) has called 'contest mobility' than is the British system.[54] In other words, the values of achievement are stronger in American society and are more deeply entrenched in the educational system. An indication of this can be seen in the fact that a larger proportion of the relevant age cohorts are enrolled in higher education in America than Britain.[55]

Access to education however, is probably not the most distinctive difference between Britain and America in the area of education. One of the biggest differences lies in the content of the knowledge that is transmitted within the system. American education has nearly always concentrated upon the transmission of essentially practical knowledge. The prime questions about the curriculum have always been, 'Of what use is it?', 'What can you do with it?' The view developed that classical education, or a liberal education in the humanities, was suitable only to the leisured classes, to the European past. Even pure science as a subject of study had its dissenters whilst few denied the obvious relevance of applied science.[56] The most important spur to the stress upon practical knowledge in education in America, is to be found in the importance of business interests in the development of education. The businessman's interest in education, even of the practical American variety, came slowly. Initially, the self-help philosophy of this group preferred the 'school of hard knocks' to the more formal attempts of the schoolroom. Yet the very success of the self-made man, in transforming the family business into a company and later a corporation, soon made his type virtually extinct. However reluctantly, businessmen began to appreciate the value of formal instruction, particularly for the more stable careers now being followed in bureaucratic business.

The businessmen, at least in the early years, were as much interested in elementary education as they were in anything more directly related to the business enterprise. After the Civil War, northern capitalists were particularly anxious to impose the ideas and values of their economic

47

order upon the South and West. Education was seen as the main weapon in this attempt, and the ideas of the business class were purveyed via two main channels. First, businessmen largely controlled the educational publishing houses, and as Cochran and Miller (1961) note, 'Standard textbooks, written to a large extent by people associated with city schools and distributed by publishing houses in New York, Boston and Philadelphia were bound to convey urban mores and business ideas, and it early became a matter of policy for educational agencies to see that contrary ideas were shut out'. [57] Secondly, as Baron and Tropp (1961) have pointed out, in America the local community is crucially important in determining what is taught in the schoolroom. Now it has already been shown that the local community in America is more likely to be dominated by business interests and so business was able to exercise considerable control over education by being the dominant force on the lay boards of control. [58] It was not just at the ideological level that business interests wished to win the battle of course, they had a more direct interest. Thus in the late nineteenth century business led the drive for the training of skilled artisans and mechanics in the public schools and at the public's expense. Their objective was education for industrial efficiency.

The same story can be repeated as far as the universities are concerned. In his classic study of university control, Beck (1947) clearly stated his findings. [59]

> Altogether, the evidence of major university-business connections at high levels seems overwhelming. The numerous high positions of power in industry, commerce and finance held by at least two-thirds of the members of the governing boards of those thirty leading universities would appear to give a decisive majority more than ample grounds for identifying their personal interests with those of business.

Businessmen themselves are quite unequivocal about the relationship. Domhoff (1967) quotes the chairman of the board of the University of Rochester, who is also president of Xerox, on the reason for heavy business involvement in university affairs: 'To put it as crassly as possible, it's a matter of sheer self-interest—dollars and cents. Xerox will live or die by technology'. [60]

In view of the stress on practical subjects in American education, and of the strong influence of business interests in the control of education, it should not be surprising to find that America has a very well-developed system of business and management education. America possesses a well-developed system in support of business at all levels. At the level of the manual worker, it must be remembered that America did not have the tradition of apprenticeship that existed in England. Indeed many of the immigrants into the United States, especially those from southern Europe, did not even possess an industrial background. This, of course, is the correct context in which to understand F.W. Taylor's revolutionary ideas on scientific management—it was an efficient solution to the problem of the ill-educated immigrant. Today there are special training schools for workers relating to particular types of industry and these stand in marked contrast to the almost pre-industrial system of apprenticeship that operates in Britain.[61] At another level there are business colleges (what in England would be called commercial colleges) that have been developed from the trade schools of the nineteenth century. In these schools secretarial and accounting skills are taught. There are also junior colleges offering non-degree courses of up to two years' duration and leading to supervisory and junior management positions. The most common educational root for someone aiming at a management career, however, is through the university system.

Vocational or 'professional' education has always occupied an important place in the American university system compared with the British. Undergraduate teaching of business was present even by 1900, although it was a relatively small proportion of all undergraduate teaching.[62] By 1971 however, approximately one in seven of all bachelors' degrees were in business, and this figure rises to one in five if one takes the figure for men only. Only social science and education can produce bigger figures.[63] Even these figures are probably underestimates because of the vast amount of 'business' that is taught in the context of other degrees, especially engineering. Graduate programmes in business can also be traced back a long way, in fact almost as far as the founding of the first business school itself, the Wharton School of Finance and Commerce, in 1881. Although at one time the proportion of masters' degrees to bachelors' degrees was relatively low, by 1971 only masters' degrees in education were more numerous.

The English educational system represents an altogether different tradition. These differences are particularly marked when one examines the stated goals of the system, access to education, and the content of education. One of the most important points to grasp about education in England in the nineteenth century is that it is very difficult to talk of a national system of education for the whole of the population. It was inconceivable in such a hierarchical society that the different social classes should receive a similar form of education when they had such different stations in life. Education very largely followed status distinctions rather than being a determinant of them.

For the mass of the working class there was no effective elementary education before 1870. Up to this date elementary education, apart from the Dame schools, was dominated by the charity schools organised chiefly by the church. This educational provision was largely controlled by the aristocracy, whose main motive it would appear, was to encourage the deference and passivity of the masses to the accepted orders of society. The rising bourgeoisie appeared to concur with this purpose because it very largely suited their own goals. The maxim that 'the Devil finds employment for idle hands', was one on which both landowner and entrepreneur could easily agree. [64] Neither group doubted the view that the children of the labouring classes would themselves become manual workers and that they should receive an education appropriate to their station in life.

The education of the working classes outlined above, which one might parody as 'teaching children to read the Bible and be industrious', would not on the face of it appear to be sufficient to fire the increasing complexity of the industrial revolution. Why did the rising power of the men of industry not press for a more technical and vocational education? The main reason is that, by and large, the owners of industrial capital were simply not persuaded of the importance of education in the profitability of their own companies or of the nation at large. [65] The reasons why they held this view can be at least partly found in the origins of these 'men of capital'. They were essentially 'practical tinkerers' to use David Landes celebrated phrase. Their own businesses had been successfully built up, not by the systematic application of scientific techniques, but by the age-old techniques of 'rule of thumb'. These men were in no position to appreciate the possibilities of a scientific or technical education. Few of them probably appreciated what was really happening in the industrial revolution that they had created. Coleman (1973) suggests that, 'the majority probably saw innovation as a once-and-for-all event rather than the beginning of an era in which invention and innovation were to be built into the whole process of business life.' [66] Not only were industrialists not really in a position to appreciate the potential contribution of scientific and technical education but they rarely saw the need for it. They had been successful without it. As Aldcroft (1964) puts it: 'Fifty years of industrial pre-eminence had bred contempt for change and had established industrial traditions in which the basic ingredients of economic progress, science and research, were notably absent. And the longer this change was delayed the more difficult it became for manufacturers to sanction and their workers to accept a break with established tradition'. [67] Another reason for the apathy and even active hostility to the technical education of workers in industry can be related to the class system. Simply put, some manufacturers believed that technical education for their workers might give them ideas above their station. [68] Finally, one might note the fact that British manufacturers were, and arguably still are, very secretive. This is partly a reflection of general cultural traditions in British society and partly a reflection of the dominance of the family firm in the British economy, at least in the nineteenth century. The connection between this and technical education is reported in evidence given to the Royal Commission on Technical Instruction in 1884. The employers argued 'that they were not going to encourage something which would bring all the workmen from the different works together to discuss matters in which *trade secrets* were involved' (this author's emphasis). [69]

The education of the children of the aristocracy and the rising middle class was naturally rather different from that of the working classes. The key institution was the public school which although initially only for the well connected gradually admitted members of the rising middle class. Yet even the public schools did not totally escape the influence of the world of business; their inefficiency and exclusionist entrance policies led the middle class to set up rival institutions (by 1864 Perkin (1969) estimates that there were probably 10,000 private schools in existence). The aristocracy met this challenge as they met most challenges in the nineteenth century, by accommodating it. Arnold and his followers rejuvenated the public schools and embraced some of the features of these new 'joint-stock schools', in particular the principle of academic competition, itself a reflection of bourgeois ideals. Yet the public schools retained much of their aristocratic tradition, they still excluded many 'sons of tradesmen', and they refused to abandon classics as the foundation of their curricula and substitute science and modern studies.

Businessmen were happy to send their sons to these schools, if they could because this was their route to real social respectability. These schools acted like a club, to use Turner's metaphor, which conferred status and prestige upon its members. The education these schools offered was primarily fitted to the traditional faculties of Oxford and Cambridge, the Church, the Army and the higher professions. Some certainly went into business, particularly some of the grand companies that were engaged in business in the colonies, [70] and indeed Reader (1966) has shown that by about 1900 considerable numbers of public school boys were entering business. Yet perhaps, above all, the public schools were a route *out* of business for the sons of successful businessmen.

The universities followed a similar path to the public schools. At the beginning of the nineteenth century, the two English universities at Oxford and Cambridge were small, expensive, closed to Dissenters for all practical purposes, and very largely the preserve of the aristocracy. The curriculum was antiquated in the extreme, being largely dominated by the constituent parts of a classical education (in 1834 even a proposal to teach mathematics was turned down). A little pure science was taught, but no applied science, and certainly no commercial subjects. Reform in the universities came at about the same time as it did in the public schools: Dissenters were admitted, modern subjects including science were encouraged, and examinations and open scholarships given a new emphasis. Yet the universities were still chiefly intended for the landed classes and the older professions. The shock of the 1867 Paris Exhibition, which once more demonstrated that England was falling behind in the application of science and technology to manufacturing industry, led to renewed pressure for the establishment of institutions to teach science and technology at a high level. The outcome was[the creation between 1871 and 1881 of seven new colleges, ultimately to become universities, in which science, technology, and in most of them economics and commerce came to be taught in the same institution as the traditional arts subjects. Several of these colleges owed their foundation to the energy and munificence of provincial businessmen.

This account of certain aspects of the English education system in the nineteenth century does not denote a very strong adherence to the values of achievement when compared to America. Yet in a way the system fitted in with the perceived needs of the business community. British industry seemed to value loyalty and certain ascribed qualities rather than more universalistic achieved qualities. Many writers, for example, have mentioned the British business tradition of vertical mobility—promotion to various supervisory and managerial levels of those who have begun on the shop floor. Such individuals are thus free of other loyalties and can learn the particular ways of the firm. Public schools contributed to this selection process, because the school background hopefully guaranteed the presence of certain sorts of qualities, among them loyalty, which made early selection safer. At the other end of the scale, the apprenticeship system performed a similar function, via the personal tutelage of an old established company employee.

This disdain for the needs of the world of work displayed by the British system of education did not go completely unchallenged even in the nineteenth century. Indeed as soon as the British economy came under serious challenge from other industrial nations, from about the middle of the century, then it is possible to identify groups of people who did argue the strong connection between scientific and technical instruction on the one hand, and industrial prosperity on the other. As the jolts to British industrial complacency grew increasingly severe (the depression of 1870, the war of 1914—1919 significantly called the engineer's war, the depressions of 1924—5, 1930—32 and the war of 1939—45) so the numbers of government reports and commissions pointing out the need for more and better scientific and technical education grew. Yet the British tradition of the autonomy of the universities allowed these institutions to resist many of these pressures. The universities which themselves largely controlled the public examination system and thus the curriculum of schools and colleges, were largely controlled by men who believed in the supremacy of the classics and natural science as the most appropriate training for the able minds of the young. Certainly subjects like engineering were eventually admitted to the universities, even into Oxbridge, but this did not change the value system of the society at large, which still tended to devalue subjects connected with the world of trade and industry. [71]

It is perhaps in the area of business and management education however, that one finds the greatest differences between England and the United States. The English universities have always been exceptionally wary of entering a field so very close to the world of trade and industry, and the progress of business-related courses has been very slow and sporadic. The universities situated in the heart of industrial England, and therefore subject to more business pressure and patronage, admitted some form of degree level teaching at an early period. [72] By the beginning of the Second World War however, one could still only find a handful of courses in business/management studies in the university sector.

After the war interest in management education increased and Rose (1970) charts a number of reasons for this. First, there were changes within the structure of British business which led to a more favourable view being taken of management education. For example, the increasing scale of business operations and the concomitant decreasing importance of family businesses paved the way for more 'professional' managers. Further, within the business world the promotion of men with a certain amount of professional training gained by study, like accountants, chemists etc., meant that those in positions of executive power were more likely to appreciate the benefits of managerial education. Thirdly, the post-war emphasis upon productivity, and the increasing use of international comparisons of economic performance, particularly with the United States, pointed out Britain's relatively poor performance and also noted her lack of investment in management education. The interest in education as a form of human capital investment was further heightened by the passing of the 1944 Education Act. Finally, Rose (1970) notes the effect that returning ex-servicemen more interested in business than many 'ordinary' undergraduates, had on the universities themselves.

Despite this greater interest in business/management education, the amount of educational provision in the area did not greatly increase. The universities were still somewhat reluctant to teach subjects which they did not regard as being wholly academically respectable, [73] whilst on the other side, business was not wholly convinced that any form of training that was not firmly industry-based could be of any value. As a consequence of these barriers very little headway was made in the universities by the beginning of the 1960s, and there were no under-graduate degree courses at all. The private sector had made some provisions with the creation of a number of independent management centres, notably the Administrative Staff College at Henley, which together with management consultants (mainly American), provided courses for various levels of existing managers. The most significant feature of the whole system of management education however, was that the main support for such education came from the lowest status colleges in the tertiary sector, the technical colleges. It was in these colleges, for example, that the National Scheme for Management Studies was launched in 1947, following the publication of the Urwick Report. When the scheme was rejuvenated in 1964, and the old National Diploma replaced by the Diploma in Management Studies, it still remained in the technical colleges.

Since 1960 the only major change in the field of management educa-tion that has occurred in England, the establishment of two postgraduate business schools, has been the result of American influence. In 1963, the National Economic Development Council, in its report on economic growth in Britain, called for a growth in management education and this initiated a discussion about the need for a 'British Harvard'. A subsequent enquiry culminated in the 'Franks Report' (1963), which recommended the setting up of two British business schools attached to the universities of Manchester and London. A third has subsequently been added in Scotland.

One can also detect a slight shift in the attitude of companies in favour of more business and management education. Partly this has been spurred on by the increasing indictment of the English education system as one of the causes of slow growth.[74] Perhaps the most important influence however, has been the rapid extension of certain logical and mathematical techniques for planning and controlling business enterprise. Linear programming, operational research etc., are not things, management has realised, that can be learned very efficiently from the 'school of life' or even by 'sitting next to Nellie'— apart from anything else they require a firm foundation in basic mathematics. The extension of these techniques has given an indisputable role to formal education institutes in business and management training in England.[75]

The development of the system of management education in America has been increasingly the subject of attention by those students of the British economy who believe that such a system contributes to economic growth. The majority of the commentators are also aware, however, of the old adage that educational systems are not easy to export. The vast development of business-related education in America reflects the American value system. It is fair to say that the same caution has not been exercised by all those who have surveyed the American industrial relations system from across the Atlantic. Just as the American education system has been regarded as more 'efficient' from the point of view of the needs of business, so too has the American industrial relations system been similarly regarded. [76] Yet just as the education system in America reflects certain central features of American society, so too does the American industrial relations system.

The nature of the stratification system is perhaps one of the most crucial variables affecting both the amount and the type of trade union activity. In the United States, before the turn of the twentieth century, the conditions were not those which have generally fostered the development of labour movements. First, the relative shortage of labour meant that employees were, by market forces, in a relatively good bargaining position. If a man did find it difficult to get a job he could always move west, where labour was scarcer. Of even greater importance was the strength of the value system which stressed the possibilities of advancement for every man. Failure was to be countered not by stressing the *collective* situation of all labourers in a similar position, but by the pursuit of an *individualistic* orientation, which urged the individual to drive himself forward above his fellows. Thirdly, it should be remembered that the mass of the proletariat in the United States were first generation immigrants, from a variety of backgrounds, speaking a variety of tongues. This fact, coupled with the agrarian background of many of them, made this heterogeneous group notoriously difficult to organise. One can also ask the question, to organise for what ends? Many of the wider social goals that were important objectives for the British labour movement in the nineteenth century, like the franchise and the extension of education, had already been won by Americans without organising, and it has been argued that, in terms of symbolic status, the American worker did not in general believe that he was in any way inferior to the owners of capital. [77] To these 'internal' hindrances to unionisation one can add two powerful 'external' ones. First, at the turn of the century business was all powerful in America, and business was intolerant of any interference by trade unions in the conduct of its affairs. Unions and union men were opposed in every conceivable manner, and often with a considerable degree of violence. [78] Business was aided in these shady endeavours by the government, which it completely dominated. Thus the Federal Anti-Trust legislation of 1890 and 1914 was more frequently and effectively invoked against trade unions than it was against the trusts.

In England during the same period, a rather different set of social conditions prevailed. In a society where class lines were more clearly drawn, and the hierarchical ordering of society gave the great mass of workers a clear feeling of their status in society, then a collective orientation, which fostered an 'us and them' view was always likely to provide a fertile soil on which trade unionism could grow. Although there is some debate about the influence of the feudal guilds upon British trade unionism, what does seem reasonably clear is that in every Western European country the tradition of collective grouping and collective action in social and economic life was thoroughly implanted and part of the old feudal and guild influences. In this sense, trade unionism was a more 'natural' development and more 'naturally' accepted by the workers and, ultimately, by employers, than was to be the case in the United States. The result of these structural differences are vividly shown in the density of trade union membership in the two societies, which has persisted to the present day.[79]

Not only does the density of trade unionism differ between Britain and America, but so also does its character. It has been traditional to focus upon the relative politicisation of the British labour movement compared with its American counterpart, and to stress this as a fundamental difference.[80] In the case of America, the arguments of the Wisconsin school of labour historians, most notably Commons and Perlman, have stressed the fact that American unions have largely rejected the wider concerns of socialism, for the more limited objectives of the economic improvement of union members. Thus, this view stresses the idea that American unions are essentially 'business unions', concerned not so much with the social status of the worker as with his job and the terms under which it is held; the capitalism of the proletariat, no more, no less. With a labour force substantially committed to the capitalist system, and a constitution ostensibly pledged to, 'health, happiness and the pursuit of liberty', the lack of political commitment on the part of American labour should not appear surprising.

One must be careful not to stress the differences between Britain and America too much in this area. Historically there have been times when socialist groups have been very powerful in the American labour movement;[81] equally there have been periods in Britain when British unionism looked like going the way of American business unions. Even today a commentator like Banks (1974) is prepared to argue that the difference between what he calls welfare unionism in Britain and business unionism in America are not that marked. Banks' observations are important because too many writers have attempted to draw too sharp a distinction between trade union organisation in Britain and America. It is doubtful at the political level whether the distinction has even been that great. Hardman (1964), for example, claims that the old AFL injunction, 'no politics in the union' was one which no one in the

AFL, beginning with Samuel Gompers himself, ever took seriously, except as a means to oppose the brand of politics they did not choose to play.[82] Yet when one comes to the actual operation of the unions in the setting of the industrial relations system, some fundamental differences do remain, which reflect differences in socio-cultural structure between the two societies. The biggest difference between America and Britain in industrial relations probably lies in the area of collective bargaining. First, one should observe the fact that in America collective bargaining takes place within a well defined legal framework, whilst in Britain, although there is some legal regulation, custom and practice tend to prevail. The prevalence of legal regulation in trade union affairs and collective bargaining merely reflects a more general recourse to legal provision in American society. It can be argued, following Lipset (1963), that this is because in British society the importance of membership of certain groups (collective orientation), where behaviour is controlled by unwritten codes of conduct, is of crucial significance. In the United States on the other hand, the stress upon individualism (self-orientation) that has already been discussed, can only be held in check by external, *legal* means. One can also add that in the case of labour relations the fact that many union leaders did not feel any *fundamental* difference of interest between themselves and the owners of capital, permitted the transformation of 'political' issues into legal ones. This is not the only reason for the difference between America and Britain in this area. One should also note the fact that British trade unions have managed to accomplish more for their members by putting pressure upon government to enact universal legal measures for the benefit of employees. In America the relative failure of unions on this front has meant that they have concentrated their efforts on improving the position of union members at the level of the individual employer.[83] Employers have therefore concluded much broader agreements with unions in America, and having reached agreement on complex packages have been happy to see that agreement given the status of legal provision. Such agreements fit more easily into the *laissez-faire* ideology of employers and also contribute in general terms to America's system of welfare capitalism, which arguably brings certain benefits to employers as well as employees.[84] Again however, one must be careful in not giving too much prominence to purely cultural explanations. Trade unions became an established part of the American industrial structure only in the 1930s, by which time the dominant feature of the American economy was the corporation. Now corporate bureaucracy is largely forced to utilise universalistic rationalistic methods (*pace* Weber) which give a degree of certainty to planning. The legal regulation of collective bargaining then fits in neatly with the needs of the corporation; it also happens to fit well with the cultural structure of American society. In other words, at least as important as any cultural variables in explaining legal regulation is the so-called 'late development effect'.

The more heterogeneous nature of American society which, via the stress on individualism, led to a value structure which stressed self-orientation is an important strand in the explanation of the greater prominence of the law in American society. This pursuit of self-interest has also led to a greater degree of violence in American industrial life, because action has not been held in place by an ingrained normative system. Employees have insisted on their rights to maximise their income, having greater regard for the ends rather than the means. [85] On the other side, employers have been equally strident in insisting on the 'right of a man to run his own business as he thinks fit'. In Britain, on the other hand, where norms derived from a pre-industrial and even pre-capitalist social system still retain a certain force, and where they have often been partly accepted by the new ruling class, the bourgeoisie, industrial relations, although not quiet, have not been marked by the violence of America.

Finally one should note the differences in the bargaining strategy of American unions compared with their British counterparts. In America bargaining tends to be rather more localised than in Britain, reflecting the greater geographical diversity in the United States as well as the presence of larger key companies in the mass production industries. This partly explains the American union strategy of attacking the most efficient and most profitable firm in the industry or locality, and then attempting to 'spread' the bargain. One should also note however, the consequences of this strategy: because the leading bargain is set at the level of the most efficient, this puts considerable pressure upon the marginal firm. The result is that although it will probably guarantee higher wages for the employees of the efficient firm, it could cause the employees of the least efficient to lose their jobs. In Britain, on the other hand, negotiation at the level of the industry represents protection for the marginal firm, perhaps reflecting the British trade unions' preference for maintaining work for all its members rather than attempting to maximise wages for some. [86] The less aggressive British bargaining undoubtedly has other causes, of which two are probably worth mentioning. First, the combination of a greater stress upon applied science and an ability to accept change more readily, has meant that pushing up the price of labour in America has very often been met by the substitution of labour with capital. Secondly, and arguably of greater importance, America is a much more self-sufficient country than Britain, and this has meant that the price of her *exports* has not been so crucial. In Britain, trade unions have almost grown up with a balance of payments problem accompanied by the motto of 'export or die'. This has acted as a moderating influence on bargaining strategy.[87]

The bargaining strategy of American trade unions has resulted in other differences between Britain and America, of which the most notable is the fact that wage differentials between skilled and unskilled workers are larger in America than in Britain. This result reflects in part the more narrowly self-interested orientation of American unions, which allows the more powerful groups of workers to maintain, or occasionally even improve, a relatively privileged position at the expense of the less powerful. Sturmthal (1957) argues that this difference relates to the historical origins of the two societies: 'The absence of feudal concepts of the place in society to which a worker may properly aspire may have played a part in allowing the larger wage differentials to arise in the United States, just as the heritage of the feudal concepts, may have helped maintain the highly compressed wage structure in Europe'. [88] Again one needs to stress a note of caution in not over-emphasising the differences between the two societies. Even in Britain, 'to each according to his deeds' is a more accurate rendering of the trade union slogan than 'to each according to his needs'. Recent government pay policies in Britain have only tended to underline how important differentials are to ordinary trade union members. Despite this reservation however, clear differences do remain between Britain and America in the structure of wage differentials. Indeed, one can even see such differences if one examines the remuneration of trade union officials within the respective unions of the two countries. Lipset (1963) notes that American labour unions offer financial rewards to their officials comparable to those of industrial executives, whilst in Britain the salaries of such officers are little higher than those of the workers they represent. The explanation of this difference follows the arguments above. As business unions, American unions bargain in the market place along with industrial companies for the most talented negotiators. In Britain, 'loyalty to the cause' is at least as important as any other qualification, and fear of embourgeoisement helps keep salaries down. In line with this argument, Lipset also observes that American unions have approximately seven times as many officials as the British. This cannot be explained by differences in their wealth, because something similar was noted when American unions were small and impoverished. British trade unions rely very heavily for support upon voluntary service and this can certainly be connected with the historical background of British society. As Lipset (1963) observes: 'The conception that public and social service is performed best when a leader is not paid, or is paid an honorarium, is basically an aristocratic value linked to the concept of *noblesse oblige*'.[89]

Before turning to a consideration of business administration, there are some significant differences to be noted between Britain and America in the field of public administration. In a sense there was no civil service in Britain until after the middle of the nineteenth century. There were lots of public officials, but there was no common system of recruitment or control, and it is doubtful whether the officials would have regarded themselves as belonging to a common service. In the early part of the century the aristocratic system of patronage permeated the whole system from top to bottom, even clerkships went to 'the sons of people of rank and influence, brought up in idleness'.[90]

This aristocratic system was gradually changed in the twenty years or so before the famous Northcote-Trevelyan report of 1854. The change resulted in a switch from the values of affectivity, particularism, ascription and diffuseness at least in the mode of operation of the service. The system of patronage was largely replaced by selection on merit; probationary appointments; promotion chiefly by merit, and different classes of officers inside the service performing different levels of work. The basic cause of this change was the demands made upon the state by the system of industrial capitalism. Of course these structural demands did not automatically 'cause' such a system to come about, they merely set up certain pressures for such a system, the pressures emanating from the drive towards efficiency that is present in most forms of industrial capitalism. It was these structural conditions that provided the incentive for the evolution of the principles and procedures of the service that Northcote and Trevelyan were to generalise and apply to the service as a whole. The implementation of the ensuing report was greatly aided by a timely crisis—the administrative mismanagement of the Crimean War that was revealed to the public gaze by *The Times'* correspondent, W.H. Russell.

The Northcote-Trevelyan reforms clearly changed the British Civil Service in the direction of that side of the pattern variables that have been designated as capitalist; yet as with so many British institutions the transformation was by no means total. To take but one area as an example, that of the selection process, although selection by merit replaced patronage, in so many ways it was an odd sort of merit. The essential features of the selection philosophy, which still largely hold today such is the power of institutional inertia, were clearly stated in the words of the Report on the Indian Civil Service: [91]

> We believe that men who have been engaged up to twenty-one or twenty-two in studies which have no immediate connection with the business of any profession, and of which the effect is merely to open, to invigorate, and to enrich the mind, will generally be found, in the business of every profession, superior to men who have, at eighteen or nineteen, devoted themselves to the special studies of their calling.

In India the tasks for which the civil servants were responsible were almost infinitely various, but it would be difficult to argue that the same is true in Britain today. The system still reflects some of the dominant themes in the English educational system, as outlined above, in particular the stress upon general rather than specialist, technical education.

Just as the modern British Civil Service may be dated from the Northcote-Trevelyan reforms of 1854, so the modern American system can be dated from the passing of the Pendleton Act in 1883. This Act, like its British equivalent, instituted the open competition system of selection in place of a system of patronage called the 'spoils system'. This system had rather different roots from the English system of patronage. The patronage was essentially political patronage, and its rationale was that important federal positions should not be left in the hands of career bureaucrats who had little if any connection with the popular democratic will. This and the device of rotation of office, reflected the deep-seated fear of strong central government. The basic cause of the change in the system was very similar to the situation in Britain. The dominance of the idea of free trade and perfect competition intruded as far as the system of public administration and led to a system of open competition on the basis of merit. The precipitating cause of the new system was also inspired by an incident, the murder of President Garfield by a disappointed office seeker, which had a similar effect upon America as the debacle of the Crimean War had on Britain.

Although the structure of the American Civil Service resulted from a similar economic infrastructure to that of Britain, there were, and are, a number of important differences. First, the system of political appointments to the Civil Service still remains, reflecting the American fear of a closed bureaucracy and the desire to maintain the democratic tradition in the service.[92] Secondly, emanating from the same cultural tradition, the American system of public administration is by no means such a closed bureaucracy as it is in Britain. Entry to the service is not only or even largely at the bottom, with the career stretching on and upwards for the lifetime of the appointee. There is a great deal of movement in and out of the service; in some post-Second World War years as many as 400,000 civil servants per annum have been moving in or out.[93] Thirdly, the educational requirements for potential entrants are rather different from those required in Britain. When Congress passed the Pendleton Act it added an instruction that the entrance examination should be practical in nature and related to the duties to be performed. One can see how the major features of the curriculum in American schools and colleges are reflected in this policy statement. In short, the American Civil Service is composed of technically qualified men and women recruited to perform particular tasks and assignments. [94]

In the previous sections of this chapter differences have been observed in the superstructures of Britain and America and it has been shown how these differences can be expressed in terms of the pattern variables. The explicit assumption in the analysis has been that superstructural relations, whether dependent or independent of the economic base, influence the operation of business enterprise. It is now necessary to focus attention more closely upon the historical development of the business enterprise itself in England and America, because differences that had emerged by 1900 are still important today.

By 1860 the industrial structure of both societies consisted largely of Marshallian type single-function firms, with a greater preponderance of family firms in British society than in America, but the difference was probably not marked. From this point on however, the two countries began to diverge, so that by the beginning of the First World War there was a significant difference in the two structures. Even before 1860 there were embryo differences between the two societies in terms of business structure. The most important of these was the greater preponderance of the business corporation, perhaps the dominating feature of modern industrial capitalism in America. The corporation was a device that certainly fitted the American situation in the nineteenth century. The business tasks, particularly in transportation, were large and the American people relatively poor, and the corporation helped solve these twin problems by gathering moderate sums from many investors. One can also see how the growth of freely marketable ownership shares in these corporations suited the needs of a migratory society, which needed some liquidity in its investment. In later years, many American corporations attempted to sell their shares to as wide a public as possible, not so much to raise capital, but to create a symbolic link between the private enterprise system in general and their company in particular and the public. [95] Certainly securing a charter for the corporation was an easier business in America than in Britain, in that it was easier to lobby a charter through a state legislature than through the British Parliament.

The significance of the corporation in the American economy at the dawn of the century cannot be overestimated. Its mode of arrival was perhaps as significant as its mode of operation. Many of the corporations were created in the 1880s and 1890s by mergers, which were often promoted by Eastern financiers eager to seize the opportunities offered by the creation of a truly national market by the railways. The significance of this is that the merger promotors often tended to replace the existing high level managerial personnel, many of them relatives of the founder, with managers chosen solely on the basis of their abilities to bring a quick return on the investment. Payne (1967) argues that the drag exerted by family influence and managerial 'deadwood' was probably not so great in America to start with compared with Britain. First, he notes that the merger movement came after a period of exceptionally fierce competition when many of the less efficient firms would have been driven out of business anyway. He adds, secondly, that the relative youth of many American companies at this time meant that familial control had not yet become so deeply embedded in their organisational structures.

The size and geographical spread of these corporations was considerable by British standards,[96] and they provided a real challenge to those men put in charge of administering them. The challenge was first met by the railways and public utilities, the first really large corporations, and in the case of the former the first organisations that really stretched right the way across the United States. These enormous problems forced these organisations to develop forms of control that did not need the constant attention of the top men, in short the problems fostered the development of bureaucracy and the discipline of management. It was in this situation, for example, that the American corporation began to develop accounting as a control over efficiency, rather than as a mere device for balancing the books that was to remain its lot in England for many decades.[97] These new managerial ideas and concepts were initially transmitted inside the corporations themselves via management meetings and occasionally by the odd article published in magazines like the *American Railroad Journal.* The greater openness of American society and American business helped the dissemination of such ideas in a way that British society and business never could. Later, American business schools were to promulgate further the ideas and discoveries of the American corporation within formal taught courses on management. Not only did the American corporations develop an arguably more efficient system of management but, because of the widespread acceptance of the democratic principle that one man was as good as another, capable persons were prepared initially to accept a fairly lowly status in the organisation, because they were aware that the possibility existed of their rising to the executive suite. The corporation, once it had set the pattern for management and organisational structure, continued to lead it as Chandler (1962) has shown in his seminal work on American industrial enterprises.[98] In this sense the corporation has remained almost as important as the university in disseminating management ideas in the United States. Abroad, particularly perhaps in England, American companies have often performed the function of business schools in propagating new ideas.

The American corporation also reaped all the benefits of its relatively large size. Not only did its large size necessarily promote the development of management techniques as argued above, but it was sufficiently big to train and send out overseas travellers to develop the company's export market. As early as 1900 Europeans were beginning to talk about the 'American invasion'.[99] Of greatest significance however, is the fact that large firms are in a much better position to fund and organise research and development of their products. Already ahead in techniques, methods of production and the creation of new products, American firms in their corporate form took an even greater lead. It was certainly the American corporation, for example, that realised that consumer goods go through a life-cycle, growing rapidly when they are first introduced and more slowly later, according to Engel's Law.[100] To meet the challenge of the constantly changing market demanding new products, the American corporation evolved the multidivisional structure. The new form was originated by General Motors and Du Pont shortly after the First World War, and followed by a few others during the 1920s and 1930s. It was widely adopted in the boom following the Second World War.

Not only were there important structural differences between business in Britain and America by the turn of the century, but there were also important differences in what can be termed the style of business. As Merton (1938) has argued, the structure of American society is such that there exists a greater accent in certain sectors on the goal of success than on the means of attaining it. Certainly this observation fits the American businessman at the turn of the century, the so-called age of the robber barons. None of these men had any notable scruples, nor, as Hobsbawm (1975) observes, could afford to have in an economy and an age where fraud, bribery, slander and if necessary guns were normal aspects of competition. Beard (1963) has argued that the lack of any form of moral propriety in business dealings can be traced back to the time of the British. Before the revolution the Americans were largely barred from legitimate enterprise and were thus 'forced into speculative channels, compelled to engage in such risky, not to say violent, trades as that in fur and rum.....retarded in development in the early period, kept back to a more primitive stage of methods, the American business-man began as a gambler in commodities, instead of a producer of goods tamed to toil.'[101] There is doubtless a good deal of merit in this account, in particular it attempts to stress another distinguishing fact of American business, that is that most of its successful practitioners, unlike so many of the great entrepreneurs of the Old World, who often seemed enamoured with their products and obsessed with technological construction as such, seemed uncommitted to any special way of making money.[102] Horatio Alger had urged them to 'get ahead' and that is just what they were doing. The American public appeared to accept them as well, in that the heroes of American business are not those who have behaved most graciously and scrupulously, but those who have shown initiative and struck out on new paths which have paid off. There was no 'moral' regulation of business behaviour, or any other behaviour come to that, in America in the same way that such normative regulation existed in English society at the same period. Fraud in England did not just bring legal penalties, but moral disapproval as well, whereas in America an admonition or at most an investigation was all that threatened the robber barons. Several features of this situation are claimed to have remained in the American business community which distinguish it from the British. Many commentators still claim that striving for monetary success and taking risks to attain it are more characteristic of American than British business behaviour (Granick (1962), Shonfield (1965)), whilst the accent on control by legal means remains the defining mark of American business practice against a greater reliance on informal moral control in Britain.[103]

In analysing both the structure and the style of business as it developed in England from around the turn of the century, one is struck by a series of marked contrasts. First, there were differences in the structure of firms. Despite the fact that Britain possessed a national market by the 1860s, owing to rapid urbanisation,[104] and the expansion of the transport system some decades earlier, company structure did not reflect this. Although there were no legal limitations to large public corporations after the 1860s, such firms were few and far between. The British industrial structure was still dominated by the relatively small private family firm. (In 1914 80 per cent of British companies were still private).[105] One of the reasons for this was that British firms were able to exploit the imperfections existing in the British market and still remain relatively small. After the 1860s the same firms could continue with their old practices by doing the same thing in Britain's overseas markets. Payne (1967) reports that:[106]

> By increasing specialisation designed to exploit
> marginal differences in quality, and by creating the
> impression that the differences were greater than they
> were in reality, many British firms were able to secure
> a degree of oligopoly power and to make sufficient
> profits to encourage them to resist the attractive
> offers of the promotors of combines later in the
> century.

Having performed successfully for a long period of time, and one might add, having been nourished in the belief of British industrial supremacy, the family firms were reluctant to change from their old and successful ways. They were especially reluctant to raise new capital through procedures that might have weakened their control over their own firms, and such was the magnitude of their accumulated sources of capital that the majority of firms were long able to keep pace with the demand for fixed capital investment without recourse to the domestic capital market.[107]

The small family firm in Britain suffered a number of increasing disadvantages in the increasingly competitive world market. First, such firms did not encourage the supply of outside talents into the business, and no family business could expect that after several generations it would still automatically be capable of producing from family talent a flow of competent managers. Secondly, the small firm will always find it difficult to compete on the basis of research and development. The fact of smallness only compounded the considerable disadvantages that Britain already had in this area. Thus Aldcroft (1964) reports that: 'Generally speaking, by 1914 there was hardly a basic industry in which we held technical superiority except perhaps pottery'.[108] Finally, it can be argued that the family firm structure is an inherently conservative one. The owners of such firms are usually anxious for a satisfactory living for the members of their family, and they are anxious to retain control. Stability and order are the hallmarks of such firms, rather than the more risky goals of innovation and profit maximisation.[109] This fact is probably of far greater importance than arguments about the structure of demand. Demand can be stimulated from the supply side, as it clearly was in the United States, by the initiative of manufacturers through the introduction of new products or by energetic selling methods.

It would be quite wrong to give the impression that there were no English giant companies by 1900, or that there had not been a series of mergers in the decade up to the turn of the century. Yet both the character of the merger movement and the resulting corporations were not generally characterised by the same features as their American equivalents. In Britain, numerous firms reluctantly coalesced under the spur of falling prices and profit margins; there was no Eastern financier to buy them all out as in America. One consequence of this was that the majority of the old personnel, often with family loyalties to the constituent parts of the new company, remained to jealously guard their old interests. Given this situation it is not surprising that many of these large British firms had severe organisational problems. The gentlemen at the top, still steeped in notions of patronage, ascription rather than achievement, were reluctant to promote outsiders on merit, or to develop a functional hierarchical mode of organisation that was altogether alien to the spirit of the gentlemen's club to which most belonged or aspired.

What new organisational ideas and product innovations that there were in individual firms made very slow progress inside the business community. The reason for this was the considerable stress upon secrecy that persisted in a relatively closed society like Britain compared with the more open nature of American society. This cultural pattern even impeded British firms from banding together for the foreign sales campaigns that many groups of American firms were conducting by the start of the First World War. The evidence for this particular feature of British business is widespread. Lewis and Stewart (1958), in their study of the British businessman, note that the 'business community, preserves the secrecy which so hampers the economist, the biographer, the historian, the novelist and the social research worker.....privacy is the key note of British business character; any invasion of it is intensely resented and instantly attacked as injurious to the national interest'.[110] This attitude was at least partly to blame for the failure of the development councils, set up in certain industries after the Second World War, to provide common services like research and export promotion, in an effort to help the average firm to a higher level of efficiency. The response from industry was almost uniformly negative, and two of the development councils were in fact boycotted from their inception. Even when management itself calls in assistance, as in the case of hiring management consultants, Farmer (1968) reports that they are often excluded from some managerial matters and are also often asked to concentrate on the factory floor rather than management. This accent upon secrecy by the business community should be understood as the manifestation of certain tendencies in British society as a whole. The classic analysis of this fundamental difference between Britain and America was made by Shils in 1956. Shils argues that the hierarchical nature of British society remains despite its democratic and pluralist political form, and that the populace are, in general, still deferential to the society's rulers. The ruling group in British society is, by and large, relied upon, even expected to conduct its own affairs away from the glare of publicity. Following Bagehot, he believes that this is what allows the English Constitution to work so well; the small group of rulers are trusted to act in the interests of the whole society. Shils argues that this leads to a situation where 'the British ruling class is unequalled in secretiveness and taciturnity. Perhaps no ruling class in the Western world, certainly no ruling class in any democratic society, is as close-mouthed as the British ruling class'.[111] The recent case of the Crossman diaries would appear to provide a good illustration of this argument.

In sharp contrast the United States has been committed to the principle of publicity since its origin. As already argued, the sweeping out of the British was also a symbolic sweeping out of the traditions of aristocracy, and with it the ethos of the small ruling class working on trust and in secret. The new America was decidely populist in tone and this helped lower the barriers to publicity on the government's side. Once this was institutionalised in the formative years of the Republic, by the usual process of institutional inertia it persisted, helped along by the gradual emergence of a special professional custodian in the institution of the mass media, which had vested interests in the 'open society'. This analysis of the relative closeness of the British business community compared with the American, is an additional factor which helps to explain the slow progress of business and management education in British society. Such education is unlikely to thrive in a situation where each firm regards itself as being unique with problems that are not shared with other firms. Similar arguments can be advanced about business attitudes towards science and scientific discoveries. The ethos of science is universalistic, it hardly thrives in a situation where the values of particularism are well to the fore as was clearly the case in British business around 1900.

The differences between the structure of business in America and Britain should be enough in themselves to indicate that American firms were probably more efficient and competitive than comparable British firms in 1900. Further evidence on the operation of business in Britain only serves to reinforce this conclusion. First, British firms tended to compete on the basis of product differentiation, claiming that their products were unique, rather than on the basis of price and delivery. Partly of course this reflected the structure of the market. The size of the American market was able to support a much greater number of large, efficient, competing producers. Yet this is not the whole story. America had, and arguably still has, a much greater symbolic commitment to competition than Britain. One can see an indication of this if, following Kaysen (1956) one examines anti-monopoly policy in the two societies. In America the anti-monopoly laws (the first of which was passed in 1890), whatever their actual effect, are an important symbolic statement of the commitment to competition. In Britain, on the other hand, the Monopolies and Restrictive Practices Commission was not created until 1948, and then its major terms of reference were not to do with the importance of competition per se, but were rather concerned with the notion of the 'public interest'. More recently, several observers have commented upon the style of business practice in Britain, which appears to lack the ruthlessness that is characteristic of America. Shonfield (1965) for example, writing about the Conservative Party's return to power in 1951 on a manifesto stressing the importance of private enterprise and competition, observes: 'The fact that the competition so carefully nurtured was often of a kind which involved only a handful of contenders, ending with a gentleman's agreement rather than a fight to the finish'.[112] In a business community long dominated by gentlemen, or at least by persons aspiring to be gentlemen, this should not be wholly surprising. For those that transgressed the informal rules of the game the penalties could be high.[113]

This historical analysis of the origins and development of British and American capitalism should be sufficient to indicate the importance of considering the socio-cultural environment within which the dominant mode of production operates. It has been shown that capitalism grew up in very different social structures in the two societies, and these two structures inevitably modified the working of economic forces. In Britain the long political dominance of the landed aristocracy, and the even longer dominance of the social values of the landed aristocracy, effected not only the political and social structure within which capitalistic business had to operate, but also the structure and operation of business itself. In America, on the other hand, the political and social structure was dominated almost from the beginning either by business or by values that were clearly in keeping with the demands of a capitalist economy. The differences between the two societies have been expressed by showing how different aspects of social structure could be symbolised as stressing certain values in the pattern variable structure rather than others. It has been argued that the variables of affective-neutrality, specificity, universalism, achievement and self-orientation, rather than their opposites, reflect the demands of a capitalist economy.

An important question for this work is to what extent the differences described between Britain and America have survived into the 1980s. Social structures rarely stand still and even the mode of production 'develops'. As previously noted, capitalism is by its very nature a constantly changing phenomenon. In the next chapter consideration will be given in detail to what extent it is still possible to detect differences between British and American companies operating in similar environments. It is necessary at this juncture however, to consider in very general terms the changes that have occurred in British and American societies. The values and ideals of the political elite are created by historical circumstances and the values and ideals may or may not be congruent with the 'needs' of the economy. There is no simple, mechanical relationship between the economy needs and the socio-political structure, indeed under certain circumstances there can exist considerable incongruence. British society is probably a particularly good example of this. In many ways the social structure and the cultural system were incongruent with the demands of the economy, although much in keeping with the ideals of the political elite. It was possible to maintain this incongruence because there was initially very little economic pressure to do otherwise. In other words, the economic advantages that Britain received as the first industrial nation protected her socio-political structure. It is true that by about 1900 Britain had lost most of her early advantage to some of the later industrialising nations, America included. Yet a certain amount of protection still remained. First, Britain was a great colonial power and she gained enormous economic advantages from cheap raw materials and a protected and guaranteed market for her finished manufactured products. Even when the economic system began to experience serious trouble it was by no means absolutely clear to the political and economic leaders that one of the troubles was an incongruent social structure. Businessmen, as already shown, are not always able to diagnose economic malaise with particular accuracy, especially when there are numerous potential candidates for the cause of the illness.[114]

Veblen was undoubtedly correct when he observed in 1915 that 'gentility' was economically costly for British society,[115] yet he also realised that British society up to that time could afford it for the reasons already outlined above. There is an important general point to make here. Just as micro-contingency theory at the level of the firm makes the erroneous assumption that the economic demands of the firm always push its structure and policies in a certain direction, ensuring that they are congruent with the economic demands of the company, so too-macro contingency theory, at the level of the society, is equally erroneous in making similar assumptions. It is only when the society experiences a profound crisis, particularly but not necessarily an economic one, that certain pressures are exerted upon the structure to bring it into line with economic objectives.[116] This is exactly parallel to the case of the firm; when it experiences an economic crisis a very hard look is taken at its management and its structure.

Arguably Britain has had some form of economic crisis since the turn of the century, but it is really only since the Second World War that it has become particularly acute, and a link made between her economic performance and her social structure.[117] This economic crisis also has strong ideological importance, because it has led some observers to call into question the system itself, or at the very least to compare the performance of the British capitalist system with the performance of other types of economic system. A good example of this is the 'Woodford' speech made by Churchill in 1955. Here he noted the performance of the Russian economy compared with the British and significantly noted the way in which the Russian education system had supposedly contributed to Russian economic performance. The editorial comment in the *Times Educational Supplement* made the issue clear: 'We are at war..... what started as a conflict of ideologies has now developed into an economic battle of the first magnitude'. The editorial went on to mention the reaction of the political leaders: 'Now that the full implications of these figures are properly understood, there is an anxiety approaching panic in high places'.[118] Interestingly enough this perceived crisis did result in a modification of the educational system in the direction of greater congruence between the system and the economy.[119] Since the 1960s, with Britain's comparative economic position worsening, her social structure has come under ever increasing scrutiny.[120] The British industrial relations system was researched by a Royal Commission and the findings published in 1969. The whole tenor of the report was that the system was outdated; it was formed during a different economic period and needed drastic modernising. Many of its recommendations bore the strong mark of the American industrial relations system, which was obviously thought to have greater relevance to modern capitalism. The British education system has also been increasingly indicted for its lack of economic relevance. Although the Robbins Report on higher education concluded that the supply of places should be based on the demand for places from potential entrants, rather than on the demand in the economy for the products of higher education, there have been subsequent indications that the government may well change its mind. In the school system the government has indicated that it is prepared to enter the 'secret garden of the curriculum' to ensure that greater stress is put on industrially relevant topics like numeracy and literacy as well as industry itself. The Civil Service has also received considerable government scrutiny, just as it did after the crisis of the Crimean War. In the Fulton Report (1968) the diagnosis was made that the Civil Service was not meeting the needs of a complex economy such as Britain. The committee detected the 'philosophy of the amateur' inside the service, which they saw as running counter the need for civil servants to be skilled managers.[121] Finally, one should note that the falling rate of profit of British companies combined with a high rate of inflation inside the economy has led to a severe liquidity crisis in British industry. The British banking system, never closely tied to industry anyway, was completely incapable of coping with this situation, and the only road from economic ruin was government salvation. The state therefore, via the National Enterprise Board and planning agreements, has begun to play an ever more crucial role in the economy, both in terms of managing the infrastructure and the superstructure.

It must be said that the economic crisis was not the only force making for a re-examination of British social structure in the 1960s. Britain's negotiations to enter the EEC must also be counted as an important incentive. As Shonfield (1965) notes: 'The effect of being required to state as precisely as possible the doctrine behind some British administrative practice in order to defend it against some alternative favoured by members of the European Common Market, was to prompt a wide-ranging review of the apparatus of British economic administration and law'.[122] Even here however, one can argue that the major impetus behind Britain's application to the EEC was an economic one—the economically successful market was seen by many as a potential solution to many of Britain's economic problems.

The superstructure of American society has historically been much

71

more congruent with the needs of the capitalist economy. Only in the area of the welfare state has there possibly been a significant gap between system needs and actual provision.[123] The 'fit' between the economy and such institutions as the education system, the industrial relations system etc., evolved in part as least because the structure of such systems reflected the values of the political elite. Similarly, the lack of a well-developed welfare state also reflected the values of such an elite. The performance of the American economy, although not particularly good by international comparison since the 1920s, has rarely reached the crisis situation that the British economy has found itself in since the 1950s. One consequence of this is that there has been no economic pressure to create a more extensive welfare state to counteract the strong ideological distaste for such a measure on behalf of many members of the political elite. The American capitalist system has, of course, had its crises. The worldwide depression of the 1930s was probably as catastrophic in America as in any country in the world. It did not however, with one major exception, lead to any great remodelling of the superstructural institutions in America, merely because they were all largely in keeping with the economic needs of the system. The major exception was the industrial relations system, which was substantially restructured following the passing of the Wagner Act 1935. The other significant result of the crisis was the attempt by the New Deal administration to foster a more active role in the economy for the state itself. The creation of the National Recovery Administration, whose job it was to compel industry to reorganise itself, fix prices, allocate quotas of production etc., met considerable opposition despite the economic crisis. Yet its creation shows how economic crises can compel the political elite to take decisions which cut right across important ideological considerations, providing of course that the decisions maintain the system itself in one form or another. Such corporatist policies did not last beyond the worst of the depression however, and in 1935 the NRA was wound up, after the Supreme Court had declared it unconstitutional. It could be that the strong belief in individualism in the United States, that supports some version of *laissez-faire* capitalism, may yet prove to be the biggest social hindrance to economic prosperity that the United States possesses. The ideology that was appropriate to the early days of capitalism is arguably an enormous hindrance to the very different sort of capitalism that has developed some two hundred years after the founding of the Republic.[124]

America has suffered some crises since the depression, but these have been of a relatively minor nature and certainly nothing severe enough to shake the system as such.[125] To return to the remark by Schumpeter which opened this chapter, one can only but agree with his observation that the 'coins of social structure' do not readily melt once they are formed.

and that the socio-economic conditions prevailing at the time of their formation leave their mark upon them. A severe economic crisis in capitalist society often presents the ruling elite with a choice, and if the crisis is long enough and severe enough the decision can easily be made to melt the coins of social structure and remould them. The remoulding is likely to be in the direction of a greater congruence between superstructure and infrastructure, but one should never commit the error of mistaking political choice for material necessity; the range of 'solutions' that are logically open to the elite are very large indeed, only history narrows the choice in practice.

There is one final historical legacy that has a bearing on the research findings which needs to be mentioned. Whatever the validity of this partial historical analysis conducted on Britain and America, one thing is certain. Businessmen in the two societies, like other men, have a conception of their own society's historical past and of the past of other societies. These national images are powerful spectacles through which present day reality is observed, constantly reinforced by the media. In particular one must mention that image of America and American firms that many British businessmen possess, as well as the image of Britain and British firms that many Americans possess. Although these images are interesting and important data in themselves, it is important not to confuse them with the real world which they purport to reflect.

Notes

1 Schumpeter, 1947, pp.12–13.

2 It would certainly be logically possible for a society to be perfectly attuned to the requirements of the economic system. It is merely suggested that there are no empirical cases of this occurring.

3 The fact that a society's socio-cultural structure is or is not in harmony with its economic mode of production need not be the result of conscious policy-making by the leaders of the society, nor need it reflect, in the short term at least, the strength of the economic demands. The polity may not understand the relationship between socio-cultural structure and economic performance, and even if they do, the society may be in a sufficiently powerful economic position to ignore such relationships, at least in the short run.

4 The concept of feudalism means something different depending on whether one is concentrating upon social, economic, legal or constitutional problems, and these different aspects change at different rates, cf. Cam (1940).

5 This is the traditional picture of feudalism, and it is almost certainly overdrawn. Hirshler (1954) has presented some interesting evidence to

suggest that there was a good deal of competitiveness in medieval economic life, and attributes the stress upon collectivistic social and economic institutions to the effects on scholars of nineteenth-century romanticism and the hardships caused by capitalist individualism.

6 Barrington Moore, 1973, p.30.

7 Perkin, 1969, p.45.

8 These goals were largely pursued by control over external trade which was effectively regulated by professional officials.

9 It is significant, as Perkin (1969) notes, that there is no English word for bourgeoisie, because it is difficult to find, at least until late into the nineteenth century, a permanent, self-conscious urban business class in opposition to the landed aristocracy.

10 Perkin, 1969, p.57.

11 Pitt, always lavish with his peerages, did not dare for a long time to bring the business community into the House of Lords. In 1797 however, he made Banker Smith the first exception. As Namier sourly observed in his *Structure of Politics:* Smith-Carrington was the first man actually engaged in trade whom George III, with much repugnance, was persuaded to make a British peer.

12 Barrington Moore, 1973, p.37.

13 Societies which join in the industrialisation process after its initial development naturally benefit from the great backlog of technological innovation which can be taken over wholesale from the initiating countries, usually without the retarding effects of institutions and customs which have grown up around them. For a further development of this point see Gershenkron, 1962, p.8. For an even earlier account see Veblen, 1915, p.86.

14 Miller, 1961, p.37.

15 For many of the European immigrants America was fabled for the promise of her riches. Seagull, a character in Marston's play, *Westward Ho,* showing in London in 1605, said of Virginia: I tell thee, gold is more plentiful there than copper is with us.....Why man, all their dripping pans and chamber pots are pure gold; and all the chains with which they chain up their streets are made of gold.....and for rubies and diamonds they goe forth on holy days and gather them up by the seashore. (Quoted in Cochran, 1968, p.9). Many took a more sanguine view of the situation on arrival, but in the end few would deny that the opportunities at least were greater in America, for men of their social position, than they were in European society. Tocqueville's observations over two centuries later illustrate the truth of this proposition.

16 The most celebrated exponent of this view is Turner (1920).

17 Schlesinger, 1970, p.109.

18 The amount of mobility is probably overstated in most accounts, at least in the latter half of the nineteenth century. It is probably not

true, for example, that the Western frontier acted as a 'safety valve' for the unemployed in the East. These people were not able to buy the waggons and the supplies to go West, and even after the railroad was completed it was still primarily the school teachers, marginally success-ful shopkeepers and farmers who could save enough to make the trip and start afresh.

19 Thistlethwaite, 1955, p.ll5.

20 The population of the United States in 1850 contained half a million more men than women, and the predominance of men was even more marked in the Western states which contained 529 men per 1,000 population compared with 504 for the Eastern seaboard (United States Bureau of the Census, 1969, p.93).

21 Bendix, 1964, p.ll8.

22 A very similar line of argument can be found in Checkland, 1975, p.177; Bendix, 1964, pp.118—9; Thistlethwaite, 1955, pp.127—30.

23 Shonfield, 1965, p.301.

24 Hartz, 1948, pp.290—1.

25 Shonfield, 1965, p.303.

26 Both these arguments are examined and rejected by Barrington Moore (1973). For a more modern analysis see Fogel and Engermann (1974).

27 Barrington Moore, 1973, p.152.

28 The only qualification one might want to offer to this statement is that in the late 1960s there were certain signs of discontent, particu-larly among the young. The phrase, 'The military-industrial complex', curiously enough first used by Eisenhower, took on a new meaning during the later stages of the Vietnam War for many young people. Anti-capitalist rhetoric began to grow in both quantity and quality and left its mark, albeit temporarily, on business recruitment. For an interesting collection of American anti-capitalist literature of this period, see Perrow (1972a), Quinney (1979).

29 The best analysis is to be found in Guttsman (1974).

30 Sutton et al., 1962, p.290.

31 There really is no British equivalent in power and prestige to the National Association of Manufacturers and the Chamber of Commerce with its more than 1,700 local units.

32 Miller, 1958, p.l3.

33 This is taken to be the view, in broad terms, of the functionalist theory of social stratification, see for example Davis and Moore (1945)

34 Assuming a roughly similar economic/industrial structure, and assuming that the value structure has been effectively institutionalised.

35 That is, seen from the standpoint of the participants.

36 Numerous studies still attest to the existence of these differences. For example, Alford's (1964) study of voting behaviour notes that

Britain has a much greater degree of class cleavage in voting compared with the United States. Studies also show that these differences affect the operation of business. Note for example the findings of Starbuck (1966), who in a study comparing British and American retail stores, found that the importance of specialised customer service in Britain leads to a greater number of salespeople being employed. In general terms it is perhaps interesting to note that the idea of the self-service store originated in America, where the ideas of personal service did not have such strong historical roots.

37 For a full development of these arguments, see Habakkuk (1967).

38 The explanation of this phenomenon should be clear from the previous analysis. In particular one should note that consciousness of class differences are minimised in America by the following:

(a)   the tendency not to give clear recognition to invidious distinctions;
(b)   the marked diffusion of equalitarian social manners through a wide range of occupations, income levels and positions of authority;
(c)   the wide accessability of such symbols of 'respectable' position, e.g. automobiles, clothing;
(d)   the relative ease of access to public education;
(e)   the persistent dissemination of the ideology of equal opportunity and the existence of a classless society.

39 Sutton et al., 1962, p.315.

40 In America, a well-educated member of the upper middle class will discuss politics or other such topics with a cab driver, a hairdresser, and others at that occupational level; but in Britain, a person from the upper middle class still finds it difficult to interact informally with people that far below him in the social scale. Lipset, 1963, p.319.

41 The problems that are likely to be encountered in those parts of American society where there exist more rigid hierarchical distinctions are well illustrated by Stouffer's (1949) classic study of American soldiers. This research showed that soldiers wanted privileges to be 'earned' rather than to be categorised, and that the rigidity of military deference requirements was probably a major cause of the resentment of enlisted personnel towards officers and towards the system of military rank.

42 By vertical mobility is meant the intergenerational movement from manual to non-manual occupations.

43 One point that must be emphasised about mobility in Britain in the nineteenth century is that it has to be compared to mobility in previous centuries. Perkin (1969), for example, notes that 'there is no doubt that there was a considerable amount of upward mobility in mid-Victorian England, *as in all periods of modern English history*' (p.424) (This author's emphasis.) This point must be borne in mind when considering the evidence from studies like those of Erickson (1959),

which suggests that there may well have been a contraction of opportunities for social climbing by the mid-Victorian age.

44 To enumerate merely the obvious there are the following:

(a) changes in the proportion of the population in each stratum;
(b) changes in the rank order of each stratum or substratum;
(c) changes in the birth rate within each stratum;
(d) changes in population growth.

45 Marsh, 1963, p.177.

46 Habakkuk, 1962, p.190.

47 'In the entire body of American fiction', he claimed, 'the business-man is almost always depicted as crass, philistine, corrupt, predatory, domineering, reactionary, and amoral', Chamberlain, 1948.

48 Wilson, 1965, p.195.

49 Lewis and Stewart, 1958, p.49.

50 'The third generation makes the gentleman', and 'From furnace to field in three generations', Aldcroft, 1964; 'Shirt sleeves to bishop's gaiters or barrister's wig in three generations', Jervis, 1974.

51 See for example Sampson, 1962, ch. 21.

52 Coleman (1973) notes that Reader (1970) talked about the 'management club' atmosphere that existed in the early days of ICI. His own investigation into the Courtauld archives demonstrated that it still existed. He quotes a memorandum from the chairman to four of his senior directors: 'There has been a Gentleman's club atmosphere in the Board Room, and I believe it is true to say that over the years this has spread to all the departments of our business. It is, in fact, part of the goodwill of the company which we must safeguard. On the other hand great care must be taken to avoid inefficiency' (pp.99–101).

53 As early as 1830 the private academies were denounced as 'exclusive, aristocratic, and un-American' (Hofstadter (1964)). Yet by the 1970s 15 per cent of elementary and secondary pupils were still in private schools and over one-third of college enrolments were private.

54 There is no question that Turner greatly exaggerates the differences between Britain and America. He seems to conveniently forget the fate of the blacks in America, as well as failing to point out that America has more students attending private schools than Britain (see note 53 above). He also appears not to realise that Britain has large numbers of students in tertiary education outside the universities.

55 One has to be very careful with comparisons of this sort because of the difficulty in defining 'higher education'. Lipset (1963) claims that if one compares the number of students enrolled in 'institutions of higher learning' to the size of the age cohort 20–24, then one finds that seven times as large a group was attending such institutions in the United States for the year 1956–7, as in England and Wales. One way of avoiding such definitional problems is to count the number of years

of schooling for the relevant age cohorts. If this is done, one finds that for the period 1964–6, 99 per cent of sixteen-year-olds and 76 per cent of seventeen-year-olds were still at school in the United States compared with 35 per cent and 25 per cent respectively for England and Wales *(Social Trends,* III, HMSO, 1972). Alternatively, if one takes the age group 25–34, in 1971 the United States population had one whole year more education (total 12 years) than the equivalent age group in the United Kingdom (total 11 years) *(Social Trends,* HMSO, 1975). Lipset (1963) also notes that one can see similar differences, if one compares two major Caribbean nations long under the hegemony of Britain and the United States, Jamaica and Puerto Rico. He writes: 'Jamaica, like many other former British colonies in Africa and Asia, has a higher education system which seems premised on the belief that only a tiny elite should receive such training; while the system in Puerto Rico, like the one in the Philippines, clearly reflects the continued impact of American assumptions concerning widespread educational opportunity' (p.261).

56 Hofstadter (1964) compares the acclaim given to Edison, who was 'all but canonised by the American public', with the reaction to 'our greatest genius in pure science, Josiah Willard Gibbs, who laid the theoretical foundations for modern physical chemistry, and who lived and died in obscurity' (p.25).

57 Cochran and Miller, 1961, p.270–1.

58 A study by Counts (1927) of the lay boards of control confirms that, for the period of his investigation in the nineteenth century, business interests were crucially important.

59 Beck, 1947, p.83.

60 Domhoff, 1967, p.78.

61 The British system does not impose any test of competence before a man may call himself a 'skilled' worker. What counts is the number of years that have been spent as an apprentice, there is also usually a stipulation that the apprentice be under a certain age. Shonfield (1965) notes that 'The notion behind this form of tuition in a craft, which conceives of the master's knowledge as being somehow rubbed off on to the pupil by constant propinquity, is essentially pre-industrial in spirit', (p.118).

62 There is a slight problem in defining exactly what is to count as 'business studies', but if one counts undergraduate degrees awarded in schools and departments of business, then for the academic year 1919–20 they accounted for 3 per cent of all undergraduate degrees. By the year 1939–40 this figure had risen to 10 per cent (Gordon and Howell, 1959).

63 Business degrees include degrees in business, commerce and accountancy *(Statistical Abstract of the United States,* US Department

of Commerce, 1974).

64   That this was indeed the case can be seen by examining this quotation from the annual report of the Stockport Sunday School: 'Are the proprietors of manufactories desirous of obtaining honest and industrious servants? Let them require a sound character, as indispensably requisite for their engagement, and the youth of both sexes, by availing themselves of a Sunday School education.....seek to possess the necessary qualification', quoted in Flinn (1967).

65   Ample evidence for the truth of this proposition is given in Cotgrove, 1958, see particularly chapter 1.

66   Coleman, 1973, p.104.

67   Aldcroft, 1964, p.133.

68   Cotgrove quotes several minutes from the Royal Commission on Technical Instruction (1884) in support of this view (1958, pp.24–5).

69   Ibid., p.25.

70   The Empire itself devoured a large proportion of the output of these schools. Excluding business enterprises operating in the colonies, it must be remembered that an empire of some 750 million people by 1900 required very large numbers of administrators.

71   Glover (1975) reveals an interesting indication of the relatively low status of engineering in British society. He notes that our famous museum of industrial techniques, i.e. engineering, is in fact called the Science Museum. The equivalent museum in France is called the Museum of Techniques.

72   In 1903 the University of Manchester established a Faculty of Commerce and Administration, although this offered little more than applied economics courses, which were applied as much to local government as they were to business. In 1930 the University of Hull instituted a two-year diploma course in industrial administration, and this was followed in 1931 by the foundation of a one-year postgraduate course run by the Department of Business Administration at the LSE.

73   The judgement that business studies did not represent a unitary discipline that was academically respectable, was one that was endorsed by the Robbins Committee (para. 294) and has gained support from time to time from the UGC.

74   *The Hudson Report*, 1974, was one of the last reports to offer such an indictment, and a whole series of articles in *The Guardian* newspaper of July-August 1976 repeated the familiar charges.

75   Despite these changes the volume of business and management education in Britain barely compares with the American effort. Rose (1970) calculates that in 1970 there were probably some 2,400 students on business/management undergraduate courses in Britain. The equivalent figure for the United States was 500,000. Taking postgraduate courses, if one was to count the DMS and British one-year courses as a whole

as together being roughly equivalent to one-half of the American master's degree, the result would be to equate the present number of postgraduate students in Britain with the American position shortly after the Second World War.

76 The Royal Commission on the Trade Unions (1968) makes numerous references to this effect, as did the important Labour Party document *In Place of Strife* (1969) and the equivalent Conservative Party document *Fair Deal at Work* (1969).

77 It is important to note that these remarks refer almost exclusively to the white population. In fact, fear of competition of negro labour prevented white trade unionists from attempting to enrol negroes in the unions.

78 This was the era of the private army in America. Hobsbawn (1975) reports that in 1865 and 1866 every railroad, colliery, iron-furnace and rolling mill in Pennsylvania was granted statutory authority to employ as many armed policemen as it wished to act as they thought fit. Many, including the notorious 'Pinkertons', were utilised to fight labour.

79 The following table adapted from Bagwell and Mingay (1970) makes the point well.

Percentage of Gainfully Employed Labour (excluding Agriculture) in Trade Unions in Britain and America

Great Britain		United States	
1901	13.7	1900	4.8
1911	18.2	1910	8.5
1921	37.0	1920	18.6
1931	23.5	1930	11.7
1941	-	1940	27.2
1951	43.1	1950	31.9
1961[a]	45.0	1960[b]	31.4
1976	53.8[c]	1976[d]	30.0

[a] *The Economist,* 19th June, 1971.

[b] US Bureau of Labour Statistics, 1969.

[c] *DEP Gazette, November, 1977.*

[d] *Statistical Abstract of the US, 1978.*

80 Bagwell and Mingay (1970) in their comparative study of Britain and America take this as their point of departure.

81 From 1860 to around 1880 the European tradition of socialist, even anarchist, influences were paramount, although admittedly few workers were organised (only 4 per cent by 1900). In the years to 1920, business unionism in the shape of Samuel Compers and the AFL was faced by the almost equal ranks of socialist labour groups.

82 Hardman, 1964, p.403.

83 Of course other factors also account for this, not least the greater geographical diversity of companies in America and the federal political structure, which makes national agreements more difficult.

84 It is a common argument that American employers have utilised the enormous system of fringe benefits, that are commonly bargained with unions, for their own benefits. Initially they were often used as a device for thwarting unionism itself, and when this failed they used the benefits to buy loyalty to the firm. As Kroos (1970) has argued: 'Most businessmen approached welfare capitalism from the point of view of dollars and cents and profit and loss. John J. Roskob, for example, believed that the experiences at General Motors proved that, "money paid in benefits is returned in the lower costs of production" '(p.352).

85 Merton's (1938) observations apply just as strongly to trade unionists as to anyone else in American society. The alleged greater degree of corruption amongst American union leaders is also explained in this way. The activities of the Teamster's leader, Hoffa, who once declared that he 'feared the guy who does not want to make money', exemplifies this point. It is interesting to note that, even after Hoffa's conviction for violent and corrupt practices, he was still very popular amongst the rank and file because he was above all an effective bargainer on behalf of his union.

86 This analysis appears to be correct, in general terms; it is always possible of course to find American unions and British unions which at particular moments of time have not followed these respective policies.

87 Exports as a percentage of GNP: GB–13.4; USA–4.1.(Source: *OECD Observer,* February 1966).

88 Sturmthal, 1957, p.343.

89 Lipset, 1973, p.195.

90 Perkin, 1969, p.336.

91 T.B. Macaulay et al., (1855). 'The Indian Civil Service, Report to the Right Hon. Sir Charles Wood' (1855), quoted in Chapman (1970).

92 These constitute less than 15 per cent of the total service however, and have been steadily declining.

93 Pear (1968).

94 In part, of course, this reflects the different nature of the tasks which fall to the lot of the public administrators in Britain and America.

The absence of a well-developed welfare state in America means that the service is much smaller and concentrated almost solely in specialist agencies like defence, agriculture, hydro-electricity etc.

95 For an illustration of this process see Cochran's analysis of the American Telephone Company, 1962 p.78.

96 The 1880s saw the first manufacturing companies with capital in excess of one hundred million dollars.

97 The early and more widespread public sale of securities in the United States also promoted the use of control procedures inside American companies to ensure adequate accountability.

98 Chandler also shows however, that not all American corporations were properly run along functional lines. Even by 1920 some corporations, like US Steel, did little more than form an office to help set price and production schedules for the almost completely autonomous divisions.

99 See Wilkins, 1970, p.70.

100 According to Engel's law, people do not generally consume proportionately more of the same things as they get richer, but rather reallocate their consumption away from old goods and towards new goods. This non-proportional growth of demand implies that goods would tend to go through a life cycle.

101 Beard, 1963, p.49.

102 Several of the most successful businessmen 'failed' several times before they eventually made it. R.H. Macey, for example, failed several times in smaller places before he eventually succeeded in New York. Many of the others were ready to move towards the big money wherever it was. Carnegie, for example, did not concentrate his energies on steel until he was almost forty. Jay Gould was in turn cartographer and leather merchant, before discovering what could be done with railway stock.

103 Nowhere can this be seen more clearly than in the financial world. The City remains largely self-controlling, relying upon codes of practice, some of them still unwritten. This contrasts markedly with America, where the Securities Exchange Commission, in particular, possesses an enormous web of legal rules and regulations.

104 Britain was certainly ahead of America in this respect. By 1841, for example, the town population of Great Britain represented 52.3 per cent of the total.

105 Aldcroft, 1964, p.132.

106 Payne, 1967, p.525.

107 The industrialisation of England had preceded without any substantial utilisation of banking for long-term investment purposes, and the banks developed most of their commercial interests in financing international trade. In America, because of the greater need for finance, partly a consequence of the fact that America developed later as an

industrial power than England, the banks were heavily involved in industry from the beginning. For some interesting observations on the role of banking in industrialisation see Gerschenkron, 1962, ch.1.

108 Aldcroft, 1964, p.117.

109 There was so little innovative expansion that some firms with surplus funds rather than invest in their own business, invested it in others (Payne (1967)). Aldcroft (1964) also concludes that: 'Domestic capital went into gilt-edged and foreign issues not because of the inability of the capital market to finance home industrial issues, but because of the paucity of domestic issues in which to invest or because English firms were on too small a scale to attract the issue houses' (p.132).

110 Lewis and Stewart, 1958, p.29.

111 Shils, 1956, p.49.

112 Shonfield, 1965, p.100.

113 Several recent cases would appear to illustrate the general truth of this proposition. John Bentley, for example, was relentlessly hounded by the press and received a decidedly cool reception from the City, for indulging in the perfectly legal and indeed highly capitalistic exercise known as 'asset stripping'. Asset stripping merely involves buying a company, at a price calculated on its success record in a particular sphere of business. The assets are then divided and sold off for different purposes. Crucial to the whole operation is the ability of takeover companies to close their deals using share and loan stock certificates rather than cash. This activity involves pursuing profit as a goal above all others, and not being concerned with the particular products that a company manufactures or the industry it is in etc. The activities of a company such as Bentley Securities, may look rather odd by normal business standards, but this merely reflects what the sole focus upon profit does to a company profile. (For an interesting American example of what can perhaps be termed 'pure capitalism', see Rieser (1962)). The other recent British example which illustrates the strong moral code of gentlemanly practice inside the upper reaches of British business is the Lonhro affair. Although the final report by HM Inspectors from the Board of Trade did indicate that there had been some legal transgressions, they appeared to be of a relatively minor kind. The great significance of the company's activities was that they transgressed certain important informal rules of conduct for British business. It was on this issue of 'business style' that half the directors eventually resigned and led the British Prime Minister at the time, Edward Heath, to talk about the 'unacceptable face of capitalism'. More accurately, he should have inserted the qualifying adjective, British, in front of capitalism, for there is no doubt that such activities would have been perfectly acceptable in the United States. Finally, one should note the ultimate fate of those

who play the game just a little too hard. Sir Arnold Weinstock, one of Britain's leading industrialists, had his application to join Brook's, one of London's oldest and most exclusive clubs, blackballed. Although the club never divulges reasons for refusing a candidate, *The Sunday Times'* correspondent wrote the following: 'Judging from the grumbles when Sir Arnold's name was first suggested, it seems that by cutting a rapid path through British industry Sir Arnold displeased some of the traditionalists' (*The Sunday Times,* 6th May 1973).

114 There are good reasons why the capitalist should turn first to economic causes of economic crises. First, until relatively recently the economist has been the only person to offer diagnosis and remedy. It is only recently that there has developed a sociology of economic life. Secondly, a social diagnosis may not fit very well with the interests of the capitalist himself. For example, if it was believed that a far greater emphasis upon achievement and universalism should be made in the education system, then this might have unfortunate results for his own children, particularly if they were unable to enter the business because of their special ascribed status.

115 Veblen put it in his own characteristic way: 'Doubtless, the English today lead the christian world both in the volume of their gentility and in its cost per unit', 1915, p.141.

116 Even here one has to add *ceteris paribus.* In particular, one has to make the assumption that there is both belief and knowledge about what effect particular configurations of social structure have on the economy.

117 There seems to be general agreement amongst economists that the rate of profit in British industry has been falling since about 1950. There are of course considerable differences of opinion about how this is to be interpreted.

118 *The Times Educational Supplement,* 27th January, 1956, quoted in Cotgrove, 1958, p.176.

119 Specifically it resulted in a government White Paper in which a major expansion of the technical colleges was planned (Technical Education', Cmnd, 9703, HMSO).

120 Symptomatic of this scrutiny was the launching by Penguin Books of a series of titles on 'What is Wrong with Britain?'.

121 In fact the Government rejected the view that the selection of graduate entrants to administrative work should be deliberately weighted in favour of those whose university studies had been in subjects thought clearly relevant to Civil Service Work.

122 Shonfield, 1965, p.108.

123 It is assumed here that the existence of a welfare state, particularly in terms of health and social security provisions, aids the operation of the capitalist economy in a direct sense, i.e. by providing a healthy labour

force. This author knows of no cost/benefit analysis however, that actually demonstrates the truth of this proposition.

124   Several writers, notably Shonfield (1965), Marris (1974) and Winkler (1975), have developed the argument that modern capitalism, because of its essentially international character, requires the active involvement of state governments in its management. It is notable that Britain and the United States, both with a political elite with a history of non-interference, have found it more difficult than most modern capitalist societies to perform well economically. In particular the United States in the post-war period has had more recessions than Western Europe, and each time they have cut output more sharply than in Europe, (Maddison (1964)). Although economists have offered several explanations of this phenomenon, it seems likely that the reluctance of the federal government to intervene in the economy is a major contributory factor of this result. Not only is there a strong ideological barrier to intervention in the United States, but the actual institutional arrangements of government, itself a reflection of the ideology, make it extraordinarily difficult for the government to intervene (with particular reference to the separation of powers contained in the Constitution). Although one can argue that a similar ideological stance has informed British capitalism, the fact remains that the *laissez-faire* doctrine has not been so important a phenomenon in post-war Britain, even in the Conservative Party, whilst the Labour Party has positively disavowed it. Furthermore, Britain's feudal legacy has equipped her with a unitary and hierarchical form of executive government, which is capable of long-term economic planning in the corporatist mould. Finally, as already observed, Britain's post-war economic position has forced both political parties, when in office, to adopt a much more interventionist strategy. This has not meant, as some writers seem to suppose, that capitalism has ceased to be the economic organising principle of British society.

125   The most notable event was probably the launching of the Russian sputnik in 1957. This shook America ideologically, in the sense that Communism was seen to be superior to capitalism in an important symbolic area. Secondly, the launching offered certain economic warnings, in that it appeared to show that Russian scientific research and education, both economically important, were superior to the American. Two years later, in 1959, two influential reports on American business education were published almost simultaneously (Pierson et al., 1959, and Gordon and Howell, 1959). Their diagnoses were very similar. They both pointed to the poor quality of many of the business schools and the fact that the students studying business were well towards the bottom of the ability range. These two events fostered certain changes inside the American educational system; attempts were

made for example to improve the quality of business education by basing it more firmly on academic disciplines, and secondly, more attention was focused upon science and technology.

3 British and American manufacturing organisations: organisational structure and process

The main object of this study was to discover to what extent there existed any differences between British and American manufacturing companies and, if there were differences, how far these could be attributed to socio-cultural differences between the two societies. In order to answer these questions it was necessary to design a research strategy that would compare American and British firms that were exactly matched along all dimensions except that of nationality. Only two previous studies in the cross-cultural management literature manage this difficult task. Richardson (1956) produced a neat research design in his study of British and American cargo ships, whilst Sim (1977) appears to have matched firms adequately in his study of British, American and Japanese companies operating in Malaysia.[1] The reason for the paucity of studies is unquestionably the great difficulty in getting the appropriate firms to co-operate in the research exercise. Granick (1972) is typical of researchers in this area who admit that the best research design would be to study 'matched firms from identical industries', but who confess that such a task proved too difficult for them. This research met with enormous difficulties in securing an adequately matched sample, but eventually six American manufacturing companies operating in England were matched with five British manufacturing companies.

The research began by attempting to draw a sample of American manufacturing firms operating within a twenty-five mile radius of London, in as wide a range of industries as possible. No adequate sampling frame existed for such firms, and lists were compiled from the Kompass Register of British Industry and Commerce as well as the Anglo-American Trade Directory. The nationality of the firm was checked by consulting the UK edition of *Who Owns Whom,* and only wholly-owned subsidiary companies were selected. The response rate from this sample was 38 per cent, details are given in Table 3.1. In all, six American manufacturing firms were selected for study, although as one can see from examining Table 3.1, the figure could have been as high as ten, but for the difficulty of matching with comparable British companies. Once the American firms had agreed to co-operate in the research it was then possible to work out the required characteristics of the comparable British firms. Following previous work, particularly that of the Aston school, an attempt was made to match the British and American companies upon the following variables. (a) Size of company: this was measured by the number of employees. A deliberate decision was made not to include any firm with more than 5,000 employees. There were two reasons for this. First, the research instrument that was used to measure organisational climate was found on piloting not to work well on firms over this size;[2] secondly, it was felt that it was unlikely that a single researcher with limited time and resources could gain an accurate knowledge of a very large organisation. (b) Ownership: as all the American companies were by definition subsidiaries, an attempt was made to ensure that all the British companies were of the same status. (c) Location: all the companies were in a twenty-five mile radius of London. In part this was merely convenient for the researcher, but it also meant that the labour market was very similar for all the companies, and this was important when it came to testing hypotheses about managerial employees. (d) Product: an attempt was made to compare companies manufacturing the same type of product. Precedence was given to matching the products of the firms and their sizes, as reading of previous research indicated that these two variables were of quite fundamental importance[3]

Table 3.1

Responses from American firms contacted: main sample

	N	%	
Firm agreed and was included in the sample	6	16	
Firm agreed but could not be matched with British firm	4	11	38
Firm agreed but proved to be unsuitable for research	4	11	
Firm refused	9	24	
Firm failed to reply to request	15	39	
Total	38	101[*]	

[*] These percentages have been rounded up.

Table 3.2 shows the response rate from suitably matched British firms. One can see that the response rate for the British firms was only 14 per cent, less than half that of the American response. This is exactly in line with the findings of Dunning (1970), who attempted a similar comparative study of British and American firms from an economic point of view. His response rates were 8 per cent for the British firms and 45 per cent for the American firms. This finding can be related to the enormous stress upon secrecy that is characteristic of British business compared with the relative openness of American society and American business.

Table 3.2

Responses from British firms contacted: main sample

	N	%	
Firm agreed and was used in sample	5	10	}14
Firm agreed but proved to be unsuitable for research	2	4	
Firm refused	8	16	
Firm failed to reply to request	34	69	
Total	49	99*	

*These percentages have been rounded.

Full details of the main sample are given in Tables 3.3 to 3.7. The names given to the firms are realistic but fictitious descriptions of their main activities. The firms selected are listed below:

American Firms	British Firms
US Pharmaceuticals	GB Pharmaceuticals
US Print	GB Print
US Furniture	GB Furniture
US Electronics I	GB Electronics
US Electronics II	
US Consumer	GB Consumer

The reason why two American electronics firms are compared to only one British electronics firm is that two American firms agreed to co-operate, and it was felt that it would be interesting to compare similar American firms with each other as well as with a comparable British firm. As it turned out, one of the American firms happened to be

89

quite tightly controlled in nearly all its activities by its parent, whilst the other firm operated almost as an independent entity. This chance occurrence allowed a more rigorous test on the effect of American control on the company.

Table 3.3

Number of employees in British and American firms:[*] main sample

US Pharmaceuticals	550	GB Pharmaceuticals	750
US Print	587	GB Print	1,461
US Furniture	350	GB Furniture	300
US Electronics I	2,500	GB Electronics	349
US Electronics II	1,300		
US Consumer	2,635	GB Consumer	1,000

* Part-time employees were counted as half.

Table 3.4

Number of employees in owning group, British and American firms: main sample

US Pharmaceuticals	8,000	GB Pharmaceuticals	*
US Print	15,000	GB Print	2,128
US Furniture	6,000	GB Furniture	350
US Electronics I	22,000	GB Electronics	25,000
US Electronics II	9,000		
US Consumer	25,000	GB Consumer	*

*The firm was not a subsidiary.

The tables indicate that the British and American firms were well matched. The matching for size is quite good, two pairs being of an almost identical size; only in the electronics industry comparison is the match less than perfect. The other important variable, the products of the companies, are also well controlled for most companies are directly competing with their matched pair. Only in the consumer

90

products comparison does one find a situation where one of the firms, US Consumer, has a more diversified range of outputs than its British counterpart. Even here however, one of the main products of the American firm directly competes with the main product of the British firm. The preciseness of the products matching is reflected in the production technologies of the sample companies, (see Table 3.7).

Table 3.5

Main Products of British and American firms: main sample

US Pharmaceuticals	Pharmaceutical chemicals	GB Pharmaceuticals	Pharmaceutical and industrial chemicals
US Print	Printing machinery	GB Print	Printing machinery
US Furniture	Contract furniture	GB Furniture	Contract furniture
US Electronics I	Electronic control instruments	GB Electronics	Electronic control instruments
US Electronics II	Electronic control instruments		
US Consumer	Plastic, metal and chemical products	GB Consumer	Plastic consumer products

Table 3.6

Length of operation in England of British and American firms: main sample (Data to 1973)

	Years		Years
US Pharmaceuticals	13	GB Pharmaceuticals	34
US Print	40	GB Print	73
US Furniture	5 *	GB Furniture	70
US Electronics I	30	GB Electronics	50 †
US Electronics II	40		
US Consumer	37	GB Consumer	55

* This firm was legally created five years ago when it was taken over by an American company. As a manufacturing entity however, it had existed for much longer.
† This firm was legally created approximately five years ago, when it was taken over by its English parent, although it had existed for fifty years. As the nationality of the firm had not altered, the older date is shown.

Table 3.7

Production technology of British and American firms: main sample

US Pharmaceuticals	3 (2)	GB Pharmaceuticals	2 (3)
US Print	2	GB Print	2
US Furniture	3 (2)	GB Furniture	3 (2)
US Electronics I	3 (2)	GB Electronics	3 (2)
US Electronics II	3 (2)		
US Consumer	3	GB Consumer	3

Note: The numbers refer to Woodward's (1965) categorisation of production technology. The main figure represents the dominant production technology, the figure in paranthesis represents any subsidiary production technology.

Key: 2 - unit or small batch production; 3 - large batch or mass production.

The response rate for both sets of firms was poor, and this might be thought to raise some doubts about the validity of the findings. However, given the small number of firms in the sample compared with the population of British and American firms operating in Britain, even if a 100 per cent response rate had been secured it would clearly have been illegitimate to have made any firm inferences about 'British manufacturing industry', compared to 'American manufacturing industry'. One of the reasons for the small sample was the rigour of the matching process, clearly the more variables that are matched the smaller the sample necessarily becomes, and it is contended that only a sample matched as rigorously as this can really test any hypotheses about the effect of nationality upon company structure and operation. It could be argued that having relatively low levels of response actually provides for an even stricter test of the hypotheses about the effects of socio-cultural variables. It seems a reasonable assumption that this sample consists of relatively 'progressive' firms, that is firms who are proud of their achievements, have a good profit record etc. and are interested in demonstrating their 'progressiveness' to research workers.[4] If this assumption is correct then one ends up by comparing progressive American companies with progressive British companies, which from the point of view of comparing like with like is satisfactory. Furthermore, if it is possible to detect the effect of socio-cultural variables even amongst progressive companies, which are by definition more fully capitalist, then it would follow that the effect of such variables is likely to be even greater amongst the larger population of less progressive companies. In other words, if this study manages to demonstrate the importance of socio-cultural factors in influencing the structure and operation of the surveyed companies, then it could be confidently argued that such differences exist, in general terms, for the total population of British and American firms.

Most research that has set out to test the effect of cultural factors on business behaviour has tended to compare indigenous firms in country A with indigenous firms in country B, (Nash (1968); Negandhi (1974)). There are clearly many advantages in proceeding in this manner, most obviously that the respective companies will be staffed by nationals of the respective countries, who will be carriers of their culture. This study, by contrast, compares American firms operating in Britain with British firms similarly operating here. This research design offers one advantage over the more usual methodology, in that the operating environment of the companies is held relatively constant. There is yet another advantage however, which again might be thought to produce a more rigorous test of hypotheses about the relevance of cultural factors. If it can be shown that the American firms, despite operating in England and employing English nationals, still exhibited the effects of American culture upon their structures and operations, then it could be safely assumed that cultural variables are relevant explanatory variables in the analysis of company structure and operation.

Three separate but interrelated sets of data were collected on all the firms in the sample. Material was collected on the organisational structures of the companies and how they operated. This was followed by information on the managerial employees of the companies. Finally data was gathered on the organisational climate of the respective firms. Certain of the hypotheses were also checked against another set of data. The British Institute of Management kindly allowed reanalysis of two of their surveys of member companies; one on the selection of managers,[5] and the other on fringe benefits.[6] All the sample companies which were not engaged in manufacturing were discarded and the American-owned firms in the sample were compared with the British firms, matching the respondents for size. These studies are referred to throughout this research as the BIM data.

This chapter reports on the results of the investigation into the organisational structure and dynamics of the companies, whilst Chapters 4 and 5 report on the managerial personnel and the organisational climates respectively. The data on organisational structure was collected in a number of ways. After the company had replied favourably to the research approach letter, which set out the main aims of the research, the researcher visited the company, explained in more detail the purpose of the research, and gathered general information about the company. This was followed by another interview where two senior executives helped the researcher complete the organisational structure schedule (see Appendix 2). [7] The initial purpose of the schedule was to allow proper matching to take place; the schedule makes use of several of the scales developed by the Aston researchers to measure contextual variables, viz. size, dependence and technology, as well as three measures of organisational structure, formalisation, organisational autonomy and functional specialisation. [8] The measure of organisational autonomy, apart from being a useful measure of an element of organisational structure, allowed the researcher to probe the exact nature of the relationship between the American subsidiaries and their parent firms. On the basis of this information it was possible to make an assessment of how tightly controlled the American firms were from the United States, and this in turn allowed adequate testing of the hypothesis that the more tightly controlled firms would exhibit more distinctly 'American' features. The organisational structure schedule also contained a variety of other questions designed to test a range of hypotheses, derived from the theoretical analysis, about the differences between British and American manufacturing industry. Some of the questions were designed more to open up certain topics of inquiry rather than to elicit pieces of formal information, e.g. the questions on collective bargaining were used to generate a discussion about the company's attitude to and experience with trade unions. The data from the schedule was supplemented in three ways. First, confirmatory material was obtained where possible from other company sources, e.g. company booklets, advertising and public relations material, and organisation charts. In addition, certain external sources were consulted, e.g. McCarthy Information Service, as well as material stored at Companies' House. Secondly, when the managers of the companies were interviewed, considerable information about the structure and more particularly about the operation of the organisation was obtained. Finally, the questionnaire sent to the managers of the company (see Appendix 3) contained as its last section an organisational climate index, which contributed some data on the perception of the structure by the managers.

The first aspect of organisational structure that was examined was formalisation. Organisational formalisation was defined following Hall (1972) as the organisational technique of prescribing how, when, and by whom tasks are to be performed. This is somewhat broader than the Aston researchers, who defined it as 'the extent to which rules, procedures, motivations, and communications are written'. [9] Formalisation was measured using a combination of the Aston scores (see Table 3.8), the managers' statements about how the company actually worked, and a more detailed examination of procedures inside particular functional areas. In line with some other research it was not found that the more formal Aston index correlated that well with the data from the company personnel; in particular the Aston index did not provide any understanding of what formalisation actually meant inside the companies investigated. There were two main hypotheses regarding the degree of formalisation of the British and American manufacturing organisations. First, it was predicted that the American firms that were more tightly controlled from the United States would be more formalised. This should follow because making the subsidiary follow standardised procedures in a number of areas of business would certainly be one quite effective way of controlling the activities of the company. The second hypothesis was that American-owned firms would be, *ceteris paribus,* more formalised than similar British firms. This should follow from the theoretical analysis, because it has been argued that American culture places a greater emphasis upon the values of achievement, universalism and specificity. The achievement stress should lead to greater formalisation in selecting and appraising managers, a formal systematic approach being preferable to an approach which stresses vaguer and more diffuse personal qualities. The stress on universalism should reinforce the higher formalisation, with American firms looking for measures of performance which are universalistic rather than particularistic. Finally, the greater hypothesised stress on specificity should lead to far more organisational rules and controls in American organisations. These predictions are further supported by the work of other researchers. Inkson et al., (1970), using an identical measure of organisational formalisation, found in their British/American comparative study a significant difference in formalisation between the two sets of firms, indeed this was the only significant difference that they found. Richardson's (1956) study of British and American cargo ships and Granick's (1972) cross-cultural study of business firms which included British and American examples, had similar findings. Finally Sim's (1977) study of British and American firms operating in Malaya offered support for the hypothesis under test.

Table 3.8

Organisational structure of British and American firms: formalisation

US Pharmaceuticals	10	GB Pharmaceuticals	8
US Print	10	GB Print	8
US Furniture	5	GB Furniture	9
US Electronics I	4	GB Electronics	7
US Electronics II	10		
US Consumer	7	GB Consumer	9

For scale details see p.II in Appendix. A high score denotes high formalisation. Possible range: 0–10.

The first hypothesis, that those American firms most tightly controlled from America would be the most formalised was supported, although there was considerable variation in the degree of formalisation in the different functional areas. The two most tightly controlled American firms, US Print and US Electronics II, had the highest formalisation scores. The second hypothesis, that the American firms in the sample would be more formalised than their comparable British firms, also received support, with one notable exception in the furniture industry comparison. In general terms the American firms in the sample were more formalised in the sense that there were more fixed procedures for a wider range of activities than in the British firms. The American firms made far greater use of certain techniques for greater managerial control: this was especially notable in the field of financial and budgetary control, and it was in this area also that the American parent exercised its strongest control. These findings are in line with those of Granick (1972) and Sim (1977). The same phenomenon was also noticeable in the personnel area. All the American firms in the sample always drew up job descriptions when recruiting new managers, whilst this was not consistently done in the English firms. These findings are reinforced by the reanalysis of the BIM survey on selection.[10] The BIM data were analysed by nationality and then broken down by size: small firms were those employing up to 1,000 persons and large firms employing more. The full tables are reproduced in Appendix 1, but summarising it was found that holding size constant significantly more American firms drew up job descriptions than British firms ($p < 0.01$). The same study also showed that American firms were much more likely to draw up a man specification for managerial positions than were British firms ($p < 0.001$, when size was controlled for). Turning to the present sample again, it was found that American firms were more inclined to use some form of objective testing in the selection process for managers than were the comparable British firms, although testing was not widespread even in the American companies. The reanalysed BIM data produced a similar result: 44.5 per cent (n = 9) of small American firms as against 27.1 per cent (n = 48) of small British firms sometimes used managerial selection tests. For the large firms the figures were respectively 38.5 per cent (n = 13) and 29.8 per cent (n = 37). Although all these differences are in the predicted direction, none reaches levels of statistical significance. These data are further supported by the work of Seyfarth et al., (1968) in their small comparative study of British and American organisations. The interviews with the personnel officers of the American companies however, indicated that there were movements away from the use of tests in the selection procedure, apparently because of their poor predictive power. The personnel area yielded yet further indications of the greater formalisation of the American companies. All the American companies had management development programmes, whilst only two of the British companies had, GB Furniture and GB Electronics. It was found that the personnel departments of the American companies were bigger than the comparable departments of the British companies, and one of the reasons for this was simply that the task of the American departments was bigger. All the 'American' managers in the sample were being systematically appraised and trained, whilst this was happening in only two British firms. These findings are supported by the comparative observations of Stewart (1957) and Urwick (1954). Furthermore, the Acton Society Trust (1956) noted the virtual absence in their study of systematic management development programmes in British firms. Thus as far as the personnel function was concerned the American firms in the sample exhibited a greater degree of formalisation.

In the marketing function the same general pattern emerged, although the differences were not so marked. Two of the British firms, GB Furniture and GB Pharmaceuticals did not possess a separate marketing function with a force of salesmen. In the case of the furniture firm it was still sufficiently small for most of the sales work to be handled by the managing director and his assistant. The managing director regarded sales as his major function, and both he and his products were well known throughout the trade. Most of the firm's business was to offices, hotels etc., and very little went to retail outlets; a well developed sales force was not therefore required. The managing director of the British company saw marketing in the same way as he saw design, indeed he did not distinguish very closely between them. Both functions were viewed as highly creative rather idiosyncratic jobs. By comparison it is interesting to note that the American furniture company employed more salesmen and gave considerably more emphasis to marketing its products in a much more systematic way. GB Pharmaceuticals was also a relatively small firm, and it sold its main outputs very largely to other companies. Marketing was regarded as rather a routine business involving liaising with established customers. The company was not highly involved in the innovative end of the market and did not compete with other companies on the basis of new products and packaging, but rather on delivery and price. This meant that production was regarded as the key function. Again the matched American company provided a stark contrast, for enormous emphasis was placed upon the marketing of its products. The rest of the companies in the sample all possessed marketing/sales departments, and the predicted differences did emerge. Not only did the American firms put greater emphasis upon this business function, but the Americans were very much more systematic and formalised about it. This manifested itself in several ways. First, the American firms ran more and larger sales training 'schools' for their members—as one interviewee put it rather graphically. 'I seem to spend more of my time learning about selling than I do seeing customers'. This emphasis was particularly marked in US Pharmaceuticals and US Consumer. The sales training was formalised in the sense that salesmen were often taught from sales manuals, in one case an adapted version of the one used by the American parent. Some salesmen likened the training to a computer programme, they were taught how to respond to almost every conceivable situation. Of course some of the British firms exhibited some of these features, particularly GB Consumer, but there did seem to be a difference of degree between the American and the British respondents. These findings are again supported by other writers (cf. Chruden and Sherman (1972); PEP (1966), and Permut (1977)).

One company studied, GB Furniture, did not fit the pattern described above. This firm was as formalised as any firm visited and in one sense could be regarded as an anomaly in that the firm was also rather small (350) persons). The reason for the large amount of formalisation lay in the character of the managing director of the company. He was a firm believer in management science and the values of management training. He had attended numerous management training courses run by consultants, and was well versed in management techniques. It would be fair to say that the whole management of the firm was convinced of the value of the application of management science to the organisation. This conviction resulted in a large number of formal systems of control and planning as it had in the American firms. It might be argued that this is one small idiosyncrasy and that all small samples risk turning up atypical examples. In one sense this is probably correct and GB Furniture is probably an atypical firm, particularly for its size. The example should act as a cautionary note however, because it does illustrate the point that business organisations are controlled by acting human beings who can influence the structure and strategy of the company. Sometimes the contingency theorists seem to present business as being totally moulded by the external contingencies of the business environment.

There were variations between the generally more formalised American companies however, as well as between them and the comparable British companies. Furthermore, there were important differences inside certain firms, and as these differences are illuminating it is worth pursuing them. US Pharmaceuticals was one of the most highly formalised of all the companies studied, despite the fact that it was a relatively small firm, and operating in an industry which is noted for its high research and development element. Some research has indicated that firms which rely heavily on research and development should be less formalised. [11] There are two major reasons for this company's high formalisation score. First, it was very tightly controlled, as its autonomy score indicates (see Table 3.9) by its parent company, and the parent company was quite large

(8,000 employees), the size effect was therefore felt through the parent. The second major reason was connected with the nature of the industry. The pharmaceutical industry is one that is tightly regulated by the government. It regulates the industry, first by being by far its largest consumer, and therefore is in a position to exercise countervailing power (cf. the Roche affair), and secondly, by being the body legally responsible for the control of drugs, it exercises control via labelling, packaging, health and quality control legislation. Faced with so many external controls companies in this industry are themselves forced to institute a wide series of formalised controls inside their companies, particularly in the production departments. Finally, it should be noted, that although US Pharmaceuticals did have a research and development department, it was not large, most of the basic research being performed by the parent company in America and exported to the subsidiary. GB Pharmaceuticals was a larger company than its American counterpart, although the difference was not great; its products were very similar, and so it was subject to the same kind of governmental constraint. It had a larger research and development function than its American counterpart, although by the standards of the industry it was not large. The only major difference between the two was that the British firm was not a subsidiary, and whilst this could have accounted for the reported difference in formalisation, it is equally possible that nationality could have been a contributory factor.

Table 3.9

Organisational autonomy: British and American firms

US Pharmaceuticals	17	GB Pharmaceuticals	23
US Print	19	GB Print	23
US Furniture	16	GB Furniture	23
US Electronics I	21	GB Electronics	21
US Electronics II	17		
US Consumer	16	GB Consumer	23

For scale details see p. II in Appendix   A high score denotes greater autonomy in decision making. Possible range: 0–23.

There was a much greater degree of formalisation in US Print compared with GB Print, and this was reflected in their respective scores on the Aston index. The products of the two firms were identical, and they were operating in an identical market. The British firm was almost twice as large as the American, which should have lead to greater pressure to formalise on the part of the former. The only major difference apart from nationality that could have accounted for the considerable difference that was found, was the size of the parent companies; the American parent company was considerably bigger than the British one.

The comparison of the furniture firms did produce a result that was rather surprising. Although there was not a great deal of difference between the two companies from the point of view of formalisation, it is probably true to say that the British company was more formalised. It has been indicated that the major reason for this was to be found in the ideas of the managing director of GB Furniture. There is one other factor that is worth mentioning. The industry is one where the average size of firms tends to be relatively small, making for rather lower formalisation scores. It should finally be noted that the American firm had come to Britain by buying into an existing British firm, and this move had been accomplished within the last five years. The managing director of US Furniture explained that although a lot of changes had taken place since the takeover, in the direction of greater formalisation, the industry itself was not one of the most progressive, and the American parent was moving relatively slowly in the direction of imposing greater control procedures.

The comparison of British and American companies in the electronics industry provided a nice example of the effect of strong American parent control. There was a marked difference between the two American companies in the area of formalised managerial controls, US Electronics I, which had been established in Britain for thirty years, was a very large and almost independent subsidiary of an American parent. In many ways the American connection was almost superfluous, it barely affected the operation of the company, and the company did not have a very high formalisation score; this is reflected in the Aston scale. It was certainly much less formalised than US Electronics II, despite being twice its size and having a parent company more than twice as large. The British company, GB Electronics, was more formalised than US Electronics I, but not as formalised as US Electronics II. Unfortunately, the variables of both size and nationality both push in the same direction in this example, and it is thus impossible to tell whether the greater size of US Electronics II or its nationality, or of course both, account for its greater formalisation. If the size of the parent was an important variable however, one would have predicted that the relationship would have been reversed.

Finally there were the two firms in the consumer products field. Again the level of formalisation is in the predicted direction, being higher in US Consumer. In general the level of formalisation was quite high in both

100

companies, as both firms attempted to predict and control for the turbulent environment of the consumer products market. The larger size of the American company, and in particular its large parent, which exerted strong control over the subsidiary, could have accounted for the difference independently of the effect of nationality.

Although companies have been described in terms of company X being more formalised than company $Y,$ there were differences to be found even within companies. The difference varied with the function inside the company, although there appeared to be far less variation inside the American companies, with the exception of US Electronics I, than inside the British companies. Fortunately, because the companies were so well matched, these variations did not affect the general conclusion that American firms were more formalised than the British. In all companies the finance and general administrative departments seemed the most formalised, followed very closely by production. In American companies this was usually followed by personnel and marketing together, then research and development, although it should be noted that the research and development function in several American companies was very small indeed, most of the research and development being done in the United States. In British companies, personnel seemed to be the least formalised function, less so than even research and development and much less so than marketing.

The explanation of the greater formalisation of the American companies should be clear from the historical analysis presented in Chapter 2. From the time of F.W. Taylor at least, America has been the home of management science and of management education. Furthermore management consultants, who have probably played an important part in diffusing managerial techniques and control mechanisms, were an American invention and are used much more extensively by American firms. Just as research and development expertise has been exported from the American parent to the British subsidiary, so too with managerial techniques. This is why one finds so many formalised control mechanisms in use in the financial area. It is the area where the American parent tends to exert most control, and it is the easiest area in which to harmonise American/British practice. Finally, it is an area which by its very nature is easier to control, because it is dealing very largely with inanimate symbols. Once these techniques are exported across the Atlantic, they have to be operated by British nationals within the American subsidiaries. This is the main reason for another major finding in this study, that there is a significant difference in the number of managers who have undergone management training in the American compared with the British companies. Of managers working for American firms in the sample 66.9 percent (n = 97) had attended management training courses, whilst only 48.7 per cent (n = 38) of managers working for the British firms had ($p<0.05$). The American firms were also much more likely to use management consultants for these courses (32 per cent ($n = 31$)) than were the British firms (23.6 per cent ($n = 9$)). The survey also found that American firms were rather more likely to send their managers on courses that were specifically designed for the needs of their firm than were the British firms, although the difference was not great (US: 18.8 per cent ($n = 18$); GB: 13.1 per cent ($n = 5$)).

The possession of some form of management training, particularly if it stresses certain management techniques, is clearly relevant to an argument which suggests that American firms are differentiated from comparable British firms by their stress upon the application of the rational techniques of capitalism. In line with other studies, e.g. Ellis and Child (1973), it was also found that in general terms the managers working for the American subsidiaries were better qualified than their British counterparts, even when 'qualified' is operationalised as any form of post 'A' level education. (These data are discussed more fully in Chapter 4). The significance of this finding is that one consequence of having a mass of formalised managerial controls in the company is that it requires personnel with a certain amount of formalised training to operate them.

In what sense does this evidence indicate that the American firms in the sample were more attached to the values of capitalism than the British firms? The connection is one pointed out by Weber. The American firms were more rational within the context of the capitalist system. American firms were, by and large, good examples of organisations run by professional managers. The measuring rod of profit and loss was pushed into more areas of the American firms, and it was pushed deeper than in the comparable British firms. This was possible because of the greater development of analytical managerial techniques like operational research, budgetary analysis etc. in these firms. These are of course mere techniques, but the unifying character of these techniques is that they seek to apply the principles of rational problem-solving to business planning and decision making. The greater application of these tools of business rationality has potentially two far-reaching consequences, although there is no direct evidence of either in this study. First, one could argue, along with Marris (1974), that once the necessary homo-logical measuring rod of profitability has been well developed for use throughout the organisation by the creation of profit centres and other devices, then far more decisions can be assessed in a commensurate way. This should lead to decisions being made on more 'rational' criteria rather than, to take Marris' example, 'according to the relative "pull" of departmental moguls'.[12] If this condition was met, then some of the assumptions of the contingency theorists about company goals might be satisfied, and the theory might find greater applicability. The second consequence would be that the attitudes and values of the employees of such companies would become increasingly less relevant, because the jobs inside the organisation would become increasingly tightly controlled, the tasks involved ever more carefully delimited and the performance more carefully monitored. This after all is one of the effects of 'management by objectives', when one ignores its motivational aspects. Thus the individual manager, whatever his own particular attitudes and values, would have his energy channelled in the direction sanctioned by the system.

To argue that the American firms were more formalised is to say that those firms had a larger number of rules and procedures, of controls and techniques for regulating organisational tasks. While this was true, it does represent something of a paradox, because the American firms appeared, at one level, to be very informal and non-bureaucratic. There were several indices of this greater openness on the part of the United States firms. There was firstly the question of the research access itself. It has been noted that it was far easier to gain research access to the American firms than to the comparable British firms. A second indicator was the physical design of the offices of the American companies. With the exception of US Electronics I, which was not notably different from its British counterpart, all the American companies had office sections that were modelled on the open plan system. There also appeared to be a less rigid distinction between 'office' and 'works' in the American firms, although this was not as marked as expected. The British companies were more inclined to spell out status differences inside the plant, for example by issuing keys to certain personnel for the washing and toilet facilities. No noticeable differences were found inside the production sections of the various plants. The layout and operation of the various processes seemed almost totally dictated by the technology, save that some of the American plants did seem rather more modern and certainly cleaner. These observations appear to be supported by other research (cf. Richardson (1956); Lewis and Stewart (1958); Novotny (1964), and PEP (1966)). The layout of office accommodation reflects differences in the ideology and philosophy of American business, which itself reflects differences between British and American societies, particularly in the area of stratification. In America it has been argued that the values of achievement rather than ascription are dominant. This means that inside the firm the distinctions between groups of employees, like managers and managed, should not be so important, because the barriers are not so rigid or permanent. The firm, like the society of which it is partly a reflection, will be more open. The authority structure within the American firms will be less permanent and more specific. People with specific positions and possessing particular expertise will hold authority within their particular delimited areas. The communication structure of the plant will reflect this openness and it is reflected in the physical design of the accommodation. The open plan structure facilitates more communication between all members of the plant and is a symbolic affirmation of the lack of caste-like distinctions within the organisation. [13]

The second index of the relative informality of the American firms in the sample is one that is of crucial importance in understanding the nature of the formalisation of the firms, and helps to resolve the paradox. The managers working in the American firms in the sample did not regard their organisations as being particularly bureaucratic and hedged around with a lot of unnecessary 'red tape', despite the fact that, as shown, there were a much larger number of fixed procedures and controls inside these firms. The explanation for this is to be found in the work of Gouldner. Gouldner explains in his celebrated work, *Patterns of Industrial Bureaucracy*, that the 'sheer degree of bureaucracy was not as important in eliciting complaints about red tape as was the *type* of bureaucracy'. [14] The controls and procedures in the American firms can be seen as examples of what Gouldner calls 'representative bureaucracy', that is rules and regulations that are regarded as legitimate inside the company. The procedures were regarded as wholly rational devices to maximise the goals of the firm. The majority (67 per cent) of the managers in the American firms had been on management training courses, many of which were specifically designed for the firm, and the managers therefore had in some senses been trained to appreciate these procedures. To a far greater extent than their British counterparts the 'American' managers regarded themselves as 'professionals', [15] and the range of management techniques that they had mastered were seen as the tools which all professional managers should possess. The American organisations were perceived to be less bureaucratic because the systems, which the managers largely found to be legitimate, controlled their behaviour, rather than any individual bureaucrat. Furthermore, the American organisations were also very informal when it came to personal relationships.

Another reason for the fact that, with the exception of US Electronics I, the American firms felt more informal, was that the American firms were more decentralised. Centralisation was defined, following Ellis and Child (1973) as 'the extent to which the locus of authority to make decisions affecting the organisation is confined to the higher levels of authority'. The evidence for decentralisation was gathered in the interviews with the key informants and in the management interview programme. The American firms involved their managers more in the decision-making process of their organisations. There were more meetings of managers to determine particular decisions and to plan strategies. There were more informal channels of communication in the American firms, as well as the general feeling that the senior executives were more 'approachable'. These findings were more marked in US Pharmaceuticals and US Electronics II, which perhaps reflects the influence of their products and consequent technology upon their organisational climates (cf. Burns and Stalker (1961); Woodward (1965), and Lawrence and Lorsch (1967)). There is clearly no simple mechanical relationship between production technology and organisational climate however, because the two comparable British firms did not exhibit the same characteristics. Confirmatory evidence of this finding from other studies is sparse. There is impressionistic evidence from Thomas (1969) that American companies in Britain allow their managers to participate more in the decision making of the organisation and this is supported, again impressionistically, by Stopford (1972). The best confirmatory evidence perhaps comes from the work of Heller (undated), who has shown, for a closely matched sample of American and British companies, that American managers tended to have more faith in their subordinates' abilities than British managers. This would be consistent with a more decentralised structure, which would involve more participation by junior managers. The best confirmatory evidence comes from the study with the best methodology for the purposes of this analysis. Sim (1977) writes: 'American subsidiaries tended to practice an open door policy and encourage their employees to participate in the planning process. British subsidiaries tended to confine their participation and information access to their top management personnel only'. [16] In many ways one would have expected formalised organisations to have been relatively decentralised; there is no need for detailed control from the top if the control of the organisation is managed by an elaborate system of procedures. This is consistent with the findings of the Aston researchers, e.g. Pugh et al., (1968, 1969) and with Hage and Aitken (1967), and Edstrom and Galbraith (1977). Apart from this purely structural explanation, there are other reasons why one might have expected this finding. America has for long been regarded as the leading country in the field of management theory, and the dominant ideology in America, at least the dominant ideology of the management schools and the 'progressive' companies, has been that version of the human relations movement that has been termed by McGregor (1960), 'theory Y'. Theory Y stresses the importance of individuals 'self-actualising', that is realising their own potential by being allowed to take a whole range of decisions that would normally, i.e. under the misguided direction of theory X, be taken higher up the organisation. At the managerial level of the firm this has led to what Peter Drucker has called 'management by objectives'. US Pharmaceuticals, US Print and US Consumer were all operating one form or another of MBO, none of the British companies was. [17] A relatively decentralised organisational structure is clearly consistent with the theory Y view. What is also important to notice is that there is a strong body of managerial opinion that such schemes also work in the sense that they directly produce greater output, or by reducing such variables as labour turnover, absenteeism etc., they reduce costs. Given the hypothesis that American firms are likely to be more concerned with such factors, then it is quite consistent to expect to find these schemes being implemented in such firms. Finally, the whole approach of the neo-human relations movement fits very much better into the social and economic structure of American society than it does into British society.[18]

Several writers have suggested that some of the most important differences between British and American industry lie in the area of technology. One of the most influential hypotheses suggests that there is a technological gap between England and America, i.e. that American firms are more competitive than British firms because they use a more sophisticated technology. The second technological hypothesis derives from the work of Woodward (1965). Woodward argued that the most important functional area in a firm is (a) determined by the dominant production technology and (b) itself influences the structure and dynamics of the company. The hypothesis of this study is that the most important functional area of the firm will be as much a function of nationality as technology, and one should expect to see systematic differences between British and American firms, particularly in the importance given to the sales function.

Two measures of technology were used in the research. All the firms in the sample were categorised into one of Woodward's four basic modes of production: prototype production; unit and small batch production; large batch and mass production; continuous process production. The second measure of technology was the workflow integration measure, developed by Inkson et al., (1970) for their abbreviated replication of the original Aston research. This scale, apart from providing a further measure of the type of technology used by the company, also provided a good index of the sophistication of the companies' production technology. All the pairs of firms in the sample fell into Woodward's mass production category with the exception of the firms in the printing machinery industry, which were in the small batch category. The results of the analysis did not present confirmatory evidence for Woodward's view that production technology has a marked effect on organisational structure. [19] There was only a very weak and rather unstable correlation between technology and structure (structure as measured by the Aston scales of formalisation, specialisation and autonomy, and technology as measured by the Aston workflow integration measure). Technology was not significantly correlated with any aspect of structure even at the 10 per cent level of significance, the closest association being with specialisation although even here size was a better predictor. There did appear to be a closer association between technology and the three elements of structure for the British firms and this might be a significant result. Rather than make deductions about the most important functional area in the companies from the work of Woodward, it was decided instead to ask the firms themselves. Thus the key informants, and the managers that were interviewed in the respective companies, were asked what they thought was the dominant function in their organisation, i.e. the function on which the ultimate success of the business depended. In general the production function was regarded as being of greater importance in the British firms, although there were important differences between the industries examined. Amongst the American firms a greater stress was placed on marketing rather than producing. It seems possible that this finding could account for the somewhat greater association between technology and structure for the British firms.

The British stress upon production, contrasted to the American stress upon marketing, is nowhere better illustrated than in the pharmaceutical industry comparison. GB Pharmaceuticals, as suppliers of chemicals largely, but not solely, to other firms, felt that they competed on price and delivery, a function of production, rather than on brand images etc. The main managerial effort in the company was devoted to production planning and control. Marketing (they called it sales) and research and development were both rather shadowy functions. It may seem surprising that in such a research-based industry the research and development function was of such little importance, but this reflects the situation of this particular firm. It was not attempting to compete in terms of basic research with the industry leaders, but was instead concentrating on producing cheap specialised chemicals to order. The American pharmaceutical company also performed hardly any basic research, but for rather different reasons. The American parent concentrated the research activity in the United States. Production in this company was regarded as an important function, but not one that required a great deal of managerial time and effort. Many of the production processes had been perfected in the United States, much of the machinery was imported from America along with many of the specialised semi-finished chemicals. Their only real problems, they claimed, were with the British suppliers who allegedly found it impossible to deliver to time. The company regarded itself as basically a marketing company, energetically selling its products to the Health Service via general practitioners and hospitals, as well as selling patent medicines to wholesale and retail outlets. [20]

The companies in the furniture industry presented clearcut differences between the British and American situation. In the British company the emphasis was upon design and quality production, indeed the company had won awards for its innovations in both areas. The company had originally made its name in producing furniture in the craftsman tradition, and the ethos of the firm was still one where the artistic quality of the product was regarded as of supreme importance. In the American firm the accent was upon profitability at all costs and craftsmanship was regarded as a rather outmoded concept, appropriate only for rather backward industries. The American firm saw its success as being based upon an efficient production system, which was in parts highly mechanised, and by successful marketing techniques. The company heavily advertised its own brand name and certain distinctive features of its products in an attempt to distinguish it from its competitors. Whereas the British firm regarded its crucial function as its design capability, and to a lesser extent its production expertise in producing high quality products, the American firm took production for granted and believed that its success was due to the efficiency of its marketing department.

The electronics industry comparison represented a different world to that of furniture. All three firms were engaged in selling their products to other companies, and so product marketing was a different sort of exercise to the one found in the consumer industries. US Electronics I regarded production as the most important function in the firm. Its products were not quite so sophisticated as the other two companies in this sector and much of its output went to public corporations. The company therefore competed on price and reliability, i.e. its ability to meet consistently stringent requirements from other businesses. The firm competed therefore by having an efficient workflow organisation. Although the firm was American, in many ways it bore all the marks of a highly anglicised organisation from the point of view of this research. For example, it did not possess the informality and employee centredness that was characteristic of many of the American firms in the sample. On the other hand its decision-making structure was more centralised than most of the other American firms. It seems possible that part of the explanation of this pattern lies in the following set of circumstances. First, the company was not tightly controlled by its American parent. One of the reasons for this was that the subsidiary was eminently successful, the average return on assets for the years 1955–67 was 28 per cent. This meant that there were no particular business reasons to interfere in the running of the company, which was clearly doing well. Thus there tended to be fewer formal controls in this company than were found in the other American organisations. The other two firms in this sector were involved in making rather more sophisticated control equipment for other companies. Despite the relatively sophisticated nature of their products, the basic production process for both companies was that of mass production, in that basic control equipment was built for stock in very large numbers and then additional, more specialised, pieces were added to suit the requirements of individual customers. Both companies regarded production as of central importance with research and development very close behind.

In the consumer products field, although it was clear that both firms placed considerable emphasis upon production as Woodward predicted, the perfecting of high-volume competitively priced products being essential to both firms, yet it was also clear, particularly in the American firm, that marketing was of supreme importance. This was accentuated by the fact that US Consumer marketed some of the products of its parent firm that were not actually manufactured in Britain. The American firm advertised very heavily, traded on its brand name and attempted to build up brand loyalty. The British firm relied more on the price and quality of its products, more a function of its production department.

The printing machinery manufacturers presented a rather different case. The production of such machinery, and indeed the printing machinery itself, is very complex. These firms are samples, in Perrow's terms, of companies where there are many exceptions in the manufacturing process. No machine is ever quite like any other as they are made to a customer's special order, but the search procedures, i.e. the procedures for satisfying the customers' requirements, and constructing the machine are relatively routine. [21] This categorisation is more useful than Woodward's classification of the firms as being in the small batch and unit production category, because it is more informative. According to Woodward's thesis, the dominant function in these firms should be research and development, and indeed this was the unanimous answer from both the American and the British firms. Both firms however, had high scores on the Aston formalisation index, both were quite highly specialised (see Table 3.10).

Table 3.10

Organisational structure of British and American firms: functional specialisation

US Pharmaceuticals	9	GB Pharmaceuticals	8
US Print	15	GB Print	16
US Furniture	8	GB Furniture	3
US Electronics I	15	GB Electronics	10
US Electronics II	16		
US Consumer	13	GB Consumer	12

For scale details see p.II in appendix specialisation. Possible range: 0–16. A high score denotes greater functional

109

The organisational climate measures showed that the American firm was felt to be more open and flexible, more organically organised, whilst the British firm was felt to be rather bureaucratised. These data indicate perhaps the fact that the American firm had adapted much more quickly to the changes which had revolutionised the industry. Until about ten years ago the industry had been a relatively stable one and the demand for printing machinery bouyant. The British firm concentrated upon production, perfecting its production techniques in the spirit of craftsmanship that ran deep in the industry. Its sturdy well-made machines sold well and were backed by a service department which the firm regarded as being crucial to its success. The American firm found itself in a similar position, priding itself on its production and service functions. It was the necessity to provide service facilities that persuaded the company to set up in Britain in the first place. It may well be that the American firm placed a greater emphasis upon the selling of its machines than the British company. Certainly there were managers in the British company who said that in the 'old days' good machinery 'sold itself', but it is difficult to be certain that this difference existed. What is certain is that both firms were overtaken by advances in technology, particularly computer and photo-typesetting, that were largely not of their making, and their market had been severely damaged. There was still printing machinery that needed servicing, there were still smaller printers who demanded their products, but the new processes were dominant elsewhere. The firms had reacted by channelling enormous resources into research and development; attempting to retain their respective positions in the market by diversifying into the new technology. Organisational structure, like social structure, does not automatically adapt itself to pressures from the external environment however. The new importance of research and development had certainly not manifested itself in the organisational structure of the British firm. On the other hand, there was not much evidence to indicate that the organisational structure of the American firm had changed much either, it had always been a rather more flexible organisation. Indeed, there were signs that the American organisation, following poor results, was becoming more formalised as pressure was exerted by the American parent for a general tightening up of its operations. The American company was also reacting to its situation by adopting very aggressive and competitive selling techniques. This was being managed not by retraining old personnel, but by recruiting new salesmen. It was clear from the management interviews that this new policy was resented by some of the older managers as being somehow inappropriate for such an industry.

In conclusion it was found that Woodward's thesis that production was the crucial department under mass production technology was quite strongly supported in the case of the British firms studied, but not so for the American firms. In two clear cases, furniture and pharmaceuticals, marketing was thought by the firms themselves to be more important, and in a third case, consumer products, there was a marginal difference in the same general direction. In the one case of small batch production in the printing machinery industry, both firms regarded research and development as crucial although this had not always been so, and there were signs that the American firm was beginning to stress marketing more.

These differences in the dominant function in the two groups of firms can be related to long-standing differences in the socio-cultural structures of the two societies. It can be shown that the nature of the American stratification system, particularly with its stress upon the values of achievement rather than ascription, led to a more homogeneous population [22] and fostered the development of marketing as a crucial function in American business. Early British expertise was much more in production, and the highly stratified home market did not encourage marketing techniques. Although the characteristics of the British market undoubtedly changed during the early decades of the twentieth century, in terms of it becoming less heterogeneous, other features, like the existence of cartels and the predominance of an essentially sellers market, still dominated Europe. The established markets yielded relatively high profit margins and were capable of continued growth. Under these conditions marketing remained in Britain very largely the province of the very senior company executives, who acted in the tradition of the merchant traders, making alliances for marketing purposes with other traders, and whose main skills lay in their capacity to outbargain and outmanoeuvre other businesses. America, wedded more strongly to the capitalist ethic, ensured that its home market was more competitive, at least in principle, by the anti-monopoly policy. One consequence of this difference was that in America the merchant trader practices that passed for marketing in England became very dangerous, and were therefore largely superseded by a more rigorous approach. The approach stressed market research, sales forecasting and a thorough training of the sales workforce. It has been shown that these techniques were more prominent in the American firms in the sample than in the comparable British firms. Although the post-war sellers' market has disappeared as more anti-monopoly legislation has followed in Britain, the 1966 PEP report on British industry could still report that much of British industry was still dominated by the production side of the business. [23]

It has been argued above, on the basis of the present and other data, that part at least of the alleged American superiority in terms of economic performance can be seen to lie in the field of marketing. A more traditional approach has been to argue that the 'gap' was a technological one,

111

that American firms competed on the basis of superior research and development, and technology. It could well be, of course, that the two are related; heavy research investment requires extensive marketing of the final products to recoup the initial expenditure. An attempt was made to test the hypothesis that the American firms in the sample were utilising superior technology in the manufacture of very similar products. In order to test this hypothesis it was necessary to use a relatively sensitive measure of technological sophistication, as it was felt unlikely that there would exist very great differences between the two groups of firms. An appropriate measure appeared to be the measure developed by the Aston researchers from Amber and Amber's (1962) 'yardstick for automation' (the scale is contained in the organisational structure schedule, see Appendix 2). The scale attempted to do two things: first, it attempted to measure how sophisticated was the mass of the company's equipment (the measure used was the mode); secondly, it attempted to assess how sophisticated was the single most sophisticated piece of the equipment used in the company's workflow. The results of these two measures are presented in Tables 3.11 and 3.12.

Table 3.11

Automaticity of production technology of British and American firms
mode score: main sample

US Pharmaceuticals	1	GB Pharmaceuticals	2
US Print	1	GB Print	2
US Furniture	1	GB Furniture	1
US Electronics I	2	GB Electronics	1
US Electronics II	2		
US Consumer	4	GB Consumer	1

Scoring key for Tables 3.11 and 3.12: hand tools and manual machines, 0; powered machines and tools, 1; single-cycle automatic and self-feeding machines, 2; automatic, repeats cycle, 3; self-measuring and adjusting, feedback, 4; computer control, automatic cognition, 5.

The results from these two measures do not give unqualified support to the hypothesis. If one considers the modal scores presented in Table 3.11, then in two industries, pharmaceuticals and printing machinery, the British firms would appear to be using a more sophisticated technology overall. Only in the electronics and consumer fields did the Americans possess what appears to be a technological advantage.

Table 3.12

Automaticity of production technology of British and American firms (measure of most sophisticated single item): main sample

US Pharmaceuticals	2	GB Pharmaceuticals	4
US Print	4	GB Print	4
US Furniture	3	GB Furniture	2
US Electronics I	3	GB Electronics	1
US Electronics II	4		
US Consumer	4	GB Consumer	3

Table 3.12 appears to give rather more support for the hypothesis in that only in the pharmaceutical industry does the British firm appear to have a technological lead. In order to make an overall judgement however, consideration must be given to each of the cases in turn.

The American pharmaceutical company, it was clear, was not competing on the basis of advanced production technology. Its main advantage lay in two areas, one of which, marketing, has already been discussed. Its other advantage was to be found in the nature of its products, sophisticated pharmaceutical chemicals that were the end result of an intensive research and development effort, largely carried out by the parent company in the United States. These chemicals were, by and large, not difficult to produce (many of the more sophisticated intermediate chemicals were anyway imported from the parent company) so that the company did not require a sophisticated production department. The company's products were very largely covered by patents. The British company, by contrast, could not afford a very large research and development effort, and instead it competed in a narrow range of chemicals, very few of which carried any patents. Its competitive edge depended very much on the efficiency of its production department, and this is reflected in its higher score on the technology index.

In the printing machinery comparison, both firms competed on the basis of their technology and the abilities of their production and service departments. The American firm did not import any technology from the United States, all the research and development being performed in this country (the parent company was not directly involved in this business in the United States). As the American firm did not have any technological advantage over its British counterpart, indeed the index indicates that it was slightly inferior in this respect, it was, as has already been shown, turning to aggressive marketing, where it believed it did have a comparative advantage.

In the three other industries that were investigated there was some evidence to suggest that the American firms were competing with more advanced technology than their British counterparts; this was conspicuously the case in the area with the greatest research and development input, the electronics industry. Even in the furniture industry however, not an industry noted for its technological innovations, the American company did possess two very sophisticated pieces of equipment, one for producing felt and the other for covering the upholstery springs with felt. Both machines were made by the American parent and had world patents.

It should not be surprising to find that there are a number of cases where American production technology does not appear to be superior to the British. As already shown, the American comparative advantage can lie in areas other than superior technology/research and development, e.g. it can lie in marketing expertise. An examination of American direct investment in the British economy (cf. Dunning (1969), (1970) and (undated)) shows that American firms are heavily concentrated in two sectors of the economy. First, they are in the science-based research-intensive industries, supplying both producers' and consumers' goods. In this sector one might expect to find an American technological lead. The American firms are also concentrated in industries supplying consumer products, often first developed in the United States, which have a high income elasticity of demand. These firms tend to concentrate on marketing, and one should not necessarily expect to find an American technological lead. Even in the first category of companies, the science-based concerns, one would not necessarily expect to find an American lead in production technology. Much of the American technological innovation is manifested in the products themselves, not necessarily in their production. Furthermore, although it can be shown that American companies spend proportionately more than comparable British companies on research and development in the United Kingdom, [24] there is still evidence to suggest that American firms spend only a tiny percentage of their research and development budget in their European subsidiaries, and this is primarily used to monitor European research and development. [25] By and large American firms prefer to carry out their research in the United States, where centralised laboratory facilities and the supply of research workers interested in applied work is much greater.

These observations would appear to fit the data produced by this research quite well. Thus in US Pharmaceuticals and US Electronics II, and to a lesser extent in US Electronics I, much of the basic research was carried out by the American parent company; there was very little research being done in the British subsidiaries. The American pharmaceutical company, as shown, actually concentrated upon marketing, not research; successful marketing was needed to recoup the expensive overheads initially incurred in the development stage. The large and relatively stable National Health Service market was an obvious attraction for such a company. US Consumer represented an example of a company selling products which had been developed first in America for the high-income consumer market. As Europe in general has approximated to the American consumer pattern, such firms, now with substantial experience in producing and marketing such products, moved to exploit the market. Emphasis is placed on trade names and trade marks in the selling process and the greatest effort made in the area of marketing. Research and development for these companies are not concentrated, as for the electronics and pharmaceutical companies, in technological breakthroughs, rather they concentrate on 'finding' new universal human needs and desires and on better ways of satisfying existing ones—they are as much related to marketing as to production.

The last area of company structure and policy that was investigated, to compare the response of British and American firms, was that of industrial relations. Two main hypotheses were derived from the comparative historical analysis in Chapter 2. First, it was hypothesised that the American firms would be less likely to be members of the relevant employers' association, preferring the greater flexibility offered by company agreements, which anyway would reflect American practice. Secondly, it was hypothesised that American firms would exhibit a tendency not to recognise trade unions, particularly white-collar trade unions, as bargaining agents.

This area of company policy proved to be the most difficult area to investigate, managers in both groups of companies generally exhibiting particular reluctance to talk about trade union matters in anything but the broadest and vaguest of terms. It is believed that one of the reasons for this sensitivity was the fact that many of the interviews took place during the miners' strike and overtime ban of 1973/4. Certainly it is thought that this fact influenced the responses of the American executives, who unfailingly seized upon the English industrial relations system as a major cause of England's economic problems. When this group was questioned about how the working, or lack of working, of the system had actually affected their company, only two executives could produce any evidence at all, and that seemed to the researcher to be largely trivial. One can see how certain ideas about the differences between Britain and America have gained popular currency and have influenced people's judgments, despite the fact that they do not have any experience themselves to support the propositions they are advancing.

The data presented in Tables 3.13–3.15 do not appear to indicate any systematic differences in industrial relations practices between the two groups of firms.

Table 3.13

Membership of employers' federations, British and American firms:

main sample

US Pharmaceuticals	Yes	GB Pharmaceuticals	Yes
US Print	Yes	GB Print	Yes
US Furniture	Yes	GB Furniture	Yes
US Electronics I	No	GB Electronics	No
US Electronics II	No		
US Consumer	No	GB Consumer	Yes

Table 3.14

Recognition of blue-collar unions as bargaining agents,
British and American firms: main sample

US Pharmaceuticals	Yes	GB Pharmaceuticals	Yes
US Print	Yes	GB Print	Yes
US Furniture	Yes	GB Furniture	Yes
US Electronics I	Yes	GB Electronics	No
US Electronics II	No		
US Consumer	No	GB Consumer	No

The main explanatory variable would appear to be the industry in which the firm was located. The interview data broadly supported this interpretation, although it did become clear that US Electronics II and US Consumer certainly did not encourage unionisation. Both firms claimed that their employees would gain no advantages from union membership, because the conditions of service, pay and fringe benefits offered in the company were already well above the average for their industries. [26] The other firms who did not recognise trade unions as bargaining agents declared that the unions had never bothered to make an approach, but there would be no objection if they did. The main reason offered by companies for not joining the relevant employers' federation was that they preferred to negotiate their own agreements with employees, or that they could see very few benefits in joining.

Table 3.15

Recognition of white-collar unions as bargaining agents,
British and American firms: main sample

US Pharmaceuticals	Yes	GB Pharmaceuticals	Yes
US Print	Yes	GB Print	Yes
US Furniture	No	GB Furniture	No
US Electronics I	No	GB Electronics	No
US Electronics II	No		
US Consumer	No	GB Consumer	No

There is not much evidence to suggest that industrial relations policies and practices are directly a function of contextual variables like location, technology or products, although size is probably important. If this is correct then it follows that this particular sample design has no particular merits when it comes to examining industrial relations practices, yet it has all the disadvantages of being very small. Fortunately there exists a study by Steur and Gennard (1971), which investigated the industrial relations practices of foreign-owned firms in the United Kingdom, and which can be used to supplement the data in this study. Although not all the firms in their sample were American owned, it was clear that the great majority were. The authors noted that there was a tendency for foreign firms to prefer the autonomy of company bargaining, and they cited a large number of American firms which had left their respective employers' federation to bargain separately. This was by no means a universal practice however, and seemed to vary quite widely from industry to industry. They went on to analyse the frequently made claim that 'some American-owned firms are anti-union and have refused to recognise British trade unions', and although they had no difficulty in finding cases where this was unquestionably true they generally found themselves in agreement with the TUC's own findings, and suggested that: 'The general conclusion is that non-recognition of manual-worker trade unions by foreign-owned firms is no worse than amongst domestic firms'.[27] They declared that the problem seemed larger than it was, because much more publicity tended to be given to foreign firms that got involved in recognition disputes, e.g. Kodak, Mars, Heinz and Roberts-Arundel. There was some evidence to suggest that American firms were very reluctant to admit white-collar unions into the firm, indeed the Association of Scientific, Technical and Managerial Staff complained on this very point to the Royal Commission on the Trade Unions (1968),[28] but again Steur and Gennard wondered if such antipathy was really any greater than amongst domestic firms. Finally, on the question of industrial disputes, they concluded from the data presented that 'foreign subsidiaries are less subject to strikes than the domestic firms',[29] and this conclusion is also supported by Creigh and Makeham (1978). They also noted that the pattern of strikes appeared to differ. 'The comparison suggests that the very big and very small strikes are more important in the domestic total. The foreign-owned firms are given to nice (sic), medium-sized disputes'.[30] This finding may well suggest differences in the personnel policies and industrial relations procedures of the American companies. In particular one might suggest that the tendency to have company agreements, rather than industry agreements, would tend to mean that the procedure for settling disputes was much more streamlined and manageable, thus helping to cut out small stoppages. Similarly, the higher capitalisation of American firms may have led them to be wary of long drawn out stoppages, which halted expensive capital equipment. At the same time, because of their low ratio of labour costs to capital costs, they would be in a better position to 'buy their way out of trouble'.

This chapter has reported on the organisational structure and process of the matched sample of British and American firms. A number of differences between the two populations were established. First, the American firms possessed in general a much greater range of managerial techniques for controlling the affairs of the organisation; to use a rather old fashioned phrase, there was more 'scientific management' in these organisations. Secondly, the American firms tended to offset the effects of this potentially bureaucratising organisational feature with a much more informal managerial style, which was even found reflected in the design and layout of the buildings. Thirdly, there was some evidence to suggest that the American firms regarded marketing as a rather more important function than the British firms, which were more inclined to concentrate upon production. All these differences can be related to differences in the socio-cultural environment, past and present, of British and American societies, but to talk of causation would clearly be simplistic. Capitalism in both societies has been mediated through the web of social structure and the end result has clearly been rather different in the two societies. Some of these differences are reflected in the comparison of the British and American manufacturing organisations.

Table 3.16

Product moment correlations of elements of context with structural variables on British and American manufacturing organisations operating in Britain

Size of organisation	Formalisation	Specialisation	Autonomy
US	-0.28	0.64	0.24
GB	0.19	0.66	0.07
US + GB	-0.17	0.70 ‡	-0.29
Size of parent * organisation			
US	-0.16	0.59	0.39
GB	0.88 ‡	0.41	-0.92 ‡
US + GB	0.29	0.54 †	-0.64 ‡
Dependence			
US	0.36	-0.26	-0.02
GB	-0.87 †	-0.11	-0.87 †
US + GB	-0.13	0.09	-0.60 †
Operations technology			
US	-0.21	0.34	-0.25
GB	0.22	0.58	0.61
US + GB	-0.15	0.51	-0.27

* Logarithm of number of employees.

† Significant at the 10 per cent level.

‡ Significant at the 5 per cent level.

Notes

1   This study claims to have matched American, Japanese and British companies operating in Malaya on the following variables: 'product or product mix, industry, technology, level of integration, age, size, labour markets served and other environmental variables'. (p.46). Unfortunately no details of this remarkable matching were presented and so it is impossible to see just how successful the enterprise has been.

2   Full details of the organisational climate index are given in Chapter 5. When the instrument was piloted, respondents from firms with more than 5,000 employees found themselves incapable of giving meaningful answers to questions about the climate of their organisations.

3   There seems general agreement now that size is a crucial variable (Child, 1972). There is also considerable evidence to suggest that the industry that a firm is in makes a difference (Ellis and Child, 1973).

4   Several writers have argued that American firms operating abroad are by definition amongst the most progressive of the total population of American firms (Dunning (1969), Kindleberger (1969)). Furthermore, it would appear to be a reasonable assumption that those companies which respond to research requests are by definition more progressive.

5   Kingston, 1971.

6   British Institute of Management, 1970.

7   In some companies these two stages were collapsed into one. The most usual office holders present were the company secretary and the personnel officer, although for some companies the managing director or his deputy attended.

8   The Aston schedules used were based on those developed by Pugh et al. (1968, 1969) and abbreviated by Inkson et al., (1970).

9   Hall, 1972, p.196.

10   Kingston, 1971. For full details see Appendix 1.

11   This is a reference to the work of Burns and Stalker (1961), Woodward (1965) and Lawrence and Lorsch (1967). In contrast however, one might note the findings of Aitken and Hage (1971), who failed to establish a correlation between formalisation and innovation, although their sample was of health, education and welfare organisations. It should be noted that formalisation has been defined here in a rather different way from many researchers, and on this conceptualisation it is certainly possible to be organically organised and yet highly formalised.

12   Marris, 1974, p.240.

13   Bernstein (1967) has developed a very similar argument for the connection between school architecture and educational ideologies, drawing upon the distinction made by Durkheim between organic and mechanical solidarity. The article is informatively entitled 'Open Schools, Open Society?'.

14   Gouldner, 1954, p.219.

15   This conception of managers as professionals is developed in Chapter 4.

16   Sim, 1977, p.48.

17   It should be noted that 'management by objectives' in fact requires that formalised job descriptions and targets be drawn up and put in writing.

18   The neo-human relations practitioners acting as 'change agents' in companies, demand access and co-operation from firms which are more likely to be forthcoming in the more open American business community. Furthermore, those theorists who emphasise the value of 'T group' methods stress the importance of individual personality and feelings, and recommend openness and authenticity as the route to good interpersonal relations, and to an organisational climate that will be receptive to innovation and change. It is likely that very many managers in Britain would consider such strategies as an invasion of the privacy of their personal lives.

19   The work of Donaldson (1976) provides a good review of the literature on the Woodward thesis.

20   It might be argued from the following description that the two companies were not exactly matched for their products, and therefore that it was not a fair comparison. This criticism has a certain justification, even thought the products of the two firms were very similar.

21   Perrow, 1970, ch.3.

22   At the very least it can be argued that this was perceived to be the case.

23   In many ways this finding would seem to run counter to the recent view that production management is underdeveloped in British industry. Several comments can be made on this finding. First, one should note a certain ambiguity in the question which was asked, which was what was the dominant function in their organisation. In most of the American firms the production process was controlled in one way or another by the parent company, e.g. product specifications were laid down, the type of machinery to be used was specified. The success of the company from the British point of view therefore, tended to lie in those areas of the company where they had considerable discretion on policies and practices, and marketing was the key function here. The British firms were clearly not affected by what might be described as the 'overseas subsidiary effect'. This does not explain the apparent paradox of why most of British manufacturing firms stressed production as the key function, whilst production is supposed to be the Cinderella function in Britain's manufacturing industry. It is assumed that one of the indices of Britain's allegedly underdeveloped production management is the low pay and status which accrue to that occupation. Two points can be

made here: first, it does not follow that just because a function is regarded as vital that high pay and status flow in the direction of that function (dustmen?). To believe such a proposition would be to embrace a particularly crude version of the functional theory of stratification. Secondly, some writers have wished to argue that the relatively low pay of production personnel in British industry is not a function of lack of esteem but merely of oversupply. This view is supported by the influential OECD report, *Gaps in Technology*, which found that: 'In relation to the size of the age group the UK is training 40 per cent more technologists than the US' (p.37). This view is supported by Gannicott and Blaug (1969) who demonstrated that the shortage of engineers was illusory, a function of the power of the engineering lobby in British society combined with the use of discredited manpower forecasting techniques by the Committee on Manpower Resources. This view now seems quite widely accepted (cf. Wilkinson and Mace (1973)).

24   Gruba, Mehta and Vernon, 1967.
25   Stanford Research Institute, 1963; quoted in Dunning, 1970.
26   It was not possible to check the accuracy of these particular assertions. Some general evidence about relative pay and conditions is presented in the text.
27   Steur and Gennard, 1971, p.97.
28   Donnovan, 1968, Minutes of Evidence No. 53.
29   Steur and Gennard, 1971, p.125.
30   Ibid.

4 British and American manufacturing organisations: the managers

In Chapter 3 the organisational structures of the British and American companies were compared along with certain aspects of the actual working of the respective firms. An organisation is defined not only by its products and structure however, but also by the people who create and work that structure, the management personnel. This chapter reports on the profiles of the managers employed by the two groups of companies. There were several reasons for concentrating on the managers rather than the blue-collar employees. First, it was felt that the characteristics of the population of blue-collar workers were more likely to be 'determined' by such factors as local labour market conditions, production technology etc., rather than by the operation of certain specific selection policies, which would hopefully reflect the basic goals and philosophy of the company. Secondly, it was clear that the research could not hope to obtain a clear grasp of the structures of the different companies without talking to the managers who had to operate those structures. Finally, there exists a considerable literature on the sorts of differences that one would expect to find between British and American managers and comparatively little on blue-collar workers. In short, it seemed likely that part of the difference between British and American companies might be expected to lie in the fact that the two groups of companies selected different types of people to manage the companies' affairs.

The data on the managers were collected by means of a questionnaire which was distributed to as many managers in each company as possible and from these responses a further sub-sample of managers was interviewed. Details of the sample are given in Table 4.1. [1] In attempting to see whether American-owned firms employed distinctively different persons as managers from their British counterparts, two strategies were adopted. First a number of questions were asked about selection procedures and strategies in the companies. [2] A check on these responses was possible by adopting a second strategy which involved looking at the characteristics of the resultant population of managers.

In what follows an attempt has been made to test a wide range of hypotheses developed from the theoretical arguments expounded in Chapter 1 and informed by the historical perspective presented in Chapter 2. In summary the hypotheses were that the 'American' managers would, on average, be younger, better qualified, have experienced a greater amount of inter and intra-firm mobility, would be more likely to be female, would probably show signs of being more ruthless or 'inner-directed', would work longer and harder and would in general exhibit a greater degree of commitment to the business world.

Table 4.1

Number of usable management questionnaires returned
and number of managers interviewed per firm

American firms	Managers in company	Usable questionnaires returned	Interviews conducted	Percentage of managers on which data collected (col.2 as percentage of col.1)
US Pharmaceuticals	104	51	12	49
US Print	40	18	8	45
US Furniture	11	10	5	91
US Electronics I	200	20	10	10
US Electronics II	90	20	9	22
US Consumer	180	26	10	14
Total	625	145	54	23
British Firms				
GB Pharmaceuticals	56	26	10	46
GB Print	145	15	8	10
GB Furniture	25	8	4	32
GB Electronics	25	12	8	48
GB Consumer	222	17	9	8
Total	473	78	39	16

The hypotheses about selection involved an investigation of the personnel function of the various firms and this enquiry permitted a test of a subsidiary hypothesis that the American firms would regard personnel selection and development as rather more important than the British firms. The basis of this prediction was that traditional American labour shortages had caused American companies to focus rather more attention upon labour productivity than British firms. Furthermore, the hypothesised greater stress on the values of capitalism on the part of such firms should have led them to concentrate on making every area of the firm as efficient as possible, labour included. Finally, motivational theories of management, management development programmes etc. are largely American artifacts. There was some evidence to support the hypothesis. In two instances, printing machinery and consumer products, the American firms possessed a larger personnel department.[3] There was no difference between the firms in the pharmaceutical comparison, and very little difference between the firms in the electronics industry. Neither of the furniture firms had separate personnel departments. These differences in size could not be accounted for by some of the personnel departments having responsibility for industrial relations matters and others not. It seems likely that the explanation lies in the fact that the American firms regarded the department as being of greater importance. It was certainly true, as already noted, that the American firms were more systematic in personnel selection, being more likely to draw up job descriptions and man specifications than the British firms. The re-analysis of the BIM study on management selection in Britain also revealed that, holding size of firm constant, American firms were more likely to spend more on the selection process.[4] Although none of the differences is statistically significant, all the differences are in the predicted direction. The BIM data also showed that American manufacturing firms were more likely to use a systematic interviewing technique in selection, e.g. NIIP's seven point plan or something similar.

It was hypothesised that the American firms would use more achievement-oriented and universalistic criteria in selection than British firms. This hypothesis gained some support in that British firms gave a higher priority to personal introductions, which might be thought to stress the values of particularism and ascription, than the American firms. On the other hand the American firms were more likely to use selection consultants and executive searchers than their British counterparts. This latter finding is reinforced by the re-analysis of the BIM data.[5]

Did the American firms end up with managers who possessed essentially different characteristics from their British counterparts? The most useful way of investigating this problem was found to be by examining the results of the selection process over the years by comparing the two populations on the range of dimensions outlined above. The first hypothesis about the differences between the two populations was that the 'American' managers would be found to be younger. Theoretically this should follow if the American firms were more committed to the values of achievement than British firms. Ability not age should be the defining marks of recruitment and promotion in such firms. One might also note that since 1968 all forms of age discrimination in employment have been forbidden by law in America. [6] There is considerable supporting evidence from other writers for the hypothesis: Novotny (1964), Dunning (1970), and Dubin (1970) all assert the existence of such a difference, although none of them actually cites any evidence. The only study which does furnish evidence from a reasonably matched sample, Ellis and Child (1973), fails to note any differences in this area. The present findings are consistent with Ellis and Child, and no significant differences were found between the two populations. When the age of the managers was cross-tabulated with their position within the organisation to see whether it was true that younger managers rose more quickly in American-owned companies, no significant difference was found. When the data for the paired comparisons were examined however, in the printing, consumer and pharmaceutical companies age was found to be a slightly better predictor of the managers' level in the British firms, but again the differences did not reach levels of statistical significance and were not marked. Finally, age was cross-tabulated with managers' functional area in the firm. It was found that in the American firms there was a significant correlation between age and function, the younger managers tended to be in marketing, whilst the older ones were to be found in production, finance and general administration.

In the British firms the connection between age and function was not so marked, but the younger managers tended to be in production rather than marketing. Finance and general administration were again staffed by relatively older managers. The fact that younger managers tended to be overrepresented in the marketing function within the American firms, and overrepresented in production within the British firms may well be a significant result. It has already been shown that, although there were industry differences, production was regarded as of more importance in the British firms and marketing in the American firms. If this finding is valid, it should not be surprising to find managers in these key functions appointed more on the basis of ability than on age, and one might therefore expect to find more younger managers in the crucial functions.

Just as it was hypothesised that in the American firms there should have been a weaker tendency to equate organisational rank with age grade, so too it was predicted that American firms would pay less attention to that other 'ascribed' quality, sex. In other words it was predicted that American firms would employ a greater percentage of women as managers than their British equivalents. Such national data as exists would seem to support the view that there are a greater proportion of women in administrative and managerial positions in the USA compared to the UK. [7] The results of this can be seen in Table 4.2. The number of women employed as managers in all the companies was low, only reaching

15 per cent in GB Consumer. Such small absolute numbers make any conclusions very tentative indeed, and although three of the American companies in the printing and electronics industries did employ more women than their comparative British companies, the overall picture is not one that can be said to support the hypothesis.

Table 4.2

Percentage of female managers, British and American firms

	Women managers	Percentage of management		Women managers	Percentage of management
US Pharmaceuticals	4	4	GB Pharmaceuticals	2	4
US Print	2	5	GB Print	4	2.5
US Furniture	0	0	GB Furniture	1	5
US Electronics I	14	7	GB Electronics	0	0
US Electronics II	5	5			
US Consumer	18	10	GB Consumer	33	15

The strongest test of the hypothesis that American firms stress the values of universalism and achievement more than their British counterparts comes in the area of qualifications for the job. It was predicted that 'American' managers would be better qualified than British managers. Table 4.3 summarises the main data.

Table 4.3

Percentage of British and 'American' managers with stated qualifications

Qualification	'US' managers		GB managers	
	%	N	%	N
Post 'A' level qualifications	56.0	80	33.4	26
First degree or equivalent	36.5	53	29.0	23
Management training	66.9	97	48.7	38

Some comments are necessary on this table. First, the figures are rather flattering to the British companies because of the contribution to the whole made by GB Pharmaceuticals, whose staff appeared to be particularly well qualified. If one discounted this contribution, then the difference becomes even more marked. Cross-tabulating qualification by

127

function, it was found that production managers tended to be better qualified than the managers in the other functions. This is particularly true, as one would expect, for the high technology industries of pharmaceuticals and electronics. However, production managers were found to be overrepresented in the British sample, and once this variable is controlled for, the gap between the qualifications of the managers working for the American firms and those working for the British firms widens still further. Curiously enough it is in the production area that the difference actually reverses itself. The British production managers tended to be slightly better qualified than their 'American' equivalents: 64 per cent of 'American' production managers ($n=21$) had a first degree or equivalent, while 75 per cent ($n = 21$) of British managers had. In all other areas the 'American' managers were better qualified and dramatically so in the marketing area. The British marketing managers were worse qualified, using either post 'A' level qualifications, or first degree or equivalent, as a measure of qualifications, than the managers in any other function. They also had the second smallest amount of managerial training, after the managers in general administration. This picture is very different in the American firms. Here the production managers were still the best qualified, but the marketing managers followed closely behind; 60 per cent ($n = 21$) of these managers possessed a first degree or its equivalent, compared with only 14 per cent ($n = 21$) of British marketing managers. Personnel managers in both sets of companies tended to be relatively well qualified, although better qualified in the American firms. Managers working in this function were also most likely to have had some form of management training in both the American and the British firms.

These findings, which showed the managerial personnel of the American companies to be better qualified than their British opposite numbers, are well supported by other research. Numerous studies have pointed out the comparative deficiency inside British managerial ranks,[8] indeed several writers have insisted that the major gap between British and American industry is not a technological one, but a managerial one.[9] The most interesting finding is not the general difference between British and American firms, which was perhaps predictable enough, but the nature of the observed differences. It could be argued that in the area of production the demands of a relatively sophisticated technology require well qualified managers, and thus the effects of culture are minimal. It is suggested that there are also other reasons operating in the case of the British companies. It has already been shown that the production department was regarded as the most crucial area for most of the British firms and, if this is correct, it should follow that it was in this area that the firms were attempting to maximise efficiency. One of the ways of doing this would be to hire managers with obvious formal technical qualifications for the job. By contrast, an area like marketing was regarded by many of the British companies as something which did not require much, if any, technical expertise, certainly nothing that could be learned formally from the textbook or college. What it did require was a creative approach, and certain personality features like extroversion, flair, drive, 'feel for the product' etc. These features were not seen by the British companies as being necessarily correlated with academic qualifications—much better correlates were experience and the 'right type of person'. The American companies were in a rather different position. Production was regarded in most cases as being rather more routine, most of the processes were developed and perfected in the United States, and the American parent often issued strict instructions about the type of machinery to be used, exact product specifications, quality control etc. What was required at the British end of the operation was managers who could routinely manage the process, and this did not require men with the highest academic qualifications. This interpretation is reinforced by Steur and Gennard (1971), who note somewhat similar findings in their comparative study of the electrical engineering industry. They observed that: 'The knowledge input into the subsidiary of a foreign parent company need not all be embodied in the men on the spot'. Just as the British companies tended to concentrate on production, so the American companies tended to concentrate on marketing as the most important function. Marketing does not directly require highly qualified personnel in quite the same way as sophisticated technology might require qualified people to manage it, and so one finds, even in the American companies, that the qualifications of the marketeers are not so high as their fellow managers in production. Yet the American method of marketing does involve a whole range of sophisticated techniques which do require, at the managerial level, certain intellectual abilities, of which academic qualifications might be thought as good an index as any other.

One of the most often cited differences between British and American industry, is the fact that American managers exhibit very much higher rates of inter-firm mobility than the British. Certainly this prediction would follow from the theoretical analysis here. As Burrage (1969) has argued, in the more ascriptive British culture one would expect to find rather less inter-organisational mobility, British firms preferring to recruit potential managers at an early age and retain them for a long period of service, loyalty being of crucial importance. Thus one would expect the more particularistic relationships in British firms to be far more permanent than the more universalistic relationships that allegedly pertain inside American firms, where anybody who fits the universalistic criteria could fill the role. This line of reasoning is pursued by Dubin (1970) as well as Burrage, although the former does add that a part of the reason for this greater rate of inter-firm mobility may simply be one of scale. The number of business firms in the United States far exceeds that of Britain, and it follows that the opportunity to move among organisations is correspondingly greater. A study by Stewart and Duncan-Jones (1957) would appear to confirm this general view of greater mobility in the United States. They showed that only 27 per cent of top American managers in manufacturing industry had spent all of their working life in the same company, compared with 40 per cent of corresponding British top managers. Yet the data in general do not present a totally unambiguous picture. Studies by Wright Mills (1953), Newcomber (1955) and Brua (1973) all claim to show that one of the distinguishing features of top management in America has been its conspicuous lack of inter-firm mobility. The editors of Fortune (1956) describe this second view well when they summarise their own study of the 900 top managers in American industry in 1952: 'The typical 900 man committed himself to the company he now manages when he was between the age of twenty and thirty. For most industries the formula is start young and stick; the hiring away of executive talent is diminishing'.[10] It could be argued that this ambiguity is the result of differing definitions of 'top managers', and/or whether the studies bother to count the number of 'exploratory' moves that many young managers make in the first few years of their business life. If one considers the mass of managers below the top ranks in both societies however, the picture is just as confused. Granick (1972) declares, admittedly on the basis of one British company and an undisclosed number of American companies, that 'the British managerial turnover between companies is even greater than the American after the first few years of the individual's total career',[11] although he does add that he has the feeling that the British company might not be fully representative of British industry. Sofer (1970) reports in his study of 'Autoline' (US) and 'Octane' (GB) that the 'Autoline' men had experienced a greater amount of inter-firm mobility, but on several counts this comparison is not a good one. The best study of differential inter-firm mobility rates of managers in British and American industry is probably the Ohio/Midlands study of Inkson et al., (1970). They conclude that there was only a 'fractional difference between the two managerial samples'.[12] One of the problems with all this literature, and one that is quite common in the area of British and American industrial differences, is that 'impressions' are taken as substitutes for evidence. This fault is heightened by the fact that much of the literature is self-citing. Table 4.4 summarises the data on inter-firm mobility for this sample of managers. The evidence is not consistent with the view that the managerial employees of American firms had experienced greater mobility than the similar group employed in the British firms.

Table 4.4

Number of firms in the career of managerial respondents: main sample

Number of firms	'US' managers		GB managers	
	%	N	%	N
1	17.2	25	15	12
2 - 4	56.6	82	62	48
5 +	26.2	38	23	18·
Total	100.0	145	100	78

There are other sorts of managerial mobility besides inter-firm mobility in which one might have expected to find differences between the two samples. Not only can managers move between firms, but they can also move between functions during their careers and between jobs within the same firm. Table 4.5 summarises the data on the number of jobs that managers have held within their present firm. These findings, which show some differences in intra-organisational job mobility were predictable enough from an earlier finding that whilst all the American firms were operating some form of management development programme, only two of the British firms were doing so. These management development programmes involved, amongst other things, making sure that each manager went through a programme of different jobs. This finding is supported by other workers (cf. Granick (1962); Novotny (1964); Inkson et al., (1970), and Ellis and Child (1973)).

Table 4.5

Number of jobs held in present firm, British and American managers

Number of jobs	'US' managers		GB managers	
	%	N	%	N
1	19	28	29	23
2 - 4	60	87	61	47
5 +	21	30	10	8

The managers were finally asked about moves between functions in their business career. Granick (1972) amongst others, had pointed to the fact that advancement for British managers was largely within a single function, compared with considerable functional movement within American firms. Sofer (1970) also noted how this was characteristic of the American firm 'Autoline' operating in Britain, which he investigated. Three of the American firms, US Pharmaceuticals,

US Furniture and US Consumer did practise functional rotation as part of their management development policy, and so it was thought that there would be differences between the 'American' and the British managers on this variable. The managers were asked if they had changed functions during their career, and the result showed there to be no differences between the two populations. Exactly the same percentage, 44, reported that they had changed functions during their career. On reflection a better question might have been to have asked the managers about functional moves within their present firm, and it is likely that this would have revealed differences. What is noticeable is that the figure of functional moves is relatively high compared with that of other British studies. Clark (1966) for example, reports that only 28 per cent of his sample had changed functions during their career. Perhaps this is evidence to suggest that the stereotype painted by Granick, of the British manager who remains in one function throughout his career, is declining.

The analysis has so far concentrated on whether the two groups of companies selected different types of people to become managers. It is possible to reverse the question and ask whether there were any systematic differences in the features of the firms that attracted the managers in the first place. Two findings are worthy of comment. In the first place a small but significant group of managers working for the American firms cited the fact that the firm was American as a reason for joining. It is tempting to interpret this response as evidence of the prestige of American business inside management circles in Britain. It is probably wise to exercise a certain amount of caution in this interpretation however, because it was noted that many of the American firms made much of their 'American connection' in employee magazines, induction programmes etc. This clearly could have had an effect on the responses obtained in the form of *post hoc* rationalisations. The reasons for this response were pursued in the interview programme with interesting results. Some respondents argued that it was self evident that American firms were better. A more illuminating response was obtained from some of the younger managers who believed that their American firms offered a very good, and widely recognised training in certain areas of business; marketing and finance being most often mentioned.

Very few managers in either group of firms mentioned pay or fringe benefits as a factor attracting them to the firm. This was surprising in view of the widespread belief that American firms pay more and offer a more generous set of fringe benefits to their employees. No information on the relative pay or fringe benefits of the sample firms was collected because it was felt that this was too sensitive an area to broach in a piece of research that was already demanding a considerable amount of co-operation from the firms concerned. Two secondary sources of information throw light on the general matter of the relative pay and fringe benefits of American firms operating in Britain. The best evidence on pay is supplied by Dunning (undated) who shows that for the years 1970/1 US affiliates paid 23 per cent more wages and salaries per employee in UK firms. Only in eight of the thirty-nine industries investigated did the UK firms pay more. In attempting to see whether American companies were more generous with their fringe benefits than British companies, as is claimed for example by Seyfarth et al., (1968), the data were reanalysed from a BIM study on fringe benefits for executives. [13] A total of forty-seven American manufacturing companies were compared with 150 British manufacturing companies, suitably matched for size, on a variety of fringe benefits, e.g. 'top hat' pensions, bonuses, provision of company car etc. Although such a sample which does not match products has some limitations, it is interesting to note that although the American firms tended to be more generous in all areas, except for the provision of company cars, in no case did the differences reach a level of statistical significance.

Another part of the pervasive folklore about American companies, is that American firms are particularly good at providing job satisfaction for their employees. There are several reasons for believing that this might in fact be the case. First, as already noted, America is the unquestioned home of a vast body of managerial theorising on the subject of the correlates of job satisfaction. The neo-human relations school of thought, heavily centred on the work of Abraham Maslow and his hierarchy of needs, argues that the need for self-actualisation is crucially important for white-collar employees, and that its satisfaction requires certain forms of organisational structure. The most 'appropriate' organisational form from this point of view contains several features which it is already shown were more likely to be found in the American firms. These include a more decentralised decision-making structure, which stimulates more participation in the decisions of the organisation, and from one point of view, a more informal managerial style. It should also be noted that three of the American firms were operating a managerial device, 'management by objectives', that was directly descended from the theoretical tradition of the neo-human relations movement. Finally, all the American firms were operating a management development programme, which it might be argued is more likely to consider the needs of managers than no programme at all. Finally, there seems general agreement that the main route through which schemes like MBO get into companies is through the work of managerial consultants, and evidence has been presented to show that American firms are more likely to use the service of such agencies.

The relative job satisfaction of the British and 'American' managers was assessed in a number of ways. First, the managers were asked a

Likert type question: 'Do you think that your present job gives you the opportunity to use your abilities to the full?' The response categories ran from 'completely' to 'not at all'. Secondly, the sample was asked which of a series of statements best described how they felt about their job (see question 18 on the management questionnaire in Appendix 3). Thirdly, these responses were probed and discussed in the interview programme. In broad terms the results of the inquiry into the relative job satisfaction of the British and 'American' managers did not reveal any differences between the two populations. In both groups the best predictor of the managers' response was their age and position in the organisational hierarchy of the firm. There was a clearer relationship between the level of the manager and his feelings about his job in the British firms; those near the top of their respective organisations tending to regard their job as rather more important to them than those nearer the bottom. This result reached the $p<0.01$ level of significance. In the American firms by contrast, although there were tendencies in the same direction, they did not reach levels of statistical significance. This finding could reflect the more participative style of American firms, which attempted to involve far more managers in the general decision-making process of the organisation. The British firms, by contrast, were in general more hierarchical.

During the interview programme both groups of managers were asked to elaborate on their answers to the questions about job satisfaction. One must treat these responses with extreme caution because the size of the interviewee sample was even smaller than that of the main questionnaire (GB:N=39; US:N=54). Although there were some interesting differences between the two groups of employees, again one was struck more by the similarities than the differences. The main points of contrast between the British and 'American' managers related to the areas of pressure of work, working conditions and level of involvement. More managers working for the American firms complained of the pressure of work compared with the corresponding British firms. This was partly because some of the American firms, particularly those that were using schemes like MBO, had put a greater structure on managerial jobs, had set targets and deadlines on projects where none had previously existed. These feelings of work pressure mentioned by the 'American' managers were backed up by the answers that they gave to the question on how many hours they worked on company business per week (question 28 on the management questionnaire). Controlling for managerial level and the function of managers, those working for American firms worked longer hours than those working for the British firms, although the differences did not reach a level of statistical significance. The average hours worked per week by 'American' managers on company business was 50.85, whilst the corresponding figure for the British managers was

47.91. Those managers working for the smaller firms appeared to work the longest hours, which perhaps offers further support for Ingham's thesis that smaller size generates a greater moral commitment on the part of employees. There was a predictable and significant relationship between the manager's level in the company and the number of hours he worked, the higher the level the more hours worked ($p < 0.01$), and managers working in the marketing function tended to work longer hours than those working in other areas of the business ($p < 0.05$). These findings, of greater pressure of work and longer hours for managers in American firms, find more general support in the literature. Granick (1972) comments upon the 'reduced pressure of work' to be found in the management of British firms compared with American enterprises,[14] although Dickson and Bucholz (1977), in their study of managerial attitudes in Scotland and America, found that the Americans valued leisure more highly.

Data on the comparative length of the working week must be treated with a certain amount of caution for a number of reasons. First, the questions asked in the various studies have not always been exactly the same; it clearly makes a difference if you include work done at home, as in the present study. Secondly, studies often do not give enough details of their sample for proper comparisons to be made. This is crucial information, because the function and level of the managers makes a difference to the result. Despite these reservations the available literature does strongly support the view of Child and MacMillan (1972), who argue that: 'Managers as a whole in the United States work very much longer hours than their British counterparts'. [15] The British managers complained more about their physical conditions of work than their 'American' counterparts, and the American firms were, by and large, much neater, cleaner and brighter than the British firms, despite the fact that the organisations were set up at roughly the same period of time. It could be that part of the explanation of these differences can be found in the fact that American companies are probably more concerned about their 'image' than British companies, and this concern for image manifests itself even in physical structure.[16] Finally, the British managers were more inclined to complain about the remoteness of the decision making in their firms than were the 'American' managers, and this fits in well with the data on organisational structure, which showed that the American firms were more participative and authority relationships were more informal. These differences are also supported by the results of the organisational climate index (see Chapter 5). There were some complaints in the American firms, especially from those managers at the top of the organisational structure, about control from the parent company limiting decision making, particularly in the area of expenditure, where elaborate formal justification had to be made

135

for capital or revenue expenditure over certain limits. As one would expect, these complaints were greater in the more tightly controlled companies.

It was expected that some of the managers working for the American firms might have complained about their jobs being insecure, but this was not the case. The reason for this expectation was that it is often argued that American firms are more ruthless than British firms in dealing with managerial 'failures'. Chruden and Sherman (1972) talk of the 'hire and fire' reputation of American firms in Europe, and Sofer (1970) in his comparative study of the American firm 'Autoline' with the British 'Octane Ltd', notes the 'unusually high risk of becoming a casualty at some point' in the American firm [17] and the propensity to retain 'dead wood' on the part of the British firms. [18] These features are supported by the observations of Farmer (1968) and Thomas (1969). This hypothesis was tested by asking the personnel managers about their policies on this matter, and the United States personnel managers did, by and large, give the impression of greater ruthlessness. Analysis of the managerial labour turnover figures for the two groups of companies however, did not appear to substantiate their claims. By and large the majority of managers in both the American and British companies said that they felt relatively secure, and did not feel that their companies pursued a 'hire and fire' policy. The only exceptions to this generalisation were some of the sales managers working for the American companies, who claimed that they were under considerable pressure to get results and reach certain targets. It could still be the case that at least some of the American companies were more ruthless than their British counterparts, and that this ruthlessness did not actually manifest itself in terminating the employment of managers, but in other more subtle ways that were impossible for an outsider to see. Alternatively, it could be argued that few managers were likely to admit in an interview situation that their employment was in any way at risk. Finally, one should bear in mind the buoyant employment situation at the time of the research, many of the firms in the sample reported difficulties in recruiting suitable managers to their companies. In such a situation firms are likely to be more reluctant to terminate a manager's employment, and the managers are less likely to feel insecure.

This chapter has so far looked at certain features of the two groups of managers for signs that would indicate that the American companies were more committed to the values of the capitalist economic order. The popular literature on American management has nearly always portrayed them as being more ruthless, more committed to the goal of profit than their British contemporaries. [19] Another way of testing this hypothesis was to present to the managers three different statements, derived from Nichols (1969), about the role of companies in society.

The managers were asked in the questionnaire to indicate which statements came nearest in their opinion. The results of this question are presented in Table 4.6.

Table 4.6

Responses to statements about the role of the company in society: main sample

Statement	Percentage agreeing	
	'US'	GB
A company can only have one responsibility and that is to maximise profit; only by doing this will the needs of the community, the customer and its employees be ultimately met.	9 (n = 13)	2 (n = 2)
A company conducted solely for the benefit of shareholders is unethical. The company must also consciously seek to satisfy the needs of its employees and the community.	52 (n = 75)	46 (n = 36)
A company's first consideration must be to make a profit, once this is achieved, then the company can consider the demands of its employees, its customers and the community.	39 (n = 57)	52 (n = 40)
Total	100 (N = 145)	100 (N = 78)

Several comments are worth making on these results. The major observation of course is that the managers working for the American companies did not appear to be more committed to profit-maximising values than managers working for British companies. There is some evidence to suggest that the results of this question are at least partly a function of management training. Those managers who responded positively to the second statement, the 'social responsibility' response, were more likely to have been on a management training course, although the association was not quite up to the level of statistical significance.[20] In view of the stress that such courses often place on human relations type literature, it is not difficult to see the possible underlying reasons for such an association.[21] This association between management training and the response to the question probably largely accounts for the greater response from the 'American' managers to the social responsibility category, as it has already been shown that the 'American' sample were more likely to have had some form of management training.

Brenner and Molander (1977) have shown that the 'social responsibility' concept is certainly no stronger in American management in general. Another possible reason for the result could have been that the American companies were more likely to be sensitive to their position in the host country and this could have had an effect on their managers.

Whilst support for the classical model of capitalism might be taken as one index of the hypothesised more aggressive American business style, another way of testing this view was to compare the opinions of the two groups of managers on what qualities they thought necessary for success in business. Yet when the question is phrased in this way, the literature itself reflects an ambiguous view of the American business manager. On the one hand, one has a body of material tracing its descent from the protestant ethic, which it is claimed became firmly established in New England around the middle of the seventeenth century, and gradually permeated its way through the rest of America, eventually breaking through into the South at the time of the Civil War. This historical legacy, the hypothesis states, can still be seen in the 'inner directed' American businessman devoting most of his energies to the pursuit of economic success. This view is challenged, in general terms, by David Riesman (1961) in his celebrated essay, *The Lonely Crowd,* and developed more specifically in the business environment by W.H. Whyte (1963) in his treatise *The Organisation Man.* Here the thesis is advanced that individuals are becoming increasingly 'other directed', that is, the approval of others is becoming more important than the pursuit of individual selfish goals. These apparently contradictory hypotheses can be welded together, if one attempts to locate them in periods of historical time. Indeed one does not have to look much further than Max Weber to see the intellectual origins of such theorising, and what arguably might pass for a theory of history. [22] Riesman's three categories of 'directedness' are nearly identical with Weber's types of orientation of social action. Riesman's tradition directed type is identical with Weber's traditional orientation, whilst the inner directed person follows closely Weber's value rational category. The other directed person, who chooses a given way of acting because he is anxious to receive the approval of others, is demonstrating at least one kind of purposive-rational (*zweckrational*) conduct. Finally, Riesman emphasises that his concepts are constructs, types, which appear to be identical in logical structure to Weber's concept of the 'ideal type'. Riesman's attempt to build a theory of history around these concepts by linking them to three major phases of population movement is not of direct concern here, although one might note in passing that he is rather less cautious and less successful here than Weber. Riesman's claim is that changes in the structure of the society are bringing about changes in the 'character' of the American population, tradition and inner directed people are declining at the expense of the other directed.[23] It is left to Whyte to directly apply these ideas to the business world. Although Whyte uses the term 'organisational man' instead of other directed, the similarity between the views of Whyte and Riesman seems obvious. From their respective viewpoints, the adaptable socially-attuned individual is going to succeed in business, while the creative, independent individualist is in for difficulties.

There are obvious difficulties in attempting to test such expansive theories, even so it did seem worthwhile to attempt to see whether the managers in the respective groups of companies perceived the qualities necessary for success in business in systematically different ways. Following Porter (1963), ten traits relating to business success were derived from the Riesman-Whyte hypothesis, and the managers were asked to rate them on the basis of how important they thought they were for success in business (question 16 on the management question-naire). The mean rank order of these traits for the British and 'American' managers is shown in Table 4.7.

Table 4.7

Mean rank order of traits thought necessary for success in business: main sample

	'US' managers	GB managers
Inner-directed:		
Forcefulness	5	7
Imagination	3	6
Independence	9	9
Self-confidence	2	2
Decisiveness	1	1
Other-directed:		
Tactfulness	6	5
Agreeableness	8	8
Cautiousness	10	10
Adaptability	4	3
Co-operativeness	7	5

The first conclusion that can be drawn from Table 4.7 is that the responses of the British and 'American' managers could clearly have been drawn from the same population. Although the 'American' managers did rate 'forcefulness' rather more highly than the British, whilst the British rated 'co-operativeness' rather more highly than the Americans, the results in general hardly lend support for the hypothesis that managers working for American firms felt that they had to adopt a more aggressive strategy to be successful. All managers seemed to believe that being decisive and self-confident were the two most important qualities for success, whilst being cautious and agreeable were not so important. Cross-tabulations between the rankings of traits and the manager's position in the company failed to reveal any significant differences, although there was a slight tendency for those at the higher levels of the organisation to put an even greater emphasis upon traits like 'decisiveness', 'forcefulness' and 'self-confidence', whilst those at the bottom tended to take rather more notice of traits like 'co-operativeness' and 'tactfulness'. In general however, one was struck by the very low standard deviations of the results, and the consequent picture of considerable homogeneity of feeling inside the various companies on what it took to be a successful manager.

Such results should lead one to think very hard about the value of Whyte's thesis, certainly in the form in which it is usually discussed. Ellis and Child (1973) have shown that although some stereotypes of managers may have a certain amount of empirical backing, most are rather clumsy conceptually, and in great need of being limited by a range of conditioning statements. Thus one wants to know exactly what are the basic features of the organisation man? What limits are imposed by his position in the organisation, managerial function etc.? When such analyses are done, one often finds that the sterotypes melt away. Kohn (1971) for example, investigated that close cousin of the organisation man, 'bureaucratic man', and found that men working in bureaucracies tended to be intellectually more flexible, more receptive to new experiences and more self-directed in their values than those employed in non-bureaucratic organisations, and these findings were broadly supported by Ellis and Child (1973). These findings, of course, completely contradict the usual stereotype of the bureaucratic personality.

By and large, cross-cultural studies of managerial attitudes of the kind contained in question 16, have failed to note many differences. Haire, Ghiselli and Porter (1966) in their study of 'managerial thinking', which covered fourteen countries, found that they could explain only about 25 per cent of the variance by reference to national differences, and the rest was accounted for by organisational differences. Whitely and England (1977) in a similar study report similar results. Studies which have focused more directly upon the Anglo-American dimension, including those of Heller and Porter (1966) and Heller (1968), have stressed the similarity of British and American managers, rather than their differences. One major problem with all these studies is the source of their samples. They were all drawn from institutions where managers were attending management training courses and, as already indicated, this training itself may account for some of the similarities found. Haire et al., (1966) even admit that one interpretation of some of their findings 'is that it reflects a sort of partial digestion of the exhortations of group-oriented consultants and professors of management during the past decade'. [24] Yet even these studies do note some differences that can be accounted for by reference to cultural differences. Haire et al., did find that American managers had a more favourable attitude than British managers towards the average person's capacity for leadership and initiative, whilst Heller and Porter found that American managers ranked 'aggressive' as a fairly important personality trait for success in one's job, and British managers ranked it last on a list of thirteen. It seems quite probable that the 'organisation man' syndrome is a product of a rather special set of circumstances that will be most common in certain segments of the United States business population. The key features of such a characterisation, to use Riesman's term, will be a large proportion of managers working for large corporations, [25] as well as a greater amount of geographical and job mobility than one would expect to find in England. [26] These factors will tend to create a situation where 'one does not know from what kind of family one's neighbours or one's colleagues come, or to what social class their parents belonged, or what they themselves have done in the past. They cannot be placed in a familiar social category except by observing and evaluating their manifest conduct or overt behaviour'. [27] These strains may well lead to the other-directedness of the organisation man, which Riesman and Whyte both found so striking, but it is doubtful whether their observations are common even in America. There is some evidence to suggest that the counter-stereotype of the inner-directed businessman is just as illusory. [28]

One other feature of Table 4.7 stands out, and that is that the items clearly do not fall neatly, as far as the respondents were concerned, into packages of 'inner' or 'other' directed items. Although the original article by Porter (1963) made no mention of the fact that the items drawn from Whyte and Riesman did not appear to form two scales, this was almost certainly the case. A review of the research in this area seems to indicate that human behaviour and attitudes are sufficiently complex to defy researchers' attempts to dichotomise them simply as inner- or other-directed. It would appear that for the attitudes and behaviours sampled, most people rely on criteria other than those hypothesised as the underlying dimension, or that they are employing a mixed strategy, i.e. applying an 'inner' orientation to some items, and an 'other' orientation to other items, and completely independent orientations to the rest. Thus Peterson (1964) subjected a scale developed by Kassarjian (1962), as well as several other similar scales that purported to measure inner- and other-directedness, to factor analysis, and discovered eight separate dimensions in the scales. These findings should serve as warnings to those who search for single 'basic' ideological dimensions on which people's attitudes and behaviours can be easily classified and predicted. If such single dimensions to exist, then empirical research into attitudes and values has surely been unsuccessful in locating them.

The concept of 'professionalism', which has often been central in discussions about the differences between British and American management, has so far been neglected. Part of the literature which purports to explain the relative success of American industry over its British counterpart has made considerable use of the distinction between the professional and the amateur. Burrage (1969) noted that 'amateurism' was probably the single most popular explanation of British economic failings. Granick (1962) talked of the two traditions of business, the amateur and the professional, and found that Britain was a country where the amateur dominated. Wilkinson (1964) came to very similar conclusions and was followed by Dubin (1970). At the level of the popular management magazines the term 'professional manager' is often used to denote the collection of traits that have been looked for in the 'American' manager sample, e.g. high academic qualifications, high inter-firm mobility. In short, the popular image of the American manager compared with his British counterpart is that he is more 'professional'.

Despite this apparent agreement amongst writers on the usefulness of the concept of 'professionalism' to highlight differences between British and American management, the concept itself is not self-explanatory. Different writers seem to operate with different reference points. [29] What does it mean to be a professional, particularly a professional manager? One of the major ways of answering this question has been to refer to a series of 'traits' which occupations are supposed to possess before they qualify as being professions. Amongst such trait theorists [30] the following major traits have usually been included. First a profession must involve a special skill based on theoretical knowledge which requires special training and education. Furthermore, the professional must be able to demonstrate his competence by passing a special test or examination. The profession will be organised in the form of a professional group or association, which will administer the required education and training, as well as regulate the conduct of members of the profession to make sure that professional members continue to render a service to the public in the appropriate manner. If the trait theory is accepted as legitimate for one moment, it should be clear that business management has difficulties in qualifying. [31]

The trait approach is open to a number of fundamental criticisms however, that render it unacceptable as a theory, as Johnson (1972) has persuasively shown. First, the theory begs the question, because in order to determine the defining marks of a profession, one must have some conception of what is a profession, and this of course is the very issue under consideration. It is quite clear that most of the trait theorists are working from an implicit model of the professions based upon the 'ancient professions'. Second, there is no theory which explains why particular traits are necessary for an occupation to be called a profession; why for example is the service ethic important? Third, the trait approach is ahistorical; there is no view of which traits came first or how they came. Finally, trait theory very easily falls into the trap of accepting the professionals' own definition of themselves.

Despite many of the difficulties which sociologists might have with trait theory, many of the managers in the main sample clearly adopted a rudimentary form of the theory when they talked about the idea of being professionals. Two groups of managers operated with the idea of their being professionals. The first group, consisting of (about) forty managers, considered themselves to be professional in the sense of having a specific expertise based on some particular area of knowledge that they had acquired in a (usually) public education institute. Into this category came the chemists, pharmacists, engineers, accountants etc. Very few of these managers appeared to fall into the category that Gouldner (1957) has designated as cosmopolitan however. Although they tended to conceive of themselves as professional accountants etc., their reference group was not that of their fellow professionals working for other companies or in private practice, but was rather of other members of their own company. They very rarely attended meetings of their profess-ional body, and although they nearly all read their relevant professional journal, usually taken by the company, their main interest in them was technical developments relevant to their field, job advertisements and salary reviews. The distribution of this group of managers was quite even between the British and American companies.

A second group of managers also considered themselves professionals, but their conception was not solely that of a functional specialist, they also had a conception of themselves as professional managers. Certainly this group was rather small, consisting of only twenty managers, but it was considerably larger proportionately than the group of managers interviewed by Nichols (1969) in 'Northern City'. Two features of this group stood out. First, these managers were rather more likely to be towards the top of their organisation than at the bottom and, secondly, they were much more preponderant in the American firms than in the British. An examination of this last point reveals some interesting differences between the American and the British conception of managers, and it confirms some of the previous research findings.

The heart of the matter of professionalism, as far as most of these managers were concerned, was technical competence. This trait was seen as absolutely fundamental, indeed hardly any other consideration was mentioned and only one senior manager seemed to be aware of the debate about the service ethic. Their conception was very similar to the one noted by Pahl and Winkler (1974) in their study of British directors. The abilities they stressed were a command over a range of techniques that would allow them to set and reach particular goals. They also stressed their ability to provide a whole range of information which would allow decisions to be taken with considerable accuracy and certainty. These managers were particularly likely to be located in the financial and marketing functions in the American firms, although even the personnel managers stressed the great battery of techniques at their disposal for manpower forecasting, management selection etc. If these were the key elements for the managers' conception of professionalism, it is easy to see why more of the managers working for the American companies conceived of themselves as professional, for as already shown, they were much more likely to possess such techniques. Allied with this point is the fact that the 'American' managers were much more likely to have undergone some form of management training than their British counterparts, and this potentially has a double significance. First, it is on such training courses, often designed specifically for the company, that the managers would have acquired such techniques. Secondly, the courses themselves may well have had some labelling effect, in that they introduced the notion of 'professional management techniques', such that managers emerging successfully from such courses would be more likely to conceive of themselves as professionals. The abilities that these managers possessed were not, so far as could be judged, based on a conception of theoretical knowledge that would have satisfied the trait theorists. On the contrary, most of the managers were suspicious of theory and anything that did not have a fairly immediate practical benefit. Those managers who had attended some of the broader management courses, often those run in the public sector of education, were particularly scornful of subjects like economics, which they believed to be too theoretical. They reserved their greatest scorn however for the human relations type courses that many had been 'subjected' to and there was general consensus that these were a waste of time.

The key feature of the professionalism of this small group of managers in the sample, was their technical knowledge of large aspects of the business process. This 'technicality' has been stressed by both Parsons (1939) and Johnson (1972) as being a crucial element in any knowledge-based occupation. By concentrating on this element Parsons, in his celebrated essay on business and the professions, attempted to argue that in certain respects these occupations were very similar. They were both marked by 'rationality, functional specificity and universalism', and both strove for the same goals of success; the differences lay in the different situations in which the two occupations found themselves.

It is by concentrating the analysis at this level that Parsons managed to show that there were no systematic differences between the motivations of businessmen and professional men. Thus the typical motivation of professional men was not in the usual sense 'altruistic', anymore than was the typical motivation of the businessman 'egoistic'. The behaviour of the two groups is determined by the institutional structures within which they reside, and once this is conceded any simple distinction between the professions and business management collapses. The managers in the sample who considered themselves professional managers certainly possessed technical competence. The source of this technical competence however, was not by and large, acquired by sitting an examination of an external professional body, which also regulated entry into the occupation. On the contrary, the source of much of their technical knowledge was, at least indirectly, the company for which they worked. It was often the company that organised the management training courses, or instructed the management consultants on what type of course they wanted. One should not assume from this however, that the knowledge was entirely parochial, because although it was often tailored to the needs of the particular firm, the techniques themselves were quite standard and, because of the high esteem of 'American management methods', were qualities that were often bought and sold on the open market in the form of distinctive varieties of managerial experience. What does follow from this analysis however, is that business management as an occupation possesses no 'occupational control', the managers were controlled by the companies for which they worked. Their special area of expertise did not insulate them from this control, because the source of expertise was in many ways the company itself. In other words, the occupation did not possess any barriers to intervention, there was no mystique which would create the conditions of uncertainty, or what Johnson called 'indetermination'—the occupation was totally controlled by the authority of the employer. Yet this does not mark them off from other professionals. Johnson has argued that many 'so-called' professionals are also subject to similar controls, e.g. from third parties (state or church) or corporate patronage (accountants). Indeed, in a later paper Johnson (1975) argued that the situation where the profession controls its members and their work activities, 'can arise only where the ideological and political processes sustaining indetermination coincide with the requirements of capital'.[32] In other words, all occupational groups serve the 'rationality' of the capitalist system and there are no systematic differences between business managers and other professionals.

This chapter has reported on the characteristics of the managers in the two groups of firms. A range of hypotheses were tested which predicted that the 'American' managers would differ in certain important ways from their British opposite numbers. In particular it was predicted that the 'American' managers would, on average, be younger, better qualified, have experienced a greater amount of inter- and intra-firm mobility, would be more likely to be female, would probably exhibit signs of being more ruthless or 'inner-directed', would work longer and harder, and would in general exhibit a greater degree of commitment towards the business world. In summary, it was predicted that the 'American' managers would more nearly exhibit signs of being 'professional managers', as that term has been defined.

It was obviously ambitious to expect to find statistically significant differences on all these variables, when all the firms were located inside one society, and one particular segment of the society at that—a small segment of South-East England. As noted before, this study represents a particularly stringent test of the hypothesis that socio-cultural factors influence company structure and process. Even so, it did seem possible, as much of the popular literature had suggested, that American firms located in Britain would carry with them certain patterns of behaviour, derived from their North American base, which would manifest themselves in their personnel. In particular it was felt that American firms might have attempted to select from the general population of actual or potential British managers, those individuals who best fitted their distinctive model of a manager. In other words, even if one assumed that the population of indigenous British business managers differed in important respects from the population of indigenous American managers, the distribution of such characteristics within British society would still be such that it might be possible for the American firms to select those British managers who possessed the characteristics that have been denoted as 'American'. Alternatively it could be argued that certain types of managers who possessed certain qualities popularly believed to be typical of indigenous American managers, might be attracted to American companies operating in Britain. Finally, there was the possibility that any observed differences were not to be accounted for by the selection process as such, but were the result of the effect of being employed by the American companies.

Very few differences were noted that reached levels of statistical significance, indeed only on two variables, the qualifications of the managers and the amount of intra-firm mobility, were there significant differences between the two populations. There were some tendencies in the predicted direction in some of the other areas, but the overall conclusion is that the data could have been drawn from the same population. As a consequence of this finding much of this chapter has been spent in explaining what differential response there was to the various questions in terms of individual and organisational variables, like position in the life cycle, functional location, position in the organisational hierarchy etc.—factors which clearly explain far more than any cultural variable. It is difficult to know which of the three explanations offered above account for those differences that were observed. It would be a mistake to consider them as alternatives because there was evidence of all three processes at work. There was some evidence from examination of the personnel departments to suggest that the American firms did have somewhat different priorities in selecting personnel than the British companies, e.g. they tended to stress qualifications more than the British firms, but it would be difficult to substantiate the view that their ideal-typical manager was markedly different from the 'British model'. Second-ly, there was evidence in a small number of cases which showed that certain managers were attracted to the company because of the image they had of American companies. Thirdly, there was evidence that being employed in American companies actually did make a difference to the managerial profiles, for example, the American companies were more inclined to send their managers on management training courses and to initiate job moves inside the firm.

Notes

1   There was one particular methodological difficulty in the sampling of managers that needs to be noted. It soon became clear that firms operated with different definitions of management. The majority of the British empirical workers in this area have tended to accept as managers those defined as such by the companies under investigation. This approach was followed by asking the company to include 'Anybody who has authority in the organisation and who would be counted as part of management'. It seems likely from this author's and other observations that the American firms counted rather more personnel as managers than the British firms.

2   This proved to be quite a difficult undertaking because often several people were involved in selection and they did not always agree on what the selection policy was.

3   Size was calculated as the number of managers working in the department expressed as a proportion of the total number of managers.

4   Of small US firms 66.7 per cent ($n = 9$) spent more than 10 per cent of the annual starting salary of the prospective manager on recruiting, as against only 45.8 per cent ($n = 48$) for British firms. The comparative figures for large firms were US: 61.5 per cent ($n = 13$); GB: 56.8 per cent ($n = 37$).

5   The BIM study showed that American firms of all sizes were more likely to use consultants in management selection 36.4 per cent ($n = 22$) than British firms 22.4 per cent ($n = 85$). The same data showed an even greater disparity when the question of the use of executive searchers was raised; only 8.2 per cent ($n = 7$) of British manufacturing firms used

them as against 41 per cent ($n = 9$) of American firms. This difference holds when size is held constant and is statistically significant ($p < 0.001$).

6   The law is by no means a 'dead letter'; see 'The Age of Discrimination', *Management International,* vol. 34, no. 9, September 1979, pp.19-21.

7   The 1974 ILO *Yearbook of Statistics* shows that in the UK in 1971 women formed 8.4 per cent of administrative and managerial workers, whilst in 1973 in the US the equivalent figure was 18.6 per cent.

8   A good review of the evidence is provided by the Department of Industry (1977).

9   J.-J. Servan-Screiber, 1969; Leggatt (1978) also shows that the proportion of graduates in British management is not increasing.

10   *Fortune,* the editors of, 1956, p.53.

11   Granick, 1972, p.295.

12   Inkson, Schwitter, Pheysey and Hickson, 1970, p.360.

13   British Institute of Management, 1970.

14   Granick, 1972, pp.42 and 370.

15   Child and MacMillan (1972). This excellent study gives details of numerous studies which support this conclusion.

16   Burrage (1969) notes that public relations developed earliest and has reached its fullest growth in the United States (p.123), and this author has advanced several reasons why American firms are likely to be concerned about their public image.

17   Sofer, 1970, p.257.

18   Ibid., p.4.

19   For example Thomas (1969), Granick (1962).

20   Nichols (1969) does not find any association with management training, although he does note that there was an association between those who participated in the affairs of management bodies and the 'social responsibility' response.

21   Child (1969a) reports in his small study of management teachers, that they regarded managerial responsibility as an important matter.

22   Several writers, most notably Mommsen and Kolko, have demonstrated that Weber's writings do contain a definite philosophy of history—history as the process of the progressive rationalisation/disenchantment of values. However, this 'history' is a construction based on its significance for certain values and is not the reality of history itself which is, at one level, as Weber was well aware, inexhaustible and unknowable.

23   Riesman actually concedes that even 'in our age of other directedness' there is still room for inner-directed people; that in fact, the other-directed personalities are still the exception, occurring most frequently in the metropolitan upper-middle classes, while rural and provincial city people are still, as a rule, tradition- or inner-directed.

24   Haire et al., 1966, p.24.

25   Whyte (1963) never actually says that the organisation man is only to be found in large organisations, but this is the clear implication.

26   The grestest complaint that the American executives in the study had about English personnel was the difficulty in persuading them to make geographical moves. For an analysis of the rate of geographical mobility amongst the professional and managerial classes in America see Landinsky (1967).

27   Heberle, 1956, p.36.

28   In a study of 'career striving' in male middle-level managers in five north-western business firms in the United States, Tausky and Dubin (1965) noted the relative absence of either of Wilensky's categories of 'strivers' or 'skidders'. They sagely observe: 'Perhaps these data will alert students of American society to the possibility that one of the great analytical myths carried over from popular culture is the belief that business bureaucracy is peopled by strivers' (p.729).

29   Lack of professionalism in British management seemed to Granick and Dubin to lie in a lack of a relevant technical education; Wilkinson on the other hand worked with a much broader conception of traits, not all of them entirely consistent one with another.

30   Examples of this approach are legion. Johnson (1972) makes a summary of most of these studies, see pp.21—32.

31   For a development of this argument see Jamieson (1977).

32   Johnson, 1975, p.10.

5 British and American manufacturing organisations: organisational climates

The previous two chapters concentrated on the organisational structures of the British and American firms and certain features of their managers. There is a tradition in organisation theory that has attempted to consider organisational structures and the individuals who work within them as composite wholes with the use of the concept of organisational climate. As International Management (1976) noted, 'companies as well as countries (can) have distinctive cultures'. This chapter considers the organisational climates of the two sets of firms to see whether there are any distinctive differences.

Early organisation theory, in the hands of formal theorists like Taylor and Fayol rendered a concept like organisational climate unnecessary, because their view of human behaviour was the rather mechanical one that had descended from the world of classical economic theory. As soon as the psychologists began to interest themselves in the world of the organisation however, these assumptions were shown to be simplistic. Armed with one of the key postulates of psychological theory, that behaviour is a function of the interaction of an organism and its environment, there was room for the concept or organisational climate to act as part of the environment. The use of the concept in industrial settings can be traced back at least as far as the work of Elton Mayo and his colleagues at the Hawthorne branch of the Western Electric. [1] The seminal study of Lewin, Lippitt and White (1939) on leadership climates quickly followed this work. These early studies developed within the field of psychology and great attention was paid to individual qualities like leadership style and very little to the independent influence of structure. The first industrial study to specifically use the concept of organisational climate, stripped of its exclusively psychological qualities, was Argyris (1958) in his study of a bank. This interesting study noted the need for a concept to integrate the 'buzzing confusion' of an organisation, which he observed was a mixture of the formal structure, the informal structure and different individual personalities. As he wrote, although organisations are very complex the complexity is not limitless, at some point the variables do connect with one another and form a finite boundary maintaining system.

Despite its potential usefulness the concept is not without its problems. It is useful to note briefly three issues with which any research-er has to contend. First, should one conceptualise organisational climate in objective or subjective terms? Evan (1968), Barker (1962) and Lawrence and Lorsch (1967) all operationalise the concept in terms of objective measures. The problems with this approach are first, that these theorists are really only talking about a different way of conceptualising organisational structure. Although it would seem reasonable to suppose that structure influences climate, in order to test such a hypothesis it would clearly be necessary to distinguish them at an analytical level. The other problem is that it is always possible that the objective qualities of the environment will be interpreted differently by different people.

A much larger group of researchers have attempted to operationalise organisational climate in terms of participant perceptions of different aspects of the work organisation. This strategy does avoid the criticism that can be levelled at those who concentrate upon objective measures of climate, and it has the advantage that these perceptions are based upon experience that is both more extensive and more involved than that of an outside observer. This approach is also not without its problems however; Sells (1963, 1968) pointed out that if one concentrates upon an individual's perception of his environment then it is formally necessary to identify variations in each phenomenon. In other words, the organisational climate results not only from variations in the structure of the organisation, but also from variations in individual personality, as well perhaps from 'definitions of the situation', which are 'imported' from outside the organisation. [2]

Finally there is the possibility that members of the organisation differentially located within the structure will perceive the climate in rather different ways, thus vitiating the whole idea of an organisational climate. Even if there is no close association between a member's position in the organisation and his perception of its climate, it is still possible to doubt whether a single, dominant, unidimensional climate will emerge from investigation. Both these matters are of course open to empirical investigation.

The problems outlined above are indeed formidable and yet many of them can be surmounted by a carefully devised methodology. It was decided to use an instrument to measure certain aspects of the climate of the companies under investigation, which used the perceptions of the managers of those companies. There were a number of reasons for that decision. First, given the limited time available, it was felt that people who had worked in the companies for a number of years were more likely to have a veridicial picture of the company's climate than a short stay outside researcher. Secondly, some objective measures of the organisations' structures via the Aston scales had already been collected (see Chapter 3), and further considerable information upon the managers themselves (see Chapter 4). Thirdly, Payne and Pheysey (1971) had managed to reconceptualise Stern's organisational climate index, and had applied it to business organisations in the form of a business organisation climate index (BOCI). This instrument had several important qualities that made it particularly valuable for this research. First, Payne and Pheysey showed that BOCI was a psychometrically sound instrument, which had a reasonable degree of construct validity.[3] Secondly, they also managed to show that there was very little variation between the top managers and the rest of the organisation with respect to scores on the index, and concluded that 'It would thus seem a valid procedure to take the mean score of the individuals in the organisation as an indication of the general climate in the organisation, at least at the managerial level'.[4] Although the two organisations on which they tried the index were rather small, 350 and 412 people respectively, this did seem a hopeful finding. BOCI was composed of twenty scales, each containing eight items. This was too big an imposition to place on the sample of managers, and so six scales were selected from BOCI that, on the basis of previous research findings and this author's own theoretical analysis, should have discriminated between British and American firms. The BOCI scales chosen were the following:

1 Leaders' psychological distance: a scale designed to measure the degree to which senior managers maintain psychological distance from their juniors.

2 Egalitarianism: a scale designed to measure the degree to which the organisation is felt to be egalitarian.

3 Employee involvement: a scale designed to measure the degree to which senior management is felt to show concern for employees.

4 Scientific and Technical orientation: a scale designed to measure the degree of concern with scientific and technical matters.

5 Innovation: a scale designed to assess the degree to which there is felt to be a readiness to innovate in the organisation.

6 Community: a scale designed to test the degree of concern for relations with the wider community.

Full details of these scales can be found in Appendix 3.

The use of scales to measure specific aspects of organisational climate gets round the problem of conceptualising it as a unidimensional whole. One final reason should be mentioned which influenced the decision to use some of the BOCI scales. In the original article by Payne and Pheysey reporting the use of the scale, very little information on the two firms investigated was reported, but in a later article by Pheysey, Payne and Pugh (1971) it was revealed that one of the two firms was American. Thus the original study had tested BOCI in a way that provided a useful comparison to this research. Unfortunately, although the two firms, 'Aston' and 'Brum', were well matched for size, they had very different products (details not specified), which made the study rather less than perfect from the standpoint of this research.

The results of the specified aspects of organisational climate as measured by certain of the BOCI scales are detailed in Table 5.1. The first point to examine is whether it was legitimate to use the aggregate score of individual managers to represent the climate of the firms in the sample. In general terms the findings of this study coincide with those of Payne and Pheysey (1971), in that there were no significant differences on any of the scales between managers located at the top of their organisations and those at the bottom, despite the fact that the organisations in this study were, on average, considerably larger than those used in the latter study. Inspection of the standard deviation scores also shows that the amount of variation is, in general, sufficiently small to permit the use of the term organisational climate. It should be added however, that although there were no significant differences between the level of the respondents and their responses to the scale, there was a greater association in the British companies, particularly GB Print, than in the equivalent American companies. This may well reflect the greater sense of community that existed in the American firms consequent upon their more participative style of management. Further evidence for this can be drawn from the Payne and Pheysey study, which consistently showed lower standard deviations for the American firm, even though it was slightly larger than the British firm in the study.[5] No association was found between the managers' functional area and their response to any of the organisational climate scales.

The scale entitled 'Leaders' psychological distance' was intended to measure the degree to which the senior members of the organisation maintained social distance between themselves and the more junior members of the organisation. A typical item from this scale was, 'Senior personnel rarely refer to one another by their first names'. The results of this scale represent an interesting test of effects of formal structure as against managerial style. As already shown, the American firms were in many ways more formally structured, in that there were a larger number of rules and procedures than in the British firms. On the other hand, it has also been stressed that in terms of 'managerial style' the American firms were more 'open'. It was predicted that the less formal style of the American firms would be more important than the structure, and that the British firms would have an organisational climate that reflected greater social distance within the organisation. The results of

Table 5.1

Organisational climate index (means and standard deviations): main sample

Firm	Leaders' psychological distance		Egalitarianism		Employee involvement		Scientific-technical orientation		Innovation		Community	
US Pharmaceuticals	2.26	0.99	6.2	1.84	6.28	1.72	6.90	1.49	4.73	1.70	4.80	1.52
GB Pharmaceuticals	2.65	1.37	6.04	2.00	5.65	1.74	5.54	1.88	4.61	1.90	3.12	1.47
US Print	1.81	0.87	6.18	2.23	6.17	1.59	3.91	2.26	3.58	2.07	3.46	1.64
GB Print	3.5	2.12	2.6	1.50	4.5	2.12	5.00	1.41	2.50	1.91	4.50	1.71
US Furniture	2.5	1.73	5.25	3.10	6.25	1.50	4.33	2.08	4.00	2.45	4.25	1.71
GB Furniture	2.5	1.29	5.75	2.22	6.50	0.58	5.50	1.92	6.75	0.50	7.50	0.58
US Electronics I	2.56	0.91	6.00	1.96	5.77	1.59	6.23	1.59	3.92	2.36	2.67	0.89
US Electronics II	2.00	1.00	5.90	1.70	5.95	1.77	6.20	1.82	4.25	1.73	4.65	2.11
GB Electronics	2.00	1.29	5.75	2.50	6.10	1.92	4.00	1.83	4.00	2.06	5.50	2.52
US Consumer	2.29	1.29	6.04	2.07	6.40	1.50	5.31	1.91	5.42	1.92	5.85	2.19
GB Consumer	2.26	1.28	6.74	1.79	6.20	1.40	4.50	1.84	5.30	2.67	5.00	1.25

154

this scale are not entirely unambiguous. The hypothesis is upheld in the case of the pharmaceutical and printing machinery firms. The large difference in the printing machinery comparison should not be surprising, in that it has already been shown that the British firm was far more formalised and did not permit much participation. The furniture industry comparison is the one case where one would not have expected a very great difference between the British and American companies because of the great emphasis placed upon participation by the managing director of the British firm and the table reveals that the scores are identical. The scores in the electronics and consumer goods industries cannot be taken as support for the hypothesis. Inspection of these scores would seem to indicate that the size of the organisation is probably an important variable, and this view throws more light on the larger gap between the British and American firms in the printing machinery comparison. It would seem reasonable to suppose that the larger the firm the greater the degree of psychological distance between the top and the bottom of the managerial hierarchy, *ceteris paribus.* In the printing machinery case the effect of nationality and size are both in the same direction and so the difference between the two firms is magnified. In the electronics industry the largest firm, US Electronics I, has the highest score yet the other American firm, US Electronics II, although bigger than the British firm has an identical score. In the consumer products comparison the larger American firm has a very slightly higher score than its British counterpart. A further indication of the effect of size can be gained from the fact that the average scores for all the firms in this study are larger than the scores for the smaller firms investigated in the Payne and Pheysey (1971) study. It would seem reasonable to conclude from these data that nationality via its effect on 'managerial style', and the size of the organisation, both have their independent effects on the managers' responses to the leaders' psychological distance scale.

The BOCI scale entitled 'egalitarianism' was designed to measure the degree to which the organisation was felt to be egalitarian. By egalitarian was meant that the values of achievement and universalism were stressed rather than those of ascription or particularism. Typical items were: 'Family, social or financial status are necessary elements for advancement or success' and 'As long as you are good at your job you will get ahead here'. It was predicted that the American firms would tend to score higher on this scale, although given that all the firms in the sample were probably 'progressive' it was not thought that the difference would be great. The hypothesis was supported in the pharmaceutical, printing machinery and electronics industries, but not upheld in the furniture and consumer products companies. The results for the furniture industry are not that surprising in view of the analysis of the disposition of the

155

managing director of that company, with his considerable stress upon egalitarianism. The results of the consumer products comparison are more remarkable however. Compared with the other firms in the sample, US Consumer had a high score, and so perhaps it is GB Consumer which is the exceptional firm. Analysis of performance of this company in terms of growth or profitability certainly indicates an exceptionally dynamic company. All the firms in the sample, with the exception of GB Print, recorded a higher score on this scale than both the American and British firms in the Payne and Pheysey (1971) study, which is perhaps further evidence of the 'progressive' nature of the firms in this sample.

The 'Employee involvement' scale was designed to measure the extent to which the managerial controllers of the organisation were perceived to concern themselves with the needs of the other managerial members of the organisation. Typical items were: 'Policy, goals and objectives are carefully explained to everyone' and 'Senior personnel have little tolerance for complaints and protests'. It was predicted that the more open and informal structure of the American organisations, that was reflected in the physical layout of some of the offices, and the more accessible management of these firms would result in higher scores for the American firms. The prediction was confirmed in the pharmaceutical, printing machinery and consumer products comparisons, but not for the electronics and furniture industry comparisons. The reversal of the predicted results in the furniture firms once more can be safely accounted for by reference to the managerial style of the managing director of GB Furniture, and it is tempting to account for the difference in the Electronics industry by reference to the much smaller size of the British firm, which would tend to make the management more employee centred, if only because the relatively small number of managers involved meant that everyone knew everybody else reasonably well. This interpretation is strengthened by the fact that the larger of the two American electronics firms scores lower on this scale than its compatriot.

The scale entitled 'Scientific and technical orientation' was intended to measure the degree of concern with scientific and technical matters that existed within the organisation. It was predicted that the firms in the pharmaceutical and electronics industries would score highest on these scales irrespective of nationality. American firms were predicted to score higher than their comparable British firms reflecting the supposedly greater stress that American firms place upon applied scientific knowledge. The industry predictions are largely supported, although GB Electronics appears to have rather a low score. The effects of nationality are less clearcut. In the pharmaceutical, electronics and consumer products industries the relationship is as predicted, but the prediction is not upheld in the printing machinery and furniture firms. **GB** Furniture once again proved to be an exception, but one that is not altogether surprising, as the British firm is an acknowledged industry leader in technology, whilst its American counterpart receives all its technology 'ready made' from its American parent. The relatively low score of US Print reflects its precarious position at the time of the research. The American company's products had been overtaken by new technology, and the low perception of the company's scientific and technical orientation might well be taken to be both a result of its poor performance and possibly even a contributory cause.

The BOCI scale 'Readiness to innovate' is designed to assess the extent to which the organisation is perceived to be willing to bring in innovation. Examples of items included 'Policy changes occur slowly here and only after considerable deliberation' and 'Programmes here are quickly changed to meet new conditions'. It was predicted that the American firms in the sample would have an organisational climate that was more conducive to innovation than the comparable British firms. There were several reasons for this prediction. First, the more open structure of most of the American firms should have made them more receptive to new ideas. [6] Secondly, many of the innovations would come from the American parent, which should be in a powerful position to impose such innovations on its British subsidiary. Thirdly, the greater use of management consultants, management development programmes and job rotation on the part of the American companies, should all provide powerful spurs to the acceptance of innovatory behaviour. The prediction finds broad support in the pharmaceutical, printing machinery and consumer products industries. In the electronics industry the strongly American-controlled firm, US Electronics II, is found to have the most innovative climate, and this is followed by the comparable British firm. One can perhaps explain the rather low score of the other American company by reference to the fact that it was only very loosely controlled from the United States, and therefore largely cut off from the powerful innovative forces emanating from its American counterpart. The other exception is once more to be found in the furniture industry, where the British firm, organised along very organic lines and noted in the industry for its innovative designs and technology, scores considerably higher than its American counterpart.

The last element of organisational climate to be explained was the BOCI scale entitled 'Orientation to wider community'. Typical scale items were 'Service to the wider community is regarded as a major responsibility of this organisation' and 'The activities of charities and social agencies are strongly supported'. It was predicted that the American firms would stress this trait more strongly than the British firms. The major reasons for this prediction were the greater public relations consciousness of American firms, [7] allied with the greater sensitivity of

American firms operating as foreigners in the British economy. In only the pharmaceutical and consumer products industries is the prediction upheld; in all the other cases the British companies score higher on this trait. It is interesting to note that in the Payne and Pheysey (1971) study the British firm also scored significantly higher than the American firm on this scale. At one level it is difficult to square these results with the responses the managers made to the question about the role of the company in society. Here a greater percentage of American managers opted for the 'social responsibility' response. This can be resolved if one realises that the organisational climate questions specifically referred to the managers' company rather than companies in general. Inside the American companies the managers experienced the full thrust of capitalist rationality that left little room for concern with the wider community; these concerns were the responsibility of a particular official, the public relations officer, or sometimes an outside consultant, but their activities did not permeate the inside of the firm and were strictly for external consumption.[8] This is not to argue that such firms did not contribute to the wider community in a variety of ways; many did, but these activities did not permeate the organisation in any noticeable way. The other factor that clearly had some explanatory power was the location of the company. If the company was located in an area where it was a major employer and thereby a publicly conspicuous firm in the eyes of the local community, as in the case of US Pharmaceuticals and GB Print, then more general attention appears to be paid to the wider community. There appeared also to be an industry effect in that those firms which dealt directly with the public, for example US Pharmaceuticals and both the consumer products companies, appeared to have higher scores than the majority of other companies. GB Furniture again stands out as an exception to this statement, and illustrates once more the power of the ideas of a particular man in a small company.

It would have been naive to have expected a simple correlation between the nationality of the company and its organisational climate, even where the concept of organisational climate is conceptualised in the rather limited manner of this study. There are numerous factors which must contribute in one way or another to a manager's perception of the organisational climate of his company, and Argyris (1958) in his pioneering study did well to stress the complexity of the total system that constitutes an organisation, and which contributes to its climate. In particular one should notice the case of GB Furniture, which was consistently different from the other British firms on the majority of the dimensions of organisational climate that were tested. This indicates once more the enormous power and influence that the leader of an organisation, or in some cases a 'dominant coalition', can have upon the organisational structure and climate of a company. It was pointed out in the theoretical analysis that measuring the organisational climate via the perceptions of members of the organisation logically entailed attempting to account for the resultant climate, not only in terms of organisational structure and managerial style, but also in terms of individual personality and 'definitions of the situation' that are imported from outside the organisation. This research has made no attempt to analyse personality traits, but some considerable attention was paid to whether the American firms systematically recruited different types of people to be managers in their firms, as much of the popular management literature insists. The only relevant difference that was found was in the educational qualifications of the managers; those working for the American companies were better qualified. No other difference in terms of age, social class background, or attitudinal differences was detected and, although this evidence is not conclusive, it does seem likely that one needs to account for differences in organisational climate largely by reference to the internal variables of the companies. Finally, there did not appear to be any direct relationship between organisational structure and organisational climate, although the contextual variable of size did appear to account for some of the variance on some of the measures. This is exactly in line with Pheysey, Payne and Pugh (1971), who attempted to examine the influence of organisational structure on the climate of a British (Brum) and an American firm (Aston). They report, evidently with some surprise, the following: 'It was hypothesised that Aston's more mechanistic structure, associated with greater formality at the group level, would be associated with lower group involvement, but the hypothesis was not supported'. They concluded that: 'Any organisation with quite extreme scores on some aspects of bureaucracy could produce a stimulating and progressive climate, given the support of other aspects of its structure. For example, Aston had management appraisal and promotion procedures expressly oriented towards the development of its members'. [9]

The evidence from this study and from Pheysey, Payne and Pugh (1971) would seem to indicate that American firms do seem to generate an organisational climate that does differ, in important respects, from that to be found in comparable British companies. There is nothing mystical about how this is done. The more informal style of management, in terms of personal relationships, combined with a whole range of policies which focus upon the development of the managers themselves, all contribute towards certain aspects of the climate. The stress on formal managerial techniques and the constant labelling of the companies as progressive in the employee magazines, induction and training programmes, all helps to contribute towards the 'progressive' feel of the company. Clearly such features are not the exclusive property of American firms, but it seems likely that they are more preponderant in American firms operating in Britain than in their British counterparts. [10]

Notes

1   The Hawthorne studies referred to the 'climate' of the relay assembly test room and the bank wiring observation room.

2   See for example Goldthorpe et al., 1968.

3   For full details of its psychometric qualities see Payne and Pheysey, 1971. pp.78–83.

4   Ibid., p.83.

5   Payne and Pheysey (1971) reported a higher standard deviation in the British firm for 21 of the 24 scales of BOCI. It should be pointed out however, that on only one scale was a significant difference found between these two firms as regards differences between the top and the bottom of the organisation, and this difference was found in the American firm.

6   For a development of this argument see Haige and Aitken, 1971.

7   See Burrage, 1969, p.71.

8   This can be related to one factor of organisation structure, that of functional specialisation. The American firms were more likely to have a separate public relations officer, and this compartmentalised the function.

9   Pheysey, Payne and Pugh, 1971, p.71.

10   It seems also quite possible that these differences may also reflect the fact that the American companies were subsidiaries of quite large parents, whilst the British firms were not all subsidiaries. Further, the size of the British parent firm tended to be smaller than its American counterpart.

6 Economic performance

The majority of the literature surveyed which attempted to compare the socio-cultural structure of Britain and America at the macro level, as well as the literature which compared the structure and operation of British and American companies, has been interested in the relative economic performance of the two units. There has been remarkably little analysis that has been content just to note differences in culture, structures or processes. In view of the fact that both countries are dominated by the capitalist mode of production, which makes the economic framework the dominant one, perhaps this observation should not be surprising. Bourgeois economists do have a branch of their discipline devoted to essentially social benefits, welfare economics, but this is still set within the basic capitalist framework, and anyway suffers from a wide range of conceptual and theoretical problems. The bulk of the literature emanating from management theory, industrial psychology and industrial sociology has also largely accepted the notion of private efficiency, which the owners of capital themselves necessarily use. There have of course been exceptions; Marxist writers, from whatever discipline, have been anxious not to accept such internal definitions, and have attempted to raise the question of for whose benefits the firm or society is organised. It is probably true to say that this question has been raised with increasing frequency since the middle of the 1960s, for reasons already discussed (see chapter 2).

This study has been primarily concerned to explore the ways in which cultural factors might have affected the operation of the capitalist economic system in Britain and America. A general macro analysis has been undertaken of the interplay between culture and capitalism in Britain and America, in the belief that only by doing such an analysis can one understand the structure and operation of an important constituent part of the system, business organisations. For the purposes of this analysis the goals of the economic system described have been taken for granted and any judgments about the effects of such a system on the individual or the society in general have been suspended. Given that capitalism has its own inbuilt goal of profit, it seems reasonable to try to make some attempt to assess the effects that cultural factors might have had upon the economic efficiency of Britain and America at a macro level, as well as on the relative efficiency of British and American companies. Such an enterprise is fraught with formidable difficulties.

First, although in principle there exists a comparative unit of measurement, which can be used as an invariant measuring rod of performance, i.e. monetary return, in practice the concept of economic performance is a very difficult one to use. Secondly, even supposing that one can solve the problems of measurement, one is faced with the even more difficult problem of causally relating differential performance to specific socio-cultural factors. Socio-cultural factors are particularly intractable variables in this context, because they are not, by and large, amenable to precise numerical measurement. Furthermore, relatively little is known about the economic, let alone the non-economic, correlates of economic growth. As Habakkuk (1968) puts it: 'The conditions favourable to growth are so varied, and combined in so many different ways, that it is not possible to give a list of essential requisites that is more than a string of platitudes'. [1] If one accepts this statement, then it clearly follows that the possibility of assigning any precise weights to the importance of particular socio-cultural variables is non-existent. The reaction of many economists to this state of affairs has been to abandon the attempt to relate non-economic and non-quantifiable variables to economic growth altogether. It does seem worthwhile however, to indicate in broad terms at least the direction of influence, and some of the possible mechanisms, that the socio-cultural variables concentrated upon have had on the general economic performance of Britain and America.

There seems to be a pervasive view among popular journalists and lay commentators that American economic growth has been considerably in excess of that of Britain. Indeed it is this supposed fact that has been partially the cause of all the *post hoc* 'theorising' that has gone on about the reasons for this difference. Analysis of the available economic data does not wholly support this view however. If one looks at the annual growth rate of total output, a measure of gross domestic product, one finds the following figures (see Table 6.1).

Table 6.1

Annual rate of growth of total output (UK and US)

	1870–1913	1913–1950	1950–1960	1960–1976 [*]
United Kingdom	2.2	1.7	2.6	2.5
United States	4.6	2.9	3.2	3.5

Source: Maddison, 1964, p.28.

[*] Statistical Abstract of the US, 1978.

This shows that the United States has grown at a greater rate than the United Kingdom for a long period of time, although the gap has narrowed.

It might be thought more reasonable however, to concentrate the analysis upon industrial output, rather than the output of the whole community, as it is upon manufacturing industry that this research has concentrated. Table 6.2 presents the results of this comparison.

Table 6.2

Annual rates of growth in industrial output, 1860–1968 (compounded)

Period	United Kingdom	United States
1860–1880	2.4	4.3
1880–1900	1.7	4.5
1900–1913	2.2	5.2
1913–1938	1.4	1.7
1938–1958	2.9	5.3
1958–1968[*]	3.2	3.3

Source: Patel, 1961, p.318.
* United Nations, 1977, p.84

Ignoring the period which covers the depression, this shows that the gap between American and British productivity was even wider on this narrower measure, although it has recently closed. One has to ask a fundamental question about these types of comparative data however, that is, is it reasonable to compare the economic growth of countries of such different economic situations? In other words, to make an assessment of the effect that socio-cultural variables might have on economic growth, the very least that could be done is to attempt to match some of the economically relevant variables like size, geographical position, natural resource endowment etc. Clearly it is quite possible for a country to grow comparatively quickly, and yet possess a socio-cultural structure which does not 'fit' at all well with the needs of the economy, even if one assumes that such socio-cultural factors have some importance in economic growth.[2] Presumably it might be technically possible to construct a table of economic growth rates for Britain and America that did attempt to control for naturally occurring economic factors like resource endowment, geographical location etc., but this is clearly beyond the scope of this research. It is common in economic statistics to control for population however, and to express the growth of output per head of population. Table 6.3 shows the result of this analysis. One can see immediately that the higher economic growth rate of America evaporates entirely after the Second World War, because the United Kingdom has had a relatively lower post-war population growth. As indicated above however, unless one believes that socio-cultural variables are the most decisive influence on economic growth, in that they account for most of the variance in the economic data, then whether America has grown faster than Britain is not really a relevant consideration, given the obvious fact that the economic factors are clearly poorly matched between the two societies. The classical economists had a relatively simple theory of growth in that they viewed capital accumulation as of decisive importance. Few economists today however, would agree that growth is only determined by essentially economic factors. Most would concede that a variety of essentially social factors, particularly perhaps the quality of capital, human as well as physical, have played a large role in economic growth.

Table 6.3

Rate of growth of output per man hour: UK and US

	1870–1913	1913–1950	1950–1970	1970–1977
United Kingdom	1.1	1.5	2.8	2.4
United States	2.1	2.5	2.5	2.0

Source: Maddison, 1979.

It seems probable that America's relatively high growth rate compared with that of Britain, in the fifty years from 1870 can at least be partly accounted for by the late development effect. For each new entrant to the ranks of 'industrial' nations, there was already an accumulated body of technological progress to assimilate. America, like any newly-industrialising country did not have to follow religiously the slow and necessarily step-by-step developments in techniques common to the countries which set out early on the road to industrialisation. This was by no means the whole story however. As already shown, America made her own unique contribution to manufacturing technique, at an early period, with what was known as the 'American system of manufacture'. The development was influenced by some structural features of the labour market, that was also influenced, as shown, by the structure of American culture. It is contended that the greater stress upon the values of achievement, affective-neutrality, specificity, universalism and self-orientation is likely to lead, *ceteris paribus,* to a better economic performance than a stress upon their opposites. [3] This can be observed even within the United States where, as Rothbarth (1946) has shown, the industries of the Southern States, where the values of capitalism have been less strongly embedded, have not been as efficient as those of the North, despite the fact that both have had as easy an access to the large American market. In Chapter 2 the greater institutionalisation of the capitalist pattern of

164

values in America was compared to Britain, both at the societal, or macro, level and at the level of business organisations, or micro level. This procedure will be followed in considering the possible economic consequences for each society of this differential value stress, although this is for analytical convenience only. Clearly the institutions and values of the society largely have their effect upon the nation's economic performance, by becoming inputs to the nation's economic organisations. For example, the structure of the nation's education system makes itself economically felt by producing a certain number of people with a certain quality at the level of the individual economic enterprise.

In the analysis of the historical development of Britain and America a considerable amount of emphasis was placed on differences that were to be found in the respective systems of stratification. There are a number of ways in which the nature of the stratification system in America is likely to be comparatively economically advantageous. First, one can note the connection between the stratification system and the structure of the domestic market: because status differences are felt to be less important, this makes for a relatively more homogeneous market structure, and this in turn means that firms can benefit by securing all the advantages of mass production and consequent longer production runs. There are signs that markets in the developed world are becoming rather more homogeneous, in this sense perhaps one can subscribe to the mass society thesis. Of course there are plenty of specialised markets left, which the structure of the British economy might be thought better fitted to serve, but these appear to be declining as fast as the mass markets are growing. The greater success of the American economy has its own effect on the domestic market structure. It means, for example, that income per head is much higher than it is in Britain, and higher amounts of disposable income mean that the public spend more of their money on consumer durables with a high elasticity of demand. As American manufacturers take the lead in the production of these sorts of goods, they are able to keep selling them in foreign markets, as those consuming publics reach American levels of income.

Another important feature of the American stratification system is the widespread belief in the possibilities of upward social mobility for the individual. This might be thought to have several effects. First, it might be thought to lead to a greater competitiveness in American society, where more people believe they have a chance to become really successful.[4] This could easily lead to greater effort on the part of many (accounting perhaps for the claim that American businessmen work longer hours), as well as a greater desire for people to get on in the business world, where the greatest monetary rewards are to be had. In an institutional sense the economic system of the United States is more competitive, as one can see by examining the analysis of the amount and type of anti-monopoly legislation between the two societies.[5] It has also been indicated that the style of competition is more aggressive in America, there being relatively few 'gentlemen's agreements', and informal codes to hold back the full effect of economic forces. The stress on money as the mark of success may also have its economic advantages, because it means that companies are less likely to remain in a particular line of business if it ceases to be profitable. If one accepts the thesis that the economic world is becoming ever more volatile, because of the speed of technological advance, the development of the third world etc., this would place societies like America at a comparative advantage.

The stratification system manifestly also has an effect upon the type and structure of the industrial relations system in the two societies, as already shown. There are a number of ways in which it can be argued that the American system might lead to higher rates of economic growth. First, the American union strategy of 'attacking' the most efficient, most profitable firm, and then attempting to spread the bargain, has obvious beneficial consequences when compared with the widespread British practice of industry bargaining, which tends to protect the marginal firm. This bargaining strategy may well not protect union members from unemployment as well as the British strategy, but this is probably easier for the American system to withstand, and arguably beneficial for economic growth. The ideology of individualism in the United States means that unemployment is less likely to be seen as caused by system failure, the oppression of the proletariat by the bourgeoisie; it is more likely to be viewed as individual failure. Furthermore, unemployment is always markedly higher amongst the black population, the American underclass, who are relatively unpoliticised and who have not formed effective pressure groups to remedy their situation. Yet this higher level of unemployment in the United States means that American industry rarely finds itself in the situation in which British industry often finds itself. British industry, particularly that section of it whose demand peaks tend to be simultaneous with those of the general business cycle, finds itself unable to take on additional labour when required. Companies facing such a constraint are both reluctant to dismiss labour during periods of the business cycle down-swing, hence the alleged British overmanning practice, and are reluctant to invest in expensive capital equipment unless it is likely to be permanently manned. Labour expenditure in much of British industry therefore becomes a relatively fixed cost. This situation is greatly ameliorated in America both by the higher rate of unemployment even at the peak of the business cycle, the lower level of unionisation, the greater regional mobility of labour and the greater willingness and ability of American workers to commute long distances. It is also argued that the British

166

industrial relations system is inefficient from the point of view that it causes more costly stoppages (Garbarino (1969)). It certainly cannot be argued that America has a better strike record than Britain, if one uses the more reliable index of the number of working days lost rather than the actual number of stoppages. Yet Garbarino argues persuasively that the 'concept of "managing" industrial conflict, (however), includes affecting the character or the "quality" of conflict as well as its quantity'.[6] He goes on to argue that the fact that Britain would appear to have far more 'unofficial' stoppages, which are relatively unpredictable, is far more damaging than the less frequent, more predictable but longer conflicts in the United States.[7] Against these arguments one needs to balance two countervailing forces. First, one must take account of the fact that the direct costs of running the British industrial relations system, particularly from the trade union side, are very small indeed. As Turner (1969) points out, unpaid union officials are cheap compared to high price lawyers. Secondly, the greater political involvement of the British trade unions has encouraged the development of the British welfare state. The provision of facilities like the National Health Service which, from the point of view of capitalism, secures an able-bodied and healthy work force, as well as more general measures of social welfare, arguably provides oil for the working of the economic system, which America does not possess in anything like the British form. Whether the costs of the British welfare state are recouped by the benefits, in purely economic terms, is difficult to say.

Considerable differences were noted between Britain and America in the field of education. To summarise the differences: America had a greater percentage of her population undergoing education and training, the differences being most marked at the tertiary stage; there was a greater provision of educational opportunity in America than in Britain, although the differences in this area have probably been exaggerated; there was a difference in pedagogic style, America adopting more 'progressive' methods; finally, education in America appeared to be more vocational, in particular there was a greater provision of management and business education and, until the recent past, probably a greater emphasis on applied rather than pure science. There are probably as many studies on the role of education in economic growth as there are of any other strictly non-economic variables, with the possible exception of science and technology. The reasons for this are that economists have found it easier to quantify educational inputs to the economy and to calculate economic 'outputs'. Denison (1962) for example, calculated that education accounted for 23 per cent of the growth in total national income and 42 per cent of growth in *per capita* income in the United States from 1929 to 1957. This is in close agreement with the classic study of Schultz (1963). Certainly such results appear to be adequate at the level of meaning. Collins (1971) has dubbed this line of approach the 'technical-function theory' and has attempted to enumerate its basic propositions. First, the skill requirements of jobs in industrial society constantly increase because of technological change. Secondly, as a consequence of the first change, formal education provides the training necessary for these more highly skilled jobs. It follows from these two propositions, that as educational requirements for employment constantly rise, increasingly larger proportions of the population are required to spend longer and longer periods in education.

If the 'human capital' economists are correct, then because America invests proportionately more in education than Britain, she should get higher returns in terms of greater economic growth. Unfortunately, the assumptions and calculations on which this economic reasoning is based are so unsound that very little credence can be placed in them. [8] The only proposition that clearly stands up to research findings is that the main economic effect of education appears to occur at the level of transition to mass literacy and not significantly beyond this level. This does not mean to say that investment in other types of education has no economic effect, but that the effect is not so marked as to be easily identifiable. The American system of education is, as observed, more open and meritocratic than the British system. This is not to argue that the American system completely reflects the values of achievement over ascription, far from it, Recent studies in America have repeatedly shown that social origins have a direct effect on occupational success, even after the completion of education. Yet it does seem likely that the American system is more achievement-oriented than the British. It is interesting to note that, whilst the American system has undergone very little structural change in the last twenty-five years, the English system has moved in the direction of being more meritocratic. [9] It is arguable that one of the reasons for this is the pressure of economic circumstances; Britain's poor economic performance has resulted in pressure upon the social structure to conform more to the needs of the economy.

In the general analysis of the education system of Britain and America two other major differences were noted that could be relevant to economic performance. First, there was the difference in pedagogic style; America tended to use more student-oriented 'progressive' methods, whilst England was more wedded to the more formal 'traditional' methods. Considerable controversy surrounds the effects that these methods might have upon even such a narrow variable as educational achievement, and there would appear to be no direct evidence that links them in any way to economic performance. In the work context however, the human relations theorists have argued that the more 'participative' style leads to higher morale which very often leads to greater productivity. Although there is considerable controversy over these studies, within the context of Anglo-American culture, there probably does exist a relationship over a wide range of tasks. On a more theoretical level, it might be possible to argue that the more person-centred learning, based as it is upon learning by discovery, does result in a better grasp of fundamental principles which, in a world which is becoming more and more marked by change, is a more appropriate form of education. This statement cannot be rated as any more than a tentative hypothesis however. The other major difference that was noted was in the content of education. The American education system tended to stress the more practical vocational subjects, whilst in Britain there was a relatively greater stress upon subjects that had no clear vocational aim. The problem is which pattern of educational provision is likely to be most economically productive? There is once again very little direct evidence on the matter, although opinions lie thick on the ground. It is widely assumed, for example, that a stress upon business and management education rather than, say, classics must pay economic dividends. There are at least two separate issues here. First, one has the old argument about what sort of education offers the best 'training for the mind'? The concept of training for the mind is such an elusive one however, that it is doubtful whether such a hypothesis is in practice testable. Much must depend anyway on the content of what is taught, particularly in the area of business/management studies. There is some reason to doubt whether the content of such business/management education does in fact offer much of a training for the mind. The two major reports on business education in the United States that appeared in 1959, both commented unfavourably on the poor quality of the staff, the content of what was taught and the students. [10] There have been no directly comparable reports on the British situation, partly because this educational sector is so poorly developed on this side of the Atlantic. The Solomons Report (1974) on the British accountancy profession did conclude however, that British accountancy education 'has been too much concerned with the mechanical application of well-tried procedures to stereotype situations', [11] a criticism which mirrors the American reports on the education of American businessmen. Presumably there is no inherent reason why the content of business and management education should be so descriptive rather than analytical, and if this apparent deficiency could be remedied there is no reason why such an education should not offer just as good a training for the mind as any other sort of education. If the analytic content of the subjects were the same, it would not seem unreasonable to conclude that a more business-orientated education would be more economically productive, if only because the use of business and managerial modes of analysis and techniques are more likely to bring economic success, via their effect on the quality of decision making, [12] than the neglect of their use. The second point one can raise in this context is the effect that the ethos of a business education has upon those that undergo it, compared with the set of values associated with an education in the classics or the humanities. It is possible to argue of course, that the content of education will merely tend to confirm existing attitudes and values that led students to choose business rather than classics in the first place. In this context the really significant fact perhaps, is that English students tend not to choose business-oriented subjects to start with, compared with American students.

There is rather more evidence on the relative economic merits of a scientific education. One persistent theme expounded by Britain's post-war leaders, is that technology can be its major resource, the twentieth-century equivalent of nineteenth-century coal. In a pioneering paper, Solow (1957) estimated a 'technical change' factor that contributed about four times more than capital accumulation to the growth of output per head in the United States. The question as far as the education system is concerned is, does one get a greater amount of economically relevant innovation by concentrating on pure science, which is assumed to be the British pattern, or is it more profitable to concentrate upon applied science, which is assumed to be the American pattern? [13] No clearcut conclusions to support either view emerge from the evidence. After a comprehensive review of previous studies, Langrish et al., (1972) conclude: 'Science probably does work economic miracles, but it acts in rather mysterious ways its wonders to perform'. [14] In other words, considerable evidence can be found to support either view. Science and technology are by their very nature intimately connected and it must be impossible to know for future development what the most profitable mix would be. As already shown (note 13) there is some debate in Britain on what the mix actually is. Furthermore, it is difficult to directly link the production of scientists and technologists, or research and development expenditure with economic growth. [15]

The final difference between Britain and America at the macro level is probably one of the most difficult and certainly one of the most contentious. It is the role of the government in the management of the economy. It has been argued that the history of both societies has predisposed the political elites towards a *laissez faire* policy in economic affairs, but that since 1900 the more business-oriented government in the United States has pursued such a policy with greater thoroughness. In Britain, as both Shonfield (1965) and Winkler (1975) have shown, the government has taken an increasingly larger role in the management of the economy. It does not make any sense to argue that state planning necessarily leads to higher rates of growth or not. A very great deal must depend not only on the quality of the planning, but on the position of the economy. The author is persuaded by the arguments of Landes (1963) for example, that given the structure of the French economy after the Second World

War, with its very large number of cultural and structural impediments to growth, government intervention in the form of nationalisation and planning in the area of prices, raw materials, labour etc. was probably beneficial to that economy. There are some structural factors which would seem to indicate, in general terms, that a degree of state planning was economically desirable for all 'advanced' industrial societies. First, one has been able to talk of a global industrial economy from about the 1850s, and since that time the economies of the industrialised and capitalist West have become increasingly intertwined. As a consequence of this, several writers have talked about the change from economic to political capitalism, recognising the crucial significance of political decisions both in foreign and domestic affairs, for the operation of the economy (e.g. Tourraine (1974), Winkler (1975)). The growing percentage of world trade transacted by multinational companies has merely accentuated these existing tendencies. It can be argued that all this is more significant for Britain than America. Britain's exports contribute a far higher proportion to her GNP than do America's exports to her GNP. Secondly, the British government is far more involved in the British economy in terms of employment and investment than the American government is in the American economy. Even so the activities of the American government are still highly significant in the domestic economy of that country. Finally, it has been argued throughout this thesis that the socio-cultural structure of British society acts as a greater impediment to economic performance in this society, than does the American socio-cultural structure to American society. If this argument is correct, then it would follow that if the leaders of British society wished to pursue economic growth as a major goal, then a considerable degree of state intervention would be necessary, far more in fact than would be necessary in the American situation.

It has been argued above that although the economic performance of the nation must be related in some way to the performance of the individual business firm, the relationship is by no means a simple one and, for the purposes of analysis, the two problems can be separated. If this is done, one can avoid getting involved in discussions about the relative economic performance of Britain and America and turn instead to the comparison of the relative performance of British and American companies.[16] In view of the great weight of sociological, psychological and management literature on the subject of organisational effectiveness or performance,[17] there is surprisingly little agreement between writers on how it should be conceptualised or measured. Campbell (1973) identified nineteen different variables that have been used, the most widely used univariate measures being the following: overall performance measured by employee or supervisory ratings; productivity measured typically with actual output data; employee satisfaction, measured by self-report questionnaires; profit or rate of return, based on accounting data; withdrawal based on archival turnover and absenteeism data. Some studies, although ostensibly about the relationship between particular internal company variables and performance, seem to operate with only a sketchy view of performance. Burns and Stalker (1961), in their classic study on the *Management of Innovation,* inform the reader in a footnote that the efficiency of the firm was judged by the 'opinion of other individuals acquainted with the firm, especially of competitors'.[18] Other important studies like that of Burrage (1969) concentrate upon indirect variables like the 'rate of innovation', although in this case no attempt was made to measure this rate.

Business firms themselves have their own measures of performance, that of profit, i.e. return on assets, or occasionally return on sales, or growth in assets.[19] In a market economy business firms must be able to show a profit or, in the long run, they will go out of business. As this study has been concerned with the effect that socio-cultural variables might have had upon economic performance, it seems wholly appropriate to take an economic measure of performance rather than something like employee satisfaction, or even perceptions of performance. This procedure might be thought to have several advantages. First, there would appear to be universal measures of performance, i.e. return on assets or growth in assets.[20] Secondly, these figures are publicly available. Two major problems remain however: firstly, there are considerable problems with the published data themselves, problems of such complexity that they have led some experts to decide that they are effectively insurmountable. Secondly, there are problems in causally relating variations in internal company variables like the structure of the organisation, managerial attitudes etc., with performance data.[21]

It is traditional accounting practice to measure profitability by taking the operating profit of the company plus other income, after depreciation, but before tax and interest. All these data are readily available from published accounts. It is acknowledged that the main difficulty arises over the valuation of assets and the rate of depreciation. There was recently a salutary warning in the government publication *Economic Trends,* which underlined the problems:[22]

> Figures taken from companies' accounts do not always provide a wholly satisfactory basis of measurement; in particular the book values of fixed assets, and the depreciation on them, are based on valuations determined at different dates in the past and so at varying price levels. This factor can effect balance sheet data, *and is particularly relevant to measures of profitability* (this author's emphasis).

As the rate of inflation in Great Britain has accelerated into 'two digit inflation' since 1970, these problems have become accentuated as some companies have attempted to adopt some form of inflation accounting provision, and others have not. [23] These problems refer to the published accounts of British companies, but if one turns to the accounts of subsidiaries of American companies, the category which contains all the American firms in this study, then the problems are compounded. There are three main problems which can be identified. First, there is the problem of accounting conventions. If it could be shown that accounting conventions differed systematically between the two groups of firms, then this might have the effect of distorting the performance figures. The main danger here would appear to be that American tax laws might encourage American firms to shift profits either to or from United Kingdom subsidiaries. The second main problem is that of concealed subsidies to American subsidiary companies operating in Britain. Dunning (1970) observes: [24]

> Undercharging for products and services purchased from the US parent provides a concealed subsidy. A particular form of this is the access which US subsidiaries have to the benefits of research, development and design and, in some cases, marketing expenditures undertaken by the US parent. In so far as this access is not charged at cost at the appropriate rate, US subsidiaries operating in the UK will enjoy higher profits than they otherwise would.

The final problem is that of dollar conversions. Since the pound has been allowed to float against the dollar, the timing of dollar conversions becomes an important factor in the company's balance sheet and can affect performance figures irrespective of any changes in the actual efficiency of the firm. These problems have led many writers to conclude that comparing the efficiency of two groups of firms, when one of the groups represents subsidiaries of foreign parents, is too hazardous to be worth the effort. Wilkins (1970) argues 'that the errors in the statistics may be immense, because they are based on nonanalogous information'.[25] Dunning, who has spent a large number of years attempting to compare the economic performance of British and American companies in England and elsewhere, concludes in a recent publication that: 'Without detailed knowledge of the process and practice of intra-group pricing, accounting conventions and the extent to which market prices are distorted by market imperfections, it is difficult to imply anything from performance ratios about the efficiency of two groups of firms'.[26] It was not possible in this research to make any assessment of these highly technical matters in the firms that were investigated and indeed no such attempt is known of. From other published evidence it would seem likely that, because American firms have tended to expand rather faster than British firms in recent years, the book values of their assets would correspond more closely to current replacement value, in which case their published accounts would tend to underestimate their profitability (Dunning (1970)). Against this the Committee of Public Accounts in 1960 calculated that in two of the industries relevant to this study, pharmaceuticals and electronics/industrial instruments, there were very considerable conceal-ed subsidies in the American firms. Indeed they argued that in the pharmaceutical industry the bias in the accounts amounted to about one-half of the recorded rate of profit on capital.[27]

If one accepts the arguments outlined above, then there would clearly be no sense in examining the published accounts and comparing records of growth and profitability between the British and American companies in the sample. Furthermore, there would certainly be no justification in attempting to correlate certain distinctive aspects of structure or manage-ment in the two groups of companies with performance, because not only are the performance figures themselves of doubtful validity, but the problems involved in *post hoc* causal theorising of this nature are truly formidable. [28] Accordingly, no detailed analysis will be made of the profitability figures of the sample companies. In summary however, the published figures for the six-year period immediately prior to the research (1966–72) showed the following: US Pharmaceuticals was generally more profitable than GB Pharmaceuticals; that apart from one disastrous year, US Print was more profitable than GB Print; that US Furniture was more profitable than GB Furniture; that GB Consumer was more profitable than US Consumer. No conclusion could be drawn in the electronics industry comparison, because the accounts of the British subsidiary had been consolidated with those of the parent firm. By the standards of the industry however, both the American firms published above average figures for profitability, with US Electronics I doing noticeably better than US Electronics II. There does seem some general agreement amongst economists that, on average, American firms are more profitable than British firms if one holds geographical location and industry constant. Dunning (1970, undated) has shown this to be the case for American and British firms operating in any country in the world, and although one might have considerable reservations about the actual figures, the trend is clear enough, and the evidence of the perfor-mance of both groups of firms in third nations particularly impressive. Other data that are often used to compare the relative efficiency of British and American firms are on comparative levels of producticity in the two societies. Table 6.4 confirms the greater efficiency of American manufacturing companies. On aggregate it seems likely that American manufacturing firms probably are more efficient than equivalent British firms; although the published data is of a very poor quality, it has consistently pointed in the same direction over a long period of time and in a variety of locations. If one accepts this propostion as being true, the question arises as to what extent it can be accounted for in terms of socio-cultural variables.

Table 6.4

Comparative levels of Productivity: UK and US

	1870	1950	1977
United Kingdom	122	55	61
United States	100	100	100

US GDP per man hour = 100
Source: Maddison, 1979.

This study has shown that when American manufacturing firms are carefully matched to British manufacturing firms, in order to eliminate the effect of variables like size, product differences and geographical location, then many of the alleged differences between British and American firms evaporate. One must bear in mind however that, because the comparison is between American and British firms operating in England, this study represents a particularly stringent test of the power of cultural variables to affect business behaviour; it is almost inconceivable that some adaptation to the culture of the host society has not occurred, not least because American firms largely employ British subjects in their organisations. Despite the test being a stringent one, some of the hypothesised differences between British and American firms were confirmed, and it is important to enquire whether, on the basis of available evidence, these differences were likely to result in differences in economic performance.

It is possible to summarise the observed differences between the two groups of firms under two main headings: differences relating to the personnel area, i.e. the importance attached to the human capital of the organisation, and differences in the broad area of decision making inside the companies. These two areas are closely related, but for analytical purposes they can be treated separately. The evidence from this study and from the re-analysis of the BIM data indicates that American firms are likely to regard personnel as a more important function than the British firms. Their personnel departments were bigger, they spent more money and effort upon recruitment, and they organised the careers of the managerial recruits in a broader and more systematic way than the British companies. The American personnel departments appeared to use more universalistic criteria in selection than the comparable British firms and one result of this was that the 'American' managers

175

were significantly better qualified than their British counterparts. On the face of it one would have thought that several of these differences would have led, at least indirectly, to higher productivity. The available evidence is not wholly convincing. Berg (1970) disputes the view that better-educated employees are necessarily more productive when productivity is measured directly, although his review of evidence did not contain the occupation of business management. Perhaps this view should not be too surprising in view of the fact that Gordon and Howell (1959) had already shown, in their important survey of business employers in the United States, that such employers regarded college degrees as important in hiring potential managers, not because they were thought to ensure technical skills, but rather to indicate 'motivation' and 'social experience'. Similarly they showed that a business school education was regarded less as evidence of necessary training than as an indication that the college graduate was committed to business values. More recently Freeman (1976) has even shown a decline in the individual economic return to advanced qualifications. Against these findings one can place the work of Collins (1971), who argues that there is a relationship between educational qualifications of the type under consideration and the demands of the managerial occupation, although he concedes that the relationship is not so close as is generally assumed. There are two other factors about the qualifications of the American managers that might be thought to offer some grounds for believing that they would perform more productively. First, a greater percentage of the 'American' managers had qualifications in 'administrative science', a subject which, embraces techniques which a wide variety of managers would normally be expected to be familiar with in most modern firms. Secondly, and probably of greater importance, a significantly greater number of the American managers had attended management training courses where they had been exposed to the managerial techniques referred to above. It has often been argued that many of the courses are too general to be of any use and, if one accepts this argument, it is perhaps significant to note that the American firms were more likely to send their managers on courses that were specifically designed for the needs of the company. The evidence here supports the view that British firms are more likely to encourage management training because of a general feeling that it is 'worthwhile', whilst American firms have a more precise view of what they actually require and tend to send their managers on courses tailor made for their needs. Whilst the American firms in the sample were more likely to send their managers on training courses, it was also found that the whole area of what can be called 'management development' was given greater importance in these firms. The managerial resources of the firm were more likely to be systematically appraised within a management development programme. Furthermore, it has been shown that three of the American companies were operating some form of 'management by objectives', a scheme which, so its practitioners argue, by its systematic attempts to match managerial abilities with job content is likely to produce higher output. One direct consequence of the management development programmes was a greater degree of movement from one job to another inside the firm. Granick (1972), amongst others, has argued that this practice is likely to have beneficial consequences for companies in that it prevents departmental parochialism, forces the manager to perform well in the 'market place of the whole company', rather than attempting just to please his superior, and finally aids the cross-fertilisation of ideas throughout the company. There was no direct evidence of the effect of these schemes on managerial performance in the firms studied, although there was a general feeling amongst some of the managers that it did make them work harder. Certainly it was found that more 'American' managers complained of the pressure of work than did comparable English managers, and the 'American' managers did work longer hours, although the differences were not statistically significant. It is possible that the longer hours of the 'American' sample reflected a greater commitment to their firms, as Child and MacMillan (1972) have argued, possibly as a consequence of the MBO schemes, although the absence of any differences in the job satisfaction findings do not encourage such an interpretation. Against these views of the potentially beneficial consequences of schemes like MBO, one must also note that such schemes could lead to sub-optimising behaviour within the firm.[29]

The other area of organisation that was singled out as being significantly different between the two groups of firms is the area labelled 'decision making'. In the final analysis the performance of particular companies must be a function of the quality of the decision making inside the firm, if only because the structure and activities of organisations are 'man made'; they are not the result of autonomous forces outside the firm. In view of the crucial nature of managerial decision making it is disappointing that there exist so few studies of the process at work, although the reasons for this are obvious enough.[30] This study is no exception to the rule; the data are relevant only to the environment of decision making, not to the process itself. The most crucial difference that was observed between the two groups of firms in this area can be expressed in terms of information flow. The American firms had on average more and better quality information on which to base their business decisions. This was particularly true in the areas of marketing, personnel and finance. The range of techniques for acquiring information and processing it was, in general terms, more sophisticated than the comparable range amongst the British companies. In the personnel area this meant that in the selection process, job descriptions and man descriptions were nearly always drawn up, 'objective' testing was more common, systematic interviewing more likely. Once recruited it was more likely in the American firms that the career of the recruit would be monitored more systematically, and promotion and training done on the basis of more detailed and objective assessment. In marketing, areas like customer behaviour, product policy decisions (in so far as these were not controlled directly by the parent), pricing decisions, promotional decisions and marketing control were also subject to more objective and 'rational' analysis than were the comparable activities in the British firms, although interestingly enough some of the British sample did not even possess some of these activities. Finally, in the area of finance, there appeared to be a far greater reliance on sophisticated control techniques than was apparent in some of the British firms. One consequence of this difference, already noted, was that the 'American' managers needed much more training to allow them to cope with the techniques that were employed in these particular areas of the company. It was because the 'American' managers possessed a larger armoury of such control devices that they were described as being more professional than their British counterparts. From the point of view of the internal processes of the firm, the American firms were by and large much richer in information, yet it can also be argued that they were also much more receptive to information flow from outside the organisation as well. It was much easier to carry out research upon American firms because they were more open to the research enterprise, and this is symptomatic of their general receptivity to new ideas and research findings from the wide field of management studies. One can illustrate this point from the area of industrial relations, where American firms have certainly been in the forefront of new types of wage payment schemes and industrial relations practice, reflecting their quicker response rate to the findings of research.[31] The better qualifications of the 'American' managers, themselves partly a function of the need to generate accurate information inside the organisation, also made them more receptive to outside information in the form of academic research findings etc. One must also note in this connection that American firms were more likely to attach themselves to sources of innovatory practices like management consultants. It is assumed that there is a relatively straightforward relationship between industrial efficiency and the quantity and quality of information available to decision makers. Other things being equal, decision makers with more relevant information will tend to make better decisions than those with less information. If it is correct, as writers like Bennis (1966) and Bell (1974) are anxious to argue, that the environment within which all firms are having to operate is becoming more 'turbulent', more marked by change, then it follows that decision makers who rely on experience or some other variety of the inductive process, will increasingly be at a disadvantage, compared with those who are attempting to monitor environmental changes. [32]

The same arguments about the advantage that American firms probably have at the level of decision making can be pursued when the structures of the two sets of firms are compared. One indication that the Americans were monitoring the external environment of their firms more closely than the comparable British firms was that the American firms in general scored higher on the functional specialisation index (see Table 3.10, p.109). In other words, the American firms were more likely to appoint a particular manager to investigate and provide information on a particular aspect of the external world than were the British firms. Although the American firms were in general both more formalised, in the sense of having more set procedures for things like personnel selection and development, financial control etc., as well as having a greater degree of functional specialisation, it was also argued in Chapter 3 that in some senses the American firms were also more organically organised. The informal feel of the organisations, reflected in the generally high scores of the American firms on the relevant organisational climate indexes ('Leader's psychological distance', 'Egalitarianism' and 'Employee involvement'), was a function of the fact that the American firms tended to adopt a more 'open door' policy towards their managerial employees and tended to encourage the horizontal flow of ideas and information. These are structural conditions which are likely to produce greater information flow and aid efficient decision making. Furthermore, as far as decisions relevant to the internal working of the company are concerned, this participative style of management is likely to meet with success in securing the acceptance of such decisions.

There exist a large number of studies which purport to show that more organically structured firms are likely to be more innovative and usually more profitable. [33] There are a number of difficulties with such views however. First, as already noted, many of these studies do not actually measure innovation or profitability in any direct way or, if they do, their measurements are rather slack and vague. Secondly, there is debate about whether it makes sense to conceptualise the organisation as a totality, in terms of organic or mechanistic structures, or whether it is better to look at different segments of the organisation (cf. Lawrence and Lorsch (1967) and Child (1970)). Thirdly, one has the debate about whether organically structured organisations are always more efficient (cf. the 'theory Y' approach of the neo-human relations movement) or whether it depends on the nature of the operating environment (cf. contingency theory). This study demonstrates the futility of conceiving of organisations as being organically or bureaucratically structured *in toto*. In certain respects the American firms were more bureaucratic than the British firms, in that they were more formalised; on the other hand they also exhibited some organic features; e.g. in certain respects they were decentralised and were marked by a degree of personal informality. Organisations are totalities however, and it is important to realise that one must consider how all the various elements of organisational structure blend together and produce a functioning company. It is tempting to argue that the majority of the American companies had produced a particular combination of elements that was likely, on the basis of previous research, to be particularly productive. On the one hand they were bureaucratised in the sense of structuring the organisation, designing jobs in such a way that each task could be easily identified, separated and quantified. This could easily have produced a rather rigid, soulless organisation of the sort that is predicted to occur under 'theory X'. Yet this formalisation was at least partially offset, as the organisational climate scores indicate, by the more informal managerial style, and decentralisation of the organisational structure. It seemed clear that the first element, the exercise of control via bureaucratic procedures, was a conscious policy decision on the part of the various companies; it was much less clear that the second element, the decentralisation and the informal managerial style, was. It would appear that the less formalised British organisations needed, as a consequence of their lack of formalisation, to centralise decision making, and this 'solution' fitted in much better with the stock of values in British society. By contrast, not only did the higher degree of formalisation in the United States companies permit decentralisation, but the informal managerial style reflected American cultural values as well.

Chapter 3 attempted to show that the organisational structures of the two groups of companies were partly related to the dominant function inside the firm; marketing tending to dominate in American firms and production in the British firms. Despite the arguments of Woodward (1965), it is not possible to say, with any certainty, which function is economically more important; it obviously depends so much upon the structure of the market in which the firm is operating. However, it is reiterated that the 'choice' of dominant function is partly a reflection of socio-cultural differences between the two societies.

This chapter has made some attempt to assess whether, on the basis of the available evidence, the differences that have been noted between British and American society on the one hand, and British and American manufacturing companies on the other, are likely to have led to different levels of economic performance. Several things have stood out from this analysis. First, how little is known about the social or organisational correlates of economic success. Secondly, how difficult it is to get reliable data, at the level of the firm, about company performance. Thirdly, how perilous an exercise it is to indulge in *post hoc* theorising about the correlates of performance.

At the level of the society, a number of elements have been isolated that reflect a distinctive and different pattern of socio-cultural values in the two societies, and their economic influence has been shown. It has been argued that certain distinctive features of the stratification system, the industrial relations system and education in American society, as well as the structure of business and the business environment, have probably all led in the direction of superior economic performance, when compared with the comparable British subsystems. No attempt has been made to suggest the relative weight of such factors, either absolutely or relatively, because no way is known of calculating it. All that is known is that if we take the data of national accounts and fit them to various production functions, then the conventional economic inputs do not account for all economic growth by a very wide margin. On the other side of the scales, Shonfield (1965) has put forward a convincing case to suggest that the non-interventionist stance of the United States governments, compared with that of British governments, has probably been detrimental to economic growth in America.

At the level of the company it is just as difficult to make firm statements about the correlates of performance. The published company accounts are only very crude approximations of the companies' economic position, as indicated, and any thorough study of company performance would have to examine company accounting practice in order to determine a truly comparable set of business ratios. Ignoring any problems of access, such a task would be a massive undertaking if American subsidiaries were to be included, and would certainly require the services of a trained accountant. It has already been indicated in this chapter how hazardous an exercise it is to attempt to correlate organisational and attitudinal attributes with company performance, and indeed the literature is marked by remarkably few serious attempts to do this. In recent years only PEP (1966) and Child (1974, 1975) have made attempts in Britain. The PEP report was rather disingenuous, in that not only was it not made clear where the performance data were generated from, but neither were any of the problems of making such correlations even discussed. Child's studies did fully discuss all the problems and concluded, tellingly enough: 'The research that has been reported does not demonstrate very strong relationships between managerial and organisational variables and company performance'.[34] No attempt at any correlational analysis has been made because of the arguments about the futility of such a practice; instead there has been an attempt to point out the possible consequences for performance of some of the differences that have been found between British and American manufacturing firms. However, such a theoretical exercise is no substitute for properly designed empirical work.

Notes

1 Habakkuk, 1968, p.30.

2 Take, for example, the case of the newly rich oil-producing states. The demand for oil is so great that these countries can achieve high rates of growth with almost any configuration of superstructure.

3 For example, appointing people to positions on the basis of certain technically relevant qualifications is, within a capitalist economic system, more likely to bring success, than appointing people on the basis of certain ascribed qualities like family connections.

4 Most measures of the alleged greater competitiveness of Americans are indirect. A study by Turner (1960a), which attempted to measure whether American students were more competitive than similar British students, concluded that there were no measurable differences.

5 The underlying assumption here is that the greater the amount of genuine competition the greater the private efficiency of the economic unit. Arguably this may not be the case in certain circumstances. For example, because of the force of international competition, it may be beneficial for a country like England to allow oligopolies or monopolies to form, because only companies of a certain size will be able to compete in the international market and the domestic market cannot take more than one or two large firms.

6 Garbarino, 1969, p.333.

7 It would be very difficult to compare the economic loss caused by a larger, yet more predictable number of days lost as against a smaller but less predictable number of days lost. An added complication is that not all writers agree that Britain has a larger number of days lost through unofficial strikes than America, (cf. Turner, 1969).

8 Very briefly the major failings of this approach are as follows, although not all researchers in this field are guilty of every failing. Most of the studies use aggregate data, i.e. correlations between aggregate levels of education in a society and a measure like GNP. Sometimes the growth in GNP is attributed to education merely because conventional inputs of labour and capital cannot account for it. The assignment to education is thus quite arbitrary. Very rarely is an attempt made to measure the link between education and productivity directly, usually a proxy measure is taken, e.g. income of persons receiving x amount of education; the argument then becomes entirely circular. A study by Berg (1970) using direct measures of productivity at the level of the individual, fails to support the conclusion that the better educated are more productive in a wide range of jobs. Education is often assumed to be a continuous variable; approximately the same marginal differences in the economic values are assumed to exist between any two successive years' schooling. The available evidence does not support such an

assumption (cf. Berg. 1970, p.43). It is possible to find quite impressive correlations between education and level of economic development, and such studies show that the higher the level of economic development of a country, the higher the proportion of its population in elementary, secondary and higher education (Harbison and Myers, 1964). Such correlations beg the question of causality however. Collins (1971) argues that there are considerable variations in school enrolments among countries at the same economic level, and anyway many of these variations are explicable in terms of political demands for access to education. Time-lag correlations of education and economic development do indeed show that increases in the proportions of population in elementary school precede increases in economic development after a take-off point at approximately 30–50 per cent of the seven to fourteen-year-old age group in school. A pattern of advances in secondary school enrolments preceding advances in economic development is found in a small number of cases; only twelve of the thirty-seven examined in Peaslee (1969). Finally, a pattern of growth in university enrolments and subsequent economic development is found in twenty-one of thirty-seven cases but, as Collins (1971) notes, the exceptions, including the United States, France, Sweden, Russia and Japan, are of such importance as to throw serious doubt on any necessary contribution of higher education to economic development.

9   In particular there is the move towards comprehensive education. Formally this means that all children have an equal chance of success, in line with Turner's (1960b) concept of contest mobility. In practice of course this is unlikely to happen.

10   The two reports were Gordon and Howell (1959) and Pierson et al., (1959). Gordon and Howell concluded: 'The simple fact of the matter is that academic standards are too low in most of the business schools in the United States..... The problem is a twofold one. Admission standards are too low, with the result that too many students are accepted who do not have either the background or the innate ability to survive a rigorous college program. On top of this, most schools do not attempt to offer a rigorous program, in part because of the high attrition rates that would result, in part because the faculty is not motivated to insist on high standards' (p.136). The Pierson report concurred and noted significantly '.....that too much emphasis is placed on practical techniques, too little on analytical methods useful in all kinds of situations' (p.24).

11   Solomons, 1974, p.100.

12   It is interesting to note that Shonfield (1965) claims that the quality of economic information supplied to the British government by its Civil Service has lagged behind that of America. It is interesting to speculate whether this is related to the educational backgrounds of those that enter the British Civil Service.

13   The reasons for these assumptions should be clear enough from the historical analysis presented in Chapter 2. Furthermore, the assumptions were supported throughout the 1960s by the influential Committee on Manpower Resources for Science and Technology, first under Zuckerman and then Jackson. The analysis claimed that not only was Britain producing too many pure scientists and not enough applied scientists, particularly engineers, but the engineers were 'draining' away to other countries, especially America. There seems little doubt that this picture was correct, probably as late as the beginning of the Second World War, but despite the prevalent government assumptions the reverse is probably the case now (cf. the OECD report *Gaps in Technology*, which claimed that Britain was producing more technologists per head than America). It may be the case however, as the OECD report suggests, that the US is using its scientists and technologists more productively, in that more of its engineers are to be found in manufacturing industry for example. Peck (1968) even shows that despite the large supply of engineers certain industries still find it difficult to recruit them.

14   Langrish et al., 1972, p.39.

15   Williams (1964) notes that there is only a poor relationship between different countries' research and development, expenditure and economic growth rates. Secondly, although there is clear evidence that the United States spends proportionately more than Britain on such expenditure, not all of it is directly relevant to economic growth, indeed defence spending consumes by far the largest proportion of the American research and development budget.

16   It is curious that the debate between Burrage (1969) and Rudd (1969) about the way cultural factors allegedly affected company performance, was conducted with reference to the figures of national performance, i.e. GNP.

17   For a review of some of this literature, see Steers, 1975.

18   Burns and Stalker, 1961, footnote on p.90.

19   Evidence from Dunning (1970) clearly shows that managers working in both British and American firms operating in Britain attached primary importance to the rate of return on total assets as the main measure of the private efficiency of a company (p.351).

20   Taking the universe of capitalist countries.

21   One might add a final problem and note the debate in the economic literature about whether firms try to profit maximise.

22   *Economic Trends*, no.238, London, HMSO, August 1973, p.vii.

23   Even the accounting profession has tacitly admitted that the standards of accounting and auditing in Britain are too variable. Following the accounting scandals at Pergamon and Associated Fire Alarms in the late 1960s the profession established the Accounting Standards Steering Committee in 1969 to try to get greater uniformity of practice.

The result of this, and one might add, of further scandals in the 1970s, has been that more and more company reports have been qualified by the auditors.

24   Dunning, 1970, p.386.

25   Wilkins, 1970, p.xi.

26   Dunning (undated), p.69.

27   Committee of Public Accounts, 1959/60.

28   The most usual form of investigation is to examine the company structure/management at time 1, and at the same moment look at its financial results. This would be a valid procedure only if one assumed that company structure/management had retained the present configuration for a considerable period of time and were therefore responsible for current performance. Many writers have disputed this assumption, Granick (1972) for example, argues '.....that it is the top management of ten to twenty years ago which is most responsible for the financial results currently achieved'. (p.30). Secondly, as Child (1974) argues, it is quite erroneous to make the assumption that performance is just an end product, a dependent variable. Indeed performance data are likely to be important inputs into the information system of the company and may themselves cause changes in the structure or management of the firms. Only highly detailed case studies of particular companies are likely to reveal such processes at work. Thirdly, there is the problem of how one shows that particular features of organisation/structure have actually contributed to performance. The fact is that very different patterns of organisational structure and management seem to be equally successful/unsuccessful in a range of situations.

29   Unless there is a very well worked out overall company plan, with objectives clearly stated for each unit of the company, in itself a very difficult exercise, then MBO could lead to 'overproduction' in certain areas, to the detriment of the company as a whole. As Winkler (1972) has pointed out, it is very difficult to get knowledge about 'productive capacity' at either the level of the company or the individual, and without it exercises like MBO become meaningless.

30   The basic problem is one of access. It is not just academic researchers who realise the crucial nature of the decision-making process, and one consequence of this is that business firms are reluctant to allow outsiders to witness this most vital part of the organisation. Further, to get anything out of such research, the researcher would need access to the information upon which decision making is based, and the research would have to be of considerable duration.

31   Several writers report that American firms have been the first to see the disadvantages of 'payment by results' schemes in certain industries, and have noted the research findings in this area. As a consequence there has been a greater tendency for American firms to abandon

these systems as antiquated, and to introduce schemes like measured daywork etc. (Marriott (1961), Turner et al., (1967), Seyfarth et al., (1968)). Furthermore, Steur and Gennard (1971) report that American firms were more likely to feel that employers' associations in Britain constrained new ideas and practices. As a consequence many American firms like Chrysler(UK), Ford, Vauxhall, Esso, Mobil, Brown and Polson, Heniz, Kelloggs, Kodak and Woolworths have left these associations to pursue their own company bargaining with the unions. Finally, it should be noted that American firms were in the forefront of developments in the area of productivity bargaining, beginning with the first scheme at the Fawley works of Esso in 1960.

32   One should note those experimental studies however, which suggest that most managers would respond to turbulent environments in a manner quite opposite to that which is predicted to lead to greater effectiveness (Hall and Mansfield (1971); Bourgeois III, McAllister and Mitchell (1978)).

33   See the review of studies in Aitken and Hage (1971).

34   Child, 1975, p.25.

7 Conclusions

In the early 1970s Michael O'neil and Jeremy Seabrooke wrote a play entitled, *Skin Deep*. The play depicted the operations of an American cosmetics firm operating in Britain and was a perfect reflection of the popular image of the clash between the formal rationality of American capitalism and the inhibiting culture of British society. In the end the cultural constraints proved to be too much for 'Lorraine Inc.', and the plant was moved to another European location. These images are very powerful and they were constantly met with in the course of this research. They represent the stereotypes held by Crozier's 'men of action'. This study has attempted in some small way to probe and test these popular pictures and, almost inevitably, has found them wanting.

The research design of this study has been particularly rigorous in that it has compared American firms operating in England with similar British firms; clearly if American firms operating in England and employing English managers still managed to exhibit differences from their British counterparts then this would have been strong evidence in favour of cultural values influencing business structure and behaviour. In view of the popular stereotypes about American firms and their employees the number of differences discovered was rather small. Before the main part of this research was started some twenty American executives working for American companies in England were contacted in order to tap the views of managers who had worked in both societies. Several things stood out about this group of men. First, the ease of access to executives in very senior positions in their companies. [1] This ease of access was to be repeated with the American firms in the main sample and reflected the greater openness of American society; it was the first research finding. The other feature which stood out about this group was the hold that the 'folklore' of British-American managerial differences had on them. When these men were asked about the differences between Britain and America in this area they poured out a picture that they had digested over the years from an avid reading of the popular press on both sides of the Atlantic, a press which is very largely self-citing and devoid of hard evidence. When taxed about their own personal experiences of such differences they found the task more difficult, although not impossible. These images of the differences between Britain and America were to constantly recur during the course of this research and reaffirmed the view that only studies with an adequate methodology, which allowed one to compare like with like, would ever manage to unravel the reality from the myth.

This study, which compared American manufacturing firms operating in Britain with their British counterparts, largely failed to confirm many of the predicted differences. It is worthwhile summarising the differences that were detected. First, the view that American companies would reflect the more open culture of American society, and would be more willing to disclose information about themselves, was confirmed. The response rate from the American executive sample was exceptionally high (86 per cent), and the response rate from the American firms in the sample was over twice that of the British firms. Four major differences were noted in the structure and operation of the two groups of companies. First, the American firms tended to give greater importance to the human capital of their organisation than the British firms. They took more care in the selection and appraisal of managers, and were more inclined to train their personnel. Secondly, the American firms made far greater use of a wider range of techniques for managerial control; this was particularly true in the areas of personnel, marketing and finance. Thirdly, the American firms tended to possess an organisational climate that was more informal and employee centred; status distinctions were less evident in most of the American organisations. Fourthly, the British firms were inclined to stress production as being the most crucial area of the firm, and the ethos and methods of this function tended to influence the whole structure; whereas in the American firms the stress was more likely to be placed on marketing. These four areas of difference all refer to the organisation of the company; interestingly enough, fewer differences were found amongst the managers in the two groups of companies, and perhaps this indicates that it was easier to mould company structure from across the Atlantic than it was the management personnel, especially when they were the nationals of another country. Only two major differences were observed between the British and the 'American' managers. The outstanding difference related to qualifications; the managers working for the American companies were significantly better qualified than their British counterparts; this difference related both to formal academic qualifications and to management training. Secondly, the 'American' managers had experienced significantly more internal job mobility in their companies. The important question to be answered is to what extent these observed differences can be explained by reference to the variable of national differences or culture. It has been a common practice in cross-cultural management research to separate cultural values from other variables that might be thought to influence business structure and behaviour, e.g. economic variables, technology. Although this practice might have considerable analytic use, in practice it remains to be seen just how useful it is. This thesis has attempted to show, particularly in the historical analysis in Chapter 2, that the economic mode of production is inextricably entwined with the superstructure of the society, each influences the other in a variety of complex ways, although eventually the economic demands are strongest. To take a practical example, is the more informal employee-centred structure of American companies to be explained by reference to the lack of status distinctions inside American society, themselves a reflection of the values of achievement, universalism etc., which had the sorts of historical origins that have been described? Or alternatively, is one to argue that such an organisational strategy is adopted by many American firms, particularly perhaps the more 'progressive' ones, because it is believed to be more efficient and profitable? The explanation is couched in terms of the demands of capitalism. It is hoped that this example demonstrates the futility of counterposing culture or capitalism. The demands of the capitalist economic system are mediated through the web of the socio-cultural structure, which is an historical product.

It has also been traditional in much socio-economic writing to try to separate the effects of the culture of the society (or the values, or 'national character') from the structure of the society. Thus the distinction is made between the structure of the society, which is denoted by such things as the system of stratification, the family etc., and some notion of the values, or 'ways of seeing the world' or some other sort of mental construct. It is doubtful whether this distinction between the 'subjective' and the 'objective' can be held even at the analytical level, and its use for the empirical researcher is even less clear—after all at one level the family is no more than a set of rules of behaviour. A rather behaviourist stance has been taken on these matters in the course of this research, in that there has been close adherence to observable features of the two societies and the two groups of companies and their managers. There may be a sense in which culture exists as an entity separate from the social structure, as Parsons wishes to maintain, but in this particular research project it did not seem to be a useful exercise to distinguish between culture and structure. [2] This thesis has stressed throughout therefore the socio-cultural structure and its influence upon economic behaviour.

It is also necessary for more to be said about the pattern variables used to 'describe' the socio-cultural structure, and more particularly about the claim that the pattern of affective-neutrality, specificity, universalism, achievement and self-orientation are in some sense the 'values of capitalism'. First, if one wishes to undertake comparative work between two societies it is necessary to have an appropriate framework for analysis. Although the Parsonian pattern variables are clearly not 'universal categories' and certainly not culture free, it seems that

they are appropriate for a comparison of two western industrial capitalist societies, because the pattern variables represent the value choices
faced by such societies. Secondly, the inbuilt goals of the capitalist mode
of production do set up certain pressures towards formal rationality. As
argued in Chapter 1, in the ideal-typical model of capitalism it is
necessary to relate to people on the basis of their achievement rather
than their ascribed qualities. Decisions cannot be made on the basis of
emotional considerations (affectivity), but rather on the basis of rational
calculation (affective-neutrality). Relations inside the ideal-typical
capitalist economy are dominated not by ill defined obligations to people
(diffuseness), but on the basis of the specific roles they play in the
division of labour (specificity), and a response is made to people on the
basis of their membership of specific categories (universalism) like
employee or consumer. Finally, the ideal-typical model stresses self-
orientation for its harmonious working. There are two powerful objec-
tions to this line of reasoning. First, although it might be possible to
argue that capitalism, via its inbuilt goal of profit, does set up certain
distinct strains towards the pattern of values that have been suggested,
indeed this point is largely conceded even by the critics of such a system
(cf. Gunder Frank, 1971), it can be argued with equal force that, at the
same time, such a system sets up counterforces, which tend to stress the
opposite pattern of values. These opposing forces represent the contradictions of capitalism. Thus the forces of 'efficiency' which are released
by such a mode of production are held in check by the need for the
capitalist class to reproduce itself; the strain towards the value of achievement for example, is checked at a certain point to allow the bourgeoisie
to remain in control. This is a very strong argument, particularly if one
accepts that capitalism has changed from its highly competitive stage in
the nineteenth century,where some of the values of capitalism were
relatively strong, to a less competitive form, even perhaps monopoly
capitalism, where the counterforces offer powerful checks to such a set
of values. As many writers have pointed out, it is hardly difficult to see
the effect of values like ascription and diffuseness in either Britain or
America today. If these arguments are accepted, then there would appear
to be a fundamental problem in the explanatory paradigm of this research.
It has been argued that the extent to which the values of capitalism are
held in check can be put down to the socio-cultural structure of the
society, and that the structure of British society offers more of a check
on the private economic efficiency of capitalism than does the comparable structure of American society. In fact there is no necessary contradiction here: in Britain the values of capitalism have always been faced
with the opposite set of values emanating from the landed aristocracy;
not only did these offer a check to capitalist rationality in the nineteenth
century, but their existence has always made it easier for the capitalist

class to draw upon that tradition to protect their own interests. In America, on the other hand, the relative absence of such a tradition has made it more difficult for American capitalists to resist the forces of efficiency generated by the capitalist mode of production, they lack a cultural tradition to fall back on to protect their own interests. Again it needs to be stressed that one cannot counterpose culture or capitalism; the two forces are inextricably entwined. What one can do however, and what this book has attempted to do is to show that certain solutions to the problems of particular groups, in this case the capitalist class, are made easier by the prevailing socio-cultural structure in some societies than in others.

To talk of the capitalist class as above raises another important issue. The empirical part of this study has not of course examined the capitalist class as such, it has only examined the operation of certain privately-owned companies. Whilst a pervasive case can be made out for the contradictions of capitalism at the level of the owners of the means of production, there is very little reason why the values of capitalism that stress efficiency should not be unleashed on the operation and organisation of those businesses. It is at this level in particular where the cultural values of society can be seen to have their major effect. It has been shown that in the case of the American firms there were signs that the firms did, in certain respects at least, stress the pattern of values that were designated as capitalist, more strongly than did the comparable British firms. As Chapter 3 put it: 'The measuring rod of profit and loss was pushed into more areas of the American firms.....This was possible because of the greater development of analytical managerial techniques.....the unifying character of these techniques is that they seek to apply the principles of rational problem-solving to business planning and decision making'. This pattern of management is consistent with the demands of capitalism and is sanctioned by the cultural values of American society. The only point at which the counter values emanating from capitalism were noted in this study was in the data on performance. Capitalism generates inequality, and inequality sets up barriers to its own description; despite the relative 'openness' of American society and the American firms, it was very difficult to get adequate data about the economic performance of such companies. It is at this level of course that the interests of the bourgeoisie do oppose the cultural tradition of openness in American society. In England, on the other hand, both culture and capitalism push in the same direction—towards secrecy.

It has been argued above that the socio-cultural structure of the society can check the operation of formal rationality by providing an alternative set of values and traditions which the bourgeoisie can use for their own ends. At the level of the firm these cultural traditions can permeate the whole organisation, but they will probably only be very strongly maintained right at the top. In Britain, because of her socio-cultural structure, one is more likely to find the values of affectivity, diffuseness, particularism, ascription and a collective orientation pervading further down the firm. In American firms such a value set will tend to be maintained only near the top of the organisation, and even here it may be difficult to observe them directly, because they are not culturally legitimate. There is a sense however, as Marx pointed out, in which capitalism tends to dissolve such cultural constraints. [3] One can see this most clearly when an economic crisis occurs in either the society or the firm. The demands of the balance sheet exert considerable pressure upon the 'managers of the economy', micro or macro, to adjust the structure to the demands of the economic system. As the British economy and British firms have faced such a crisis in the last two decades, one result has been an ever greater stress on the values of capitalism, both in the society and in the firms. This point can be dramatically illustrated by the activities of the new British Conservative Government that was elected in Spring 1979. Faced with an even gloomier set of economic predictions for the 1980s, and armed with an analysis which indicted the socio-cultural structure of British society for impeding economic activity, the Government set about modifying large areas of Britain's social structure. The key to this policy was to allow economic forces to work relatively untrammelled in the society in order that the productive sector of the economy (designated as manufacturing industry) could recover. [4] The slow dissolution of the 'old' values deriving from the domination of the landed aristocracy was to be speeded up, and replaced by the values of capitalism. This process can only go so far of course; eventually such abrasive values will be checked by the capitalist class. Even in a country like America, where it has been argued the socio-cultural system is more in accordance with the demands of ideal-typical capitalism, there are checks exerted by such a structure, indeed the structure of any particular nation state is likely to exert a certain drag upon the economy. It is because of this factor that one has seen the development of the corporation that attempts to free itself from the constraints of the culture of any particular nation state—the multi-national company. There is a sense in which such companies are, at least potentially, 'culture free'. In the sample of American executives that were interviewed, three were drawn from what Perlmutter (1969) calls 'geocentric' firms, [5] and although such firms are still relatively rare, they can be said to represent the ultimate stage of capitalist rationality. Such a stage is a natural evolution for those American firms which have allowed the fullest play for the values of capitalism inside their home-based organisations, but are still constrained by the activities of their own nation state. Multinational companies, because they are not attached to any particular country also offer further advantages to the capitalist class; it is difficult both to observe their activities in detail, and to control them.

The managers in these geocentric firms represent the epitomy of professional management: highly mobile; technically well qualified in an extensive range of managerial techniques; possessing few loyalties, except to formal rationality itself—as Webber (1969) puts it, the international executive is a 'man for all countries'.[6] It is to these sorts of men that the label 'professional managers' was applied by some of the managers in the main sample of firms. Chapter 4 attempted to show that, as capitalism increasingly forces firms to apply formal rationality to the business of profit making, technocrats become more prominent inside business organisations. As the techniques of administration become more specialised and increasingly require formal training, it becomes ever more difficult to distinguish between business managers and other 'professionals'. There is probably now no more guesswork and hunch involved in running a large geocentric multinational corporation, than there is in running a medical practice. One possible consequence of this fact is that the image of 'business manager' may become much more clearly defined; the job may entail a certain minimum of technical knowledge, and this may take the occupation out of the category of 'residual occupation' in terms of career choice, that it still seems to be in, in Britain. Indeed, as the activities of the state and the large corporations become ever more closely entwined, and business bureaucracy becomes increasingly indistinguishable from state bureaucracy, then the job of 'administrator' could emerge clearly for the first time. Of course there is still some way to go before this becomes a reality; the British Civil Service is still a curious mixture of ascription and achievement, particularism and universalism, diffuseness and specificity, whilst the American civil service, although it is more 'professional' in one sense, is still tainted by relatively low status. On the other side, American business would appear to be more professional than British business practice, although the new predictive tools of management science, particularly techniques like operational research, could soon transform even British business.[7] Again it must be stressed that given the present structure of the capitalist mode of production, this formal rationality is likely to be checked when it reaches the owners of the enterprise.

One of the problems of a value system which stresses affective-neutrality, specificity, universalism, achievement and self-orientation, as both Weber and Durkheim were well aware, is that it can lead to a sense of alienation. Although the American firms in the sample were in general marked by a greater degree of formal rationality, their managers did not exhibit any more signs of alienation than the British managers. The reason for this was that the formal rationality was embedded in a set of informal personal relationships. This informal style is clearly partly to be explained by the value structure of American society; as Sutton et al., (1962) put it: 'If "capitalism" is still respectable in the United States, the fluidity of "informal" social relations has greatly contributed'.[8] It could be argued anyway, that the cultural values of American society, by offering greater legitimation to the protestant values of hard work in a business setting, would be less likely to produce feelings of alienation amongst such managers. In Britain there might be a greater problem: ignoring any difficulties involved in the application of the formal techniques of managerial control in British business, the greater formality of British society and hence British business life could well lead to 'soulless corporations'. Furthermore, several writers have claimed to have detected a 'middle class reaction to the values of the competitive society' within Britain.[9] Certainly there is a strand in the culture of British society that would legitimate this adaptation, although it is not strong, and the fact that almost 50 per cent of all managers in the sample opted for what was called the 'social responsibility' response, when asked about the role of the company in society, is food for thought. Perhaps the most dramatic evidence for this view is that business itself is not a high status and popular career choice in England anyway.

These are large speculations for such a small study and the author is acutely aware of the difficulties involved in generalising about British and American industry on the basis of this study. Indeed one of the findings of this study has been the variation within the American and British firms as well as between them. Even though the sample of firms was rather small, there was one firm in each group that did not fit the general pattern: GB Furniture and US Electronics I. Business organisations are influenced not just by the economic and cultural framework of the society of which they are a product, but also by contextual variables like size, product and technology. The example of GB Furniture also stresses the enormous importance that a key figure or a dominant coalition of managers can have upon the structure and climate of a firm. Similarly the characteristics of the managers in the two groups of firms were to be explained more by reference to variables like position in the life cycle, functional location, position in the organisational hierarchy etc., than by reference to the fact that they worked for British or American firms. It would be interesting to replicate a study such as this in a third country, i.e. to compare British and American manufacturing countries operating outside of Britain or America. Such a study design would get round the problems that this study has had whereby both groups of firms had to draw upon the same population of managers. Studies like the one reported, which attempt to carefully match up companies on a range of variables will be increasingly difficult to do however, as companies increasingly diversify their product ranges, making industry and product matching extremely difficult.

Notes

1 Seven managing directors, one deputy managing director, one vice president, and the rest in senior management posts.

2 One of the most interesting attempts to distinguish culture and structure is that of Bernstein (1971) (especially chapters 7 and 8). Drawing on the work of Weber, Durkheim and Marx, Bernstein attempts to sketch the way in which linguistic codes 'transmit the culture and so constrain behaviour'. This way of viewing culture as being embodied in language is one that could well prove to be a very fruitful line of enquiry, particularly if it was linked to some of the current work in semiotics.

3 'Capital develops irresistibly beyond national boundaries and prejudices.....it destroys the self satisfaction confined within narrow limits and based upon a traditional mode of life and reproduction', Marx,1953, p.313.

4 The justification of this policy is derived from a combination of monetarist policies, i.e. the view that the control of the money supply is the key variable in the management of the economy, combined with the proposition that there is too much public spending and not enough concentration on manufacturing industry (cf. the influential work of Bacon and Eltis, 1976). As a consequence of this view public sector spending in Britain has come under very close scrutiny and all those elements of the welfare state which are not regarded as directly contributing to the general economic well being of the society are being cut back. One can illustrate this from the field of education, thus whereas things like nursery classes and school meals are being cut, greater emphasis is being placed on the teaching of basic skills and 'industry'.

5 Perlmutter (1969) has evolved a three stage model of the multinational company. Initially, there is the ethnocentric organisation, where the minimum of autonomy is allowed to subsidiaries. This form of organisation evolves into a polycentric type where the parent company recognises that local conditions are different from those faced by the parent company and those of other subsidiaries. Rather more autonomy of decision making is allowed. Finally, at the top of the evolutionary tree, and in Perlmutter's view the most desirable organisational type, is the geocentric company. In this type of multinational organisation there is the fullest co-operation between the subsidiaries and the parent on the basis of full equality. The guiding principle for decision making is 'culture free rationality'.

6 Webber, 1969, p.9.

7 This author does not wish to argue that we will see 'rule by technocrats', merely that these more formal methods are likely to be used by the bourgeoisie because they are more efficient. The incentive to use such methods will be provided by falling rates of profit (cf. Glyn and Sutcliffe, 1972).

8 Sutton et al., 1962, p.315.
9 Pahl and Pahl, 1971; Williams and Guest, 1973.

Appendix 1

The re-analysis of the BIM data

Table A. 1

Number of manufacturing firms which used job descriptions
in management recruitment: BIM sample (1971)

Small (1-1,000 employees)				Large (1,000+ employees)			
US firms		GB firms		US firms		GB firms	
%	N	%	N	%	N	%	N
33.3	3	54.2	26	100	13	54.4	19

Table A. 2

Number of manufacturing firms which used man specifications in
management recruitment: BIM sample (1971)

Small (1-1,000 employees)				Large (1,000+ employees)			
US firms		GB firms		US firms		GB firms	
%	N	%	N	%	N	%	N
33.3	3	18.8	9	76.9	10	24.3	9

Table A. 3

Number of manufacturing firms which used tests in management
recruitment: BIM sample (1971)

Small (1-1,000 employees)				Large (1,000+ employees)			
US firms		GB firms		US firms		GB firms	
%	N	%	N	%	N	%	N
44.9	4	27.1	13	38.5	5	29.7	11

197

Table A.4

Number of manufacturing firms which used selection consultants in
management recruitment: BIM sample (1971)

US firms		GB firms	
%	N	%	N
36.4	8	22.4	19

Table A.5

Number of manufacturing firms which used executive searchers in
management recruitment: BIM sample (1971)

US firms		GB firms	
%	N	%	N
40.9	9	8.2	7

Table A.6

Amount spent on the management selection process as percentage of starting
salary, British and American manufacturing firms: BIM sample (1971)

Percentage of starting salary	Small (1-1,000 employees)				Large (1,000+ employees)			
	US firms		GB firms		US firms		GB firms	
	%	N	%	N	%	N	%	N
Up to 10	33.3	3	54.2	26	30.8	4	37.8	14
11−25	55.6	5	37.5	18	46.2	6	40.5	15
26−50	11.1	1	8.3	4	23.1	3	16.2	6

Appendix 2

The organisational structure schedule

1 What is the status of this organisation?

(Please tick appropriate category)

1 Principal unit

2 Subsidiary (with legal identity)

3 Head branch (with headquarters
  on same location)

4 Branch

2 How long has this unit of organisation been in operation?   years

  (a)   If this unit of operation is not the principal unit,
how long has the principal unit been in operation?   years

3 How many employees does this unit of organisation employ?

(part-time employees count as half)

4 Total number of employees in ultimate owning group?

5 Could you list all the main outputs produced by this
organisation.

(Examples: cakes, biscuits, milk products etc.)

....

....

....

....

....

FORMALISATION

(Please tick appropriate answer)

1 Is there an organisation chart for this company?   YES   NO
   (If the answer is 'no', please move to question 3)

2 Is the organisation chart given to:

   Chief executive only

   Departmental heads

   All senior executives

3 Are there written operating instructions for direct   YES   NO
   workers?

4 Are there written terms of reference or job   YES   NO
   descriptions for direct workers?

5 Are there written terms of reference or job   YES   NO
   descriptions for line (workflow) superordinates?

6 Are there written terms of reference or job   YES   NO
   descriptions for staff (other than line superordinates)?

7 Are there written terms of reference or job   YES   NO
   descriptions for the chief executive?

8 Are there written policies for the organisation as   YES   NO
   a whole?

9 Is there a workflow (production) schedule or   YES   NO
   programme?

ORGANISATIONAL AUTONOMY

An organisation has autonomy when the decisions are taken inside it.

Please tick those decisions which the firm can take inside it.

DECISIONS

1 Supervisory establishment.

2 Appointment of supervisory staff from outside the organisation.

3 Promotion of supervisory staff.

4 Salaries of supervisory staff.

5 To spend unbudgeted or unallocated money on capital items.

6 To spend unbudgeted or unallocated money on revenue items.

7 What type or what brand new equipment is to be.

8 To determine a new produce or service.

9 To determine marketing territories covered.

10 The extent and type of market to be aimed for.

11 What shall be costed.

12 What shall be inspected.

13 What operations shall be work studied.

14 Dismiss a supervisor.

15 Training methods to be used.

16 Buying procedures.

17 Which suppliers of materials are to be used.

18 What and how many welfare facilities are to be provided.

19 The price of the output.

20 To alter responsibilities/areas of work of specialist departments.

21 To alter responsibilities/areas of work of line departments.

22 To create a new department.

23 To create a new job.

FUNCTIONAL SPECIALISATION

A function is specialised when at least one person performs that function
and no other function, and when that person is not in the direct line
command.

Please tick those activities that on the above definition are specialised
in this company.

ACTIVITIES TO:

1   Develop, legitimise and symbolise the organisation charter
    (public relations, advertising etc.).

2   Dispose of, distribute and service the output
    (sales and service, customer complaints etc.).

3   Carry outputs and resources from place to place
    (transport).

4   Acquire and allocate human resources
    (employment etc.).

5   Develop and transform human resources
    (education and training).

6   Maintain human resources and promote their identification
    with the organisation
    (welfare, medical, safety, magazine, sports and social etc.).

7   Obtain and control materials and equipment
    (buying, material control, stores, stock control etc.).

8   Maintain and erect buildings and equipment
    (maintenance, works engineer etc.).

9   Record and control financial resources
    (accounts, costs, wages etc.).

10 Control the workflow
    (planning, progressing etc.).

11 Control the quality of materials, equipment and output
    (inspection testing etc.).

12   Assess and devise ways of producing the output
     (work study, OR, rate fixing, methods study etc.).

13   Devise new outputs, equipment and process.

14   Develop and operate admin. procedures
     (registry, filing, statistics, OM.).

15   Deal with the legal and insurance requirements
     (legal, registrar, insurance, licensing etc.).

16   Acquire information on the operational field
     (market research).

TECHNOLOGY: MODE OF PRODUCTION

Tick the production technology that is central to the company.

If the firm uses a mixed type, tick all the appropriate categories.

If the company uses a mixed type but one is clearly subsidiary to the other, tick the main one twice.

1 Production of prototype units only.

2 Production of units or parts of units to
  customers individual requirements.
  Single units or very limited runs only.

3 Production of batches of units in very
  large numbers.

4 Continuous flow production of liquids,
  gases and crystalline substances.

TECHNOLOGY: AUTOMATICITY RANGE
AND AUTOMATICITY MODE

RANGE is defined by the highest scoring piece of equipment the organisation is known to use (ignore thermostatic governors).

MODE is determined by assessing the bulk of the equipment used by the organisation on its workflow.

PLEASE TICK

	MODE	RANGE

HAND TOOLS AND MANUAL MACHINES

These give mechanical advantages, but do not replace man's energy or control.

Examples: shovel, hammer, wrench, file,
                  jack, handsaw.

	MODE	RANGE

POWERED MACHINES AND TOOLS

Muscles are replaced for the basic machine function. Machine action and control completely dependent upon operator.

Examples: electric drill, air hammer,
                  spray gun, belt sander.

	MODE	RANGE

SINGLE CYCLE AUTOMATICS AND
SELF-FEEDING MACHINES

Completes an action when initiated by an operator. Feeds tool to the work by power.

Examples: piper threading machines,
                  machine tools such as grinder,
                  planer, mill shaper, lathe.

	MODE	RANGE

AUTOMATIC: REPEATS CYCLE

At this level all energy is mechanised. Carries
out routine instructions without aid of man.
Starts cycle and repeats cycle automatically.

Examples: engine production lines, automatic
copying lathe, automatic assembly
of switches.

	MODE	RANGE

SELF-MEASURING AND ADJUSTING:
FEEDBACK

Measures and compares result to desired size
or position and adjusts to minimise any error.

Examples: automatic sizing grinders, dynamic
balancing, colour matching or
blending, pattern tracing flame
cutter.

	MODE	RANGE

COMPUTER CONTROL: AUTOMATIC
COGNITION

Is cognisant of multiple factors on which
machine or process preformance is predicted,
evaluates and reconciles them by means of
computer operations to determine proper
control action.

1   Before an executive is recruited into the firm is a job description
formally drawn up?

Always   Sometimes   Never

2 Here is a list of the various sources of recruitment that a firm might use in recruiting new managers. Ignoring recruitment at the boardroom level and the recruitment of technical specialists, would you rank them, from 1 to 9, in the order in which you use them. For example, if you use newspaper advertisements more than any other source place the number 1 next to it; if you use the services of the DEP less than any other source place the number 9 next to it, etc.

Internal promotions

Personal introductions

Newspaper advertisements

Journal advertisements

Selection consultants

Executive searchers

Executive registers and agencies

Professional associations

Department of Employment

Any others (please specify)...

....

....

3 Does the company use any TESTS in its selection procedure?

Always   Sometimes   Never

If 'never',please pass to question 6.

4 Does the company use intelligence tests?

Always   Sometimes   Never

206

5   Does the company use personality tests?

Always   Sometimes   Never

6   Here is a list of attributes and qualities that might be considered
    important in selecting management personnel. Ignoring recruitment
    at the boardroom level and the recruitment of technical specialists,
    would you rank them from 1 to 10 in the order of importance
    that the company gives to them. For example, if the company
    takes least notice of educational qualifications place the number
    10 next to this quality; if the company takes most notice of
    appearance then place the number 1 next to this quality.

    Educational qualifications

    Appearance

    Type of school attended

    References

    Interests

    Speech

    Performance on selection tests (IQ,
    personality etc.)

    General attitudes

    Experience

    Manner

7   Is there a formal system of assessing the progress of
    executives (e.g. annual reports, appraisals etc.)?   YES   NO

8   Is it a matter of company policy to move
    management personnel around the various
    departments of the firm (e.g. from marketing
    to personnel)?   YES   NO

9   How many administrative staff are there in this
    organisation? (Note: for the purpose of this question,
    count administrative staff as anybody who has
    authority in the organisation and who would be
    counted as part of 'management'. Take'organisation'
    to mean the unit for which this personnel department
    is responsible.)

    ————————————————

10 What percentage of the administrative staff, as defined
    above, are female?

    ————————————————

11 How many administrative staff, on average, leave each year?

    ————————————————

12 How many administrative staff are there working in the
    personnel department?

    ————————————————

13 Does the personnel department in this organisation
    also have responsibility for industrial relations matters?

    YES   NO   PARTIALLY

14 Does the company belong to an employers'
    association?   YES   NO

15 Does the company recognise any blue-collar
    trade unions as bargaining agents?   YES   NO

Appendix 3

The management questionnaire

You are being asked to complete this questionnaire as part of a survey being carried out on a number of organisations. The researchers are interested to see how organisations, differing in size, product, technology, etc. differ in their organisational structure, and we are particularly interested in the impact that these different structures have on managers themselves.

The questionnaire comes in two parts: in the first part you are asked to answer questions about your job, your career, your education and a small number of personal details. The second part asks for your attitude towards various aspects of the organisation.

You will find that in many of the questions you are given a number of alternative answers and have to choose one of them. This simplifies the questionnaire for you so that it will take less time to complete; indeed it it not as long as it looks. We realise that often this may have the effect of over-simplifying your ideas, and that in some cases there may be no alternative answer which expresses exactly how you feel; we hope that you will bear with us in choosing the answers nearest to your feelings.

Please complete the questionnaire without consulting any of your colleagues. When you have finished, put it in the enclosed stamped addressed envelope and return it by post.

The first question asks for your name, this is because it is intended to interview a small sample, randomly chosen, of those who complete our questionnaire. If you do not wish to be interviewed, please leave this question blank. The information you supply is just as valuable to us without the name. Every answer will be treated in the strictest confidence, and all information given to us will be used in such a way as to preserve complete anonymity.

Finally, we would like to thank you for completing this questionnaire and hope you will find it of interest.

Ian Jamieson.
University of Surrey and
School of Business,
Ealing Technical College.

1 Name

1(a) When did you join this firm?

2 How many firms or organisations have you been employed by during your career?

3 Have you ever changed functions during your career (e.g. from production to sales etc.)? Please circle the appropriate answer

YES   NO

4 What is your job title?

5 Below is a list of various authority levels in an organisation. Please indicate the one nearest to your own level by placing a tick in the appropriate box.

(a) A person at this level is in charge of the whole unit of organisation, i.e. he is the chief executive of this unit of organisation.

(b) A person at this level is in charge of a whole segment of the organisation, e.g. works manager or a manager in charge of all the technical scientific activities of the organisation.

(c) A person at this level is in charge of a small segment of the organisation, e.g. a departmental manager of production, sales, accounts, method study etc.

(d) A person at this level is in junior management, he might supervise people working directly on production if he is in line management.

6 How did you enter your present firm? (Please tick).

Advertisement

Personal approach

Family contact

Ministry of Labour

Other agency (selection consultants, university appointments board etc.)

7 What features of the present firm attracted you to it?

8 Did you consciously choose a career in business? By a career in business we mean a job in the general management of a profit-oriented company rather than as a professional man, e.g. doctor, lawyer, or as an employee of central/local government etc. Please circle appropriate answer.

YES   NO

9 What were the most important influences determining your decision to enter business?

10 Did you ever consider other careers? Please circle appropriate answer.

YES   NO

If yes, please specify:

11 Would you be happy if your children chose the same career? Please circle appropriate answer.

YES   NO

12 At what age did you firmly decide upon your career?

13 If you were looking for a new job, what factors would you rank highly in making your choice?

14 What factors would you rank of low importance?

15 Here are three statements about the role of the company that have been made by various businessmen. Please tick the statement nearest to your own opinion.

(a) A company can only have one responsibility and that is to maximise profit for its shareholders; only by doing this will the needs of the community, the customer and its employees be ultimately met.

(b) A company conducted solely for the benefit of shareholders is unethical. The company must also consciously seek to satisfy the needs of its employees, its customers and the community.

(c) A company's first consideration must be to make a profit. Once this is achieved, then the company can consider the demands of its employees, its customers and the community.

16 We would like you to rank these ten traits on the basis of how important you think each trait is for success in business. Rank them by placing a number from 1 to 10 beside each trait. For example, if you think that tact is the most important trait for success in business, place the number 1 next to it. If you think that imagination is the least important, place the number 10 next to it.

Forcefulness

Tactfulness

Imagination

Agreeableness

Independence

Cautiousness

Self-confidence

Adaptability

Decisiveness

Co-operativeness

17 Do you think that your present job gives you the opportunity to use your abilities to the full? (please tick the appropriate category.)

Completely

To a major extent

To some extent

To a minor extent

Not at all

18 Which of these statements best describes how you feel about your job? (Please tick the appropriate category.)

A dominant factor in my life and as a primary source of satisfaction.

A distinctly interesting and important part of my life.

An activity separate from the rest of my life and one which must not be allowed to dominate.

A source of demand and pressure that threatens other activities.

19 Have you seriously thought of going into business on your own?

20 Do you find this idea attractive? (Please tick appropriate category.)

Very attractive

Quite attractive

Indifferent

Not very attractive

Not attractive at all

21 Do you belong to a professional association e.g. BIM, IPM?

(Please circle appropriate answer)   YES   NO

If no pass to question 24.

22 How often do you attend meetings of this professional body?

(Please tick appropriate category.)

Regularly

Quite often

Seldom

Never

23 Do you hold, or have you ever held, office in this professional body (at local or national level)?

YES   NO

If yes, please specify.

24 Do you regularly read a professional journal?   YES   NO

If yes, which one(s)?

25 Are most of your friends outside or inside the company?

(Please circle the appropriate answer)   OUTSIDE   INSIDE

26 How many of your colleagues at work would you call close friends?

27 Do you discuss matters other than business with your colleagues? (Please tick appropriate category.)

Regularly

Often

Seldom

Never

28 How many hours would you say you worked on company business per week? Include work at home in the evenings and at weekends and count lunch breaks etc.

29 What type of school did you last attend full time? (Please tick appropriate category.)

Elementary school

Maintained secondary school (excluding grammar)

Comprehensive school

Grammar school

Private school

30 At what age did you leave school?

31 Did you attend university or college?

university or college(s)	degrees/diplomas	subjects
....	....	....
....	....	....
....	....	....

32 Have you ever attended any management training courses?

                                                        YES   NO
    If yes, where?

    What was the course?

33 Year of birth

34 Marital status?
    If single, please pass to question 36.

35 How many children have you?

36 What was your father's principal occupation?
    (Please be specific)

    The second part of this questionnaire consists of 48 statements. They
are statements which refer to the environment in which people work.
The statements refer to daily activities, to rules and regulations and
policies, to typical interests and projects etc. You are asked to indicate
which statements are characteristic of your organisation and which are
not. Your answers should tell us what you believe your institution is
like rather than what you might prefer. You may not have a certain
answer to many of these statements, because there may not be any really
definite information on which to base your answers. We would like you
to answer all the questions, however. Your response will simply mean
that, in your opinion, the statement is probably true or probably false
about your organisation.

Beside each statement there appears the letters 'T' for true and 'F' for
false.

Please circle the appropriate answer.

1   Important people here are always addressed as 'Sir'   T   F

2   It's important here to be in the right club or group   T   F

3   Policy, goals and objectives are carefully explained
    to everyone   T   F

4   Applications of research, experimental analysis and
    other forms of scientific method are encouraged   T   F

5   Policy changes occur slowly and only after considerable
    deliberation   T   F

6   The organisation's activities are often featured in the
    newspapers   T   F

7   It's necessary to be polite under all circumstances to
    stay out of trouble   T   F

8   Personality and pull are more important than
    competence in getting on   T   F

9   Criticism or advice from a superior is usually welcomed T   F

10 Discussions about the latest technical developments are
    not uncommon   T   F

11 Quick decisions and actions are not characteristic of
    this organisation   T   F

12 This place has a reputation for being indifferent to the
    needs of the wider community   T   F

13 Senior personnel rarely refer to one another by their
    first names   T   F

14 Family, social or financial status are necessary elements
    for advancement or success   T   F

15 Regulations are interpreted and enforced in an
    understanding manner   T   F

16 Few people would be interested in attending a lecture
    by an outstanding scientist   T   F

17 Thinking of alternative ways in which problems might
    be solved or things done differently is discouraged   T   F

18 The activities of charities and social agencies are
    strongly supported by this organisation   T   F

19 The important people in this firm expect others to show
    proper respect for them   T   F

20 There are no favourites in this organisation; everyone gets treated alike   T   F

21 There are few opportunities for informal conversation with senior personnel   T   F

22 Few people in this organisation have any background in science   T   F

23 The latest scientific discoveries make few changes in the way this organisation is run   T   F

24 Service to the wider community is regarded as a major responsibility of this organisation   T   F

25 People here are always looking for compliments   T   F

26 Anyone who knows the right people here can progress quite quickly   T   F

27 This organisation does not concern itself with the personal problems of the people who work here   T   F

28 A discussion about the latest scientific inventions would not be uncommon here   T   F

29 New ideas are always being tried out here   T   F

30 It's easy to find people here to give talks to clubs and social groups   T   F

31 Senior personnel are frequently jealous of their authority   T   F

32 Everyone has the same opportunity to do well here   T   F

33 Senior personnel have little tolerance for complaints and protests   T   F

34 Magazines about new developments in science and management techniques are read by many people who work here   T   F

35 Unusual or exciting plans are encouraged here   T   F

36	Special events are given a great deal of publicity	T	F
37	People here are very deferential to their superiors	T	F
38	Senior personnel will go out of their way to help you with your work	T	F
39	As long as you are good at your job, you'll get ahead here	T	F
40	Senior personnel here are considered experts in their respective fields	T	F
41	There are conventional ways of doing things here which are rarely changed	T	F
42	Any form of publicity is frowned upon here	T	F
43	There is a recognised group of leaders in the organisation who receive special privileges	T	F
44	If your face fits, you're all right here	T	F
45	Senior personnel are prepared to listen to people as well as direct them	T	F
46	This organisation is research-conscious	T	F
47	Programmes here are quickly changed to meet new conditions	T	F
48	Social issues are rarely discussed here	T	F

Bibliography

Abegglen, J.C. (1958): *The Japanese Factory,* Glencoe, Illinois: Free Press.

Acton Society Trust (1956): *Management Succession.* London: The Trust.

Aitken, H.G.J. (ed.) (1965): *Explorations in Enterprise,* Cambridge, Mass.: Harvard University Press.

Aitken, M. and Hage, J. (1971): 'The Organic Organisation and Innovation', *Sociology,* 5.

Ajiferuke, M. and Boddewyn, J. (1970): 'Culture and Other Explanatory Variables in Comparative Management Studies', *Academy of Management Journal,* 35.

Aldcroft, D.H. (1964): 'The Entrepreneur in the British Economy 1870–1914', *Economic History Review, xvii, 1.*

Alford, R.R. (1964): *Party and Society.* London: Murray.

Amber, G.H. and Amber, P.S. (1962): *Anatomy of Automation.* Englewood Cliffs, N.J.: Prentice-Hall.

Argyle, M. (1967): *The Social Psychology of Social Change,* in Burns, T. and Saul, S.B.

Argyle, M. (1972): *The Social Psychology of Work.* London: Allen Lane.

Argyris, C. (1958): 'Some Problems in Conceptualizing Organisational Climate: A Case Study of a Bank', *Administrative Science Quarterly,* 2, 4.

Ashton, T.S. (1955): *An Economic History of England. the Eighteenth Century.* London: Methuen.

Bacon, R. and Eltis, W. (1976): *Britain's Economic Problem: Too Few Producers,* London: MacMillan.

Bagwell, P.S. and Mingay, G.E. (1970): *Britain and America: A Study of Economic Change 1850–1939.* London: Routledge and Kegan Paul.

Balfour, W.C. (1953): 'Productivity and the Worker', *British Journal of Sociology,* IV.

Banks, J.A. (1974): *Trade Unionism.* London: Collier - MacMillan.

Barker, R.G. et al. (1962): *Big School - Small School.* University of Kansas: Midwest Psychological Field Station.

Barnes, B. (ed.) (1972): *Sociology of Science.* Harmondsworth; Penguin.

Barrington Moore Jr. (1973): *Social Origins of Dictatorship and Democracy.* London: Penguin University Books.

Beard, M. (1963): *A History of Business, vol. II.* Michigan: Michigan University Press.

Beck, H.P. (1947): *Men Who Control Our Universities.* Kings Crown Press.

Bell, D. (1965): *The End of Ideology.* New York: Collier Books.

Bell, D. (1974): *The Coming of Post - Industrial Society.* London: Heinemann.

Bendix, R. (1964): *Nation - Building and Citizenship.* New York: John Wiley and Sons.

Benedict, R. (1946): *Patterns of Culture.* New York: Penguin Books.

Bennis, W.G. (1966): *Changing Organisations.* New York: McGraw-Hill.

Berg, I. (1970): *Education and Jobs.* London: Penguin.

Berkhofer, R.F., Jr. (1973): *Clio and the Culture Concept: Some Impressions of a Changing Relationship in American Historiography',* in Schneider, L. and Bonjean, C.

Bernstein, B. (1967): 'Open Schools, Open Society', *New Society,* 14 September.

Bernstein, B. (ed.) (1971): *Class, Codes and Control,* vol. 1. London: Routledge and Kegan Paul.

Black, M. (ed.) (1961): *The Social Theories of Talcott Parsons.* Englewood Cliffs, N.J.: Prentice - Hall.

Blumer, H. (1960): 'Early Industrialization and the Labouring Class', *Sociological Quarterly,* 1.

Bourgeois III, L.J., McAllister, D.W. and Mitchell, T.R. 'The Effects of Different Organisational Environments upon Decisions about Organisational Structure', *Academy of Management Journal,* 21 March 1978.

Brenner, S.N. and Molander, E.A. (1977): 'Is the Ethics of Business Changing?', *Harvard Business Review,* 55, 1.

British Institute of Management (1970): *Fringe Benefits for Executives,* Information Summary No. 145. London: British Institute of Management.

Brua, L.A. (1973): *'Who Are the Top Managers II',* in Taylor, B. and MacMillan, K. (eds).

Burnham, J. (1941): *The Managerial Revolution.* New York: Day.

Burns, T. and Stalker, G.M. (1961): *The Management of Innovation.* London: Tavistock.

Burrage, M. (1969): 'Culture and British Economic Growth', *British Journal of Sociology,* 20.

Cam, H.M. (1940): 'The Decline and Fall of English Feudalism', *History,* New Series, XXV, 99.

Cattell, R.B. (1950): 'The Principal Culture Patterns Discoverable in the Syntal Dimensions of Existing Nations', *Journal of Social Psychology,* 32.

Chamberlain, J. (1948): 'The Businessman in Fiction', *Fortune,* XXXVIII, November.

Chandler, A.D. Jr. (1962): *Strategy and Structure, Chapters in the History of American Industrial Enterprise.* Boston: MIT, Press.

Chapman, R.A. (1970): *The Higher Civil Service in Britain.* London: Constable.

Checkland, S.G. (1975): 'The Entrepreneur and the Social Order', *Business History,* XVII, 2.

Child, J. (1969) : *British Management Thought.* London: Allen and Unwin.

Child, J. (1972): 'Organisational Structure, Environment and Performance: The Role of Strategic Choice', *Sociology,* 6, 1.

Child, J. and MacMillan, B. (1972): 'Managerial Leisure in British and American Contexts', *Journal of Management Studies,* 9, 2.

Chruden, H.J. and Sherman, W.W., Jr (1972): *Personnel Practices of American Companies in Europe.* New York: American Management Association.

The Civil Service, (1969): *Report of the Committee, (The Fulton Report).* London: HMSO, Cmnd 3638.

Clark, D.G. (1966): *The Industrial Manager: His Background and Career Pattern.* London: Business Publications.

Coch, L. and French, J.R.P. (1948): 'Overcoming Resistance to Change', *Human Relations,* 1.

Cochran, T.C. (1962): *The American Business System: A Historical Perspective 1900–1955.* New York: Harper.

Cochran, T.C. (1968): *Basic History of American Business,* D. Van Nostrand Inc.

Cochran, T.C. and Miller, W. (1961): *The Age of Enterprise.* New York: Harper Torchbooks.

Coleman, D.C. (1973): 'Gentlemen and Players', *Economic History Review,* Second Series, XXVI, 1.

Collins, R. (1971): 'Functional and Conflict Theories of Educational Stratification', *American Sociological Review,* 36.

Conservative Political Centre (1968): *Fair Deal at Work.* London: Conservative Political Centre.

Cotgrove, S.F. (1958): *Technical Education and Social Change.* London: Allen and Unwin.

Creigh, S.W. and Makeham, P. (1978): 'Foreign Ownership and Strike Proneness: A Research Note', *British Journal of Industrial Relations,* XVI.

Crozier, M. (1964): *The Bureaucratic Phenomenon.* London: Tavistock.

Crozier, M. (1972): The Relationship between Micro and Macrosociology', *Human Relations,* 25.

Davis, K. (1966): *Human Society.* New York: Collier - MacMillan.

Davis, K. and Moore, W. (1945): 'Some Principles of Stratification', *American Sociological Review,* April.

Department of Industry, (1977): *Industry, Education a: d Management.* London: Department of Industry.

Dixon, K. (1977): 'Is Cultural Relativism Self Refuting?', *British Journal of Sociology,* 26, 1.

Dickson, J.W. and Bucholz, R.A. (1977): 'Managerial Beliefs about Work in Scotland and the USA', *Journal of Management Studies,* XIV.

Domhoff, G.W. (1967): *Who Rules America.* N. Jersey: Prentice-Hall.

Donaldson, L. (1976): 'Woodward - Technology, Organisational Structure and Performance - A Critique of the Universal Generalisation', *Journal of Management Studies,* XlII.

Donnovan, Lord (1968): *'Royal Commission on Trade Unions and Employers' Associations'.* London: HMSO Cmnd 3623.

Dore, R. (1973): *British Factory - Japanese Factory.* London: Allen and Unwin.

Dubin, R. (1970): 'Management in Britain - Impressions of a Visiting Professor', *Journal of Management Studies,* 7.

Duerr, M.G. and Greene, J. (1968): *Foreign Nationals in International Management,* National Industrial Conference Board.

Dunning, E. and Hopper E. (1966): 'Industrialization and the Problem of Convergence: A Critical Note', *Sociological Review,* New Series, 14, 2.

Dunning, J.H. (1969): 'American Growth in Britain', *Management Today,* February.

Dunning, J.H. (1970): *Studies in International Investment.* London: Allen and Unwin.

Dunning, J.H. (ed.) (1971): *The Multinational Enterprise.* London: Allen and Unwin.

Dunning, J.H. (undated): *U.S. Industry in Britain.* London: Economists Advisory Group.

Edstrom, A. and Galbraith, J.R. (1977): 'Transfer of Managers as a Coordination and Control Strategy in Multinational Organisations', *Administrative Science Quarterly,* 22,2.

Ellis, T. and Child J. (1973): 'Placing Stereotypes of the Manager into Perspective', *Journal of Management Studies,* 10, 3.

Etzioni, A. (1968): *The Active Society.* New York: Free Press.

Etzioni, A. and Dubow, F.L. (eds.) (1970): *Comparative Perspectives: Theories and Methods.* Boston: Little, Brown and Co.

Etzioni, A. (1971): 'Toward a Macrosociology' in Katz, F.E. (ed.), *Contemporary Sociological Theory,* New York: Random House.

Evan, W.M. (1968): *'A Systems Model of Organisational Climate',* in Tagiuri and Litwin (eds.).

Evan, W.M. (1975): 'Measuring the Impact of Culture on Organisation', *International Studies of Management and Organisation,* V, 1.

222

Evan, W.M. (1977): 'Social Structures and Organisational Systems', *Organisation and Administrative Sciences*, 7.

Farmer, R.N. (1968): *International Management.* California: Dickenson Publishing Company.

Farmer, R.N. and Richman, B.M. (1966): *International Business: An Operational Theory.* London: Irwin.

Fayerweather, J. (1957): 'Foreign Operations: A guide for Top Management', *Harvard Business Review*, 35.

Fayerweather, J. (1969): *International Business Management.* New York: McGraw - Hill Inc.

Ferrari, S. (1974): 'Cross Cultural Management Literature in France, Italy and Spain', *Management International*, 14, 4.

Firth, R. (1971): *Elements of Social Organisation.* London: Tavistock.

Flinn, M.W. (1967): *'Social Theory and the Industrial Revolution'*, in Burns, T. and Saul, S.B. (eds.).

Fogel, R.W. and Engermann, S.L. (1974): *Time on the Cross.* Boston, Mass: Little, Brown and Co.

Fortune, The Editors of (1951): *U.S.A.: The Permanent Revolution.* New York: Prentice - Hall.

Fortune, the Editors of (1956): *The Executive Life.* New York: Dolphin Books.

Freeman, R.B. (1976): *The Over - Educated American.* New York: Academic Press.

French, J.R.P., Israel, J. and As, D. (1960): 'An Experiment on Participation in a Norwegian Factory', *Human Relations*, 13.

Garbarino, J.W. (1969): 'Managing Conflict in Industrial Relations: United States' Experience and Current Issues in Britain', *British Journal of Industrial Relations*, 7.

Gannicott, K.G. and Blaug, M. (1969): 'Manpower Forecasting since Robbins: A Science Lobby in Action', *Higher Education Review*, 2, 1.

Gerschenkron, A. (1962): *Economic Backwardness in Historical Perspective.* Cambridge, Mass.: Harvard University Press.

Ginsberg, M. (1961): *Essays in Sociology and Social Philosophy*, vol.1. 'National Character and National Sentiments'. London: Heinemann.

Glaser, W. (1975): 'Cross - National Comparison of Organisations', *International Studies of Management and Organisation*, V, 1.

Glover, I.A. (1975): *Managers and Their Backgrounds in Britain, Germany, Sweden and France,* unpublished seminar paper. Edinburgh: Heriot - Watt University.

Glyn, A. and Sutcliffe, B. (1972): *British Capitalism, Workers and the Profits Squeeze.* London: Penguin.

Goldthorpe, J.H., Lockwood, D. Bechhofer, F. and Platt, J. (1968): *The Affluent Worker: Industrial Attitudes and Behaviour.* Cambridge: Cambridge University Press.

Goldthorpe, J.H. and Llewellyn, C. (1977): 'Class Mobility in Modern Britain: Three Theses Examined', *Sociology*, 11.

Gonzalez, F. and McMillan, C. Jr. (1961): 'The Universality of American Management Philosophy', *Journal of the Academy of Management*, 4, 1.

Gordon, R.A. and Howell, J.E. (1959): *Higher Education for Business.* New York: Columbia University Press.

Gorer, G. (1956): *'The Concept of National Character'*, in Kluckholm et al. (eds).

Gouldner, A.W. (1954): *Patterns of Industrial Bureaucracy.* Glencoe: Free Press.

Gouldner, A.W. (1970): *The Coming Crisis of Western Sociology.* London: Heinemann.

Granick, D. (1962): *The European Executive.* London: Weidenfeld and Nicolson.

Granick, D. (1972): *Managerial Comparisons of Four Developed Countries.* MIT Press.

Gruber, W., Mehta, D. and Vernon, R. (1967): 'The R and D Factor in International Trade and International Investment of US Industries', *Journal of Political Economy*, LXXV.

Gunder Frank, A. (1971): *Sociology of Development and Under-development of Sociology.* London: Pluto Press.

Guttsman, W.L. (1974): *'The British Political Elite in the Class Structure'*, in Giddens, A. and Stanworth, P. (eds.)

Habakkuk, H.J. (1967): *American and British Technology in the Nine-teenth Century.* Cambridge: Cambridge University Press.

Habakkuk, H.J. (1968): *'The Historical Experience of the Basic Conditions of Economic Progress'*, in Eisenstadt, S.N.

Habermas, J. (1972): *'Science and Technology as Ideology'*, in Barnes, B. (ed.)

Hage, J. and Aiken, M. (1967): 'Relationship of Centralization to other Structural Properties', *Administrative Science Quarterly*, 12, 1.

Hagen, E.H. (1962): *On the Theory of Social Change.* Homewood.

Haire, M., Ghiselli, E.E. and Porter, L.W. (1966): *Managerial Thinking: An International Study.* New York: Wiley.

Hall, D.T. and Mansfield, R. (1971): 'Organisational and Individual Response to External Stress', *Administrative Science Quarterly*, 16.

Hall, R.H. (1963): 'The Concept of Bureaucracy: An Empirical Assessment', *American Journal of Sociology*, 69, 1.

Hall, R.H. (1968): 'Professionalisation and Bureaucratisation', *American Sociological Review*, 33, 1.

Hall, R.H. (1972): Organisations, Structure and Process. Englewood Cliffs, N. Jersey: Prentice - Hall.

Harbison, F.H. and Myers, C.A. (eds) (1958): *Management in the Industrial World: An International Analysis.* New York: McGraw - Hill.

Harbison, F. and Myers, C.A. (1964): *Education, Manpower and Economic Growth.* New York: McGraw - Hill.

Hardman, J.B.S. (1964): *'From "Job - Consciousness" to Power Accumulation',* in Nash, G.D. (ed.).

Hartz, L. (1948): *Economic Policy and Democratic Thought: Pennsylvania 1776–1860.* Cambridge, Mass.: Harvard University Press.

Heberle, R. (1956): 'A Note on Riesman's "The Lonely Crowd" ', *American Journal of Sociology,* LXII, 1.

Heller, F.A. (undated): *A Study of British and American Managerial Skills,* unpublished paper. Tavistock Institute of Human Relations.

Heller, F.A. (1968): 'How British are Americans?' *The Director,* June.

Heller, F. and Porter, L.W. (1966): 'Perceptions of Managerial Needs and Skills in Two National Samples', *Occupational Psychology,* 40.

Heydebrand, W.V. (ed.) (1973): *Comparative Organisations.* Englewood Cliffs, N.J.: Prentice - Hall.

Heydebrand, W.V. (1973): *'The Study of Organisations',* in Heydebrand, W.V. (ed.).

Hickson, D.J. (1974): *The Grounds for Comparative Organisation Theory: Shifting Sands or Hard Core?,* paper presented to the Industrial Sociology Section of the British Sociological Association at Imperial College, London.

Hickson, D.J., Hinings, C.R., McMillan, C.J. and Schwitter, J.P. (1974): 'The Culture-Free Context of Organisational Structure: A Tri-National Comparison', *Sociology* 8.

Hickson, D.J., Pugh, D.S. and Pheysey, D.C. (1969): 'Operations Technology and Organisational Structure: An Empirical Reappraisal', *Administrative Science Quarterly,* 14, 3.

Hinings, C.R., Pugh, D.S., Hickson, D.J., and Turner. C. (1967): 'An Approach to the Study of Bureaucracy', *Sociology,* 1, 1.

Hirshler, E.E. (1954): 'Medieval Economic Competition', *Journal of Economic History,* XIV, 1.

Hobsbawn, E.J. (1975): *The Age of Capital 1848-1875.* London: Weidenfeld and Nicolson.

Hofstadter, R. (1964): *Anti-Intellectualism in American Life.* Jonathan Cape.

The Hudson Institute Europe, (1974): *The United Kingdom in the 1980's.* London: Associated Business Programmes Ltd.

Ingham, G.K. (1970): *Size of Industrial Organisation and Worker Behaviour.* Cambridge: Cambridge University Press.

Inkeles, A. (1960): 'Industrial Man: The Relation of Status to Experience, Perception and Value', *American Journal of Sociology,* LXVI, 1.

Inkson, J.H.K., Pugh, D.S. and Hickson, D.J. (1970): 'Organisation Context and Structure: An Abbreviated Replication', *Administrative Science Quarterly*, 15.

Inkson, J.H.K., Schwitter, J.P., Pheysey, D.C. and Hickson, D.J. (1970): 'A Comparison of Organisational Structure and Managerial Roles, Ohio, USA and Midlands, England', *Journal of Management Studies*, 7, 3.

International Management, The Editors of (1976): 'When Company Culture Counts', *International Management*, 31, 9.

Jervis, F.R. (1974): *Bosses in British Business*. London: Routledge and Kegan Paul.

Jamieson, I.M. (1977): *Capitalism and Culture: A Comparative Analysis of British and American Manufacturing Organisations'*, unpublished Ph.D thesis, University of Surrey, Guildford.

Jamieson, I.M. (1978): 'Some Observations on Socio-Cultural Explanations of Economic Behaviour', *Sociological Review*, 26, 4.

Jamieson, I.M. (1980): 'Capitalism and Culture: A Comparative Analysis of British and American Manufacturing Organisations', *Sociology*, 14, 2.

Johnson, T. (1972): *Professions and Power*, London: MacMillan.

Johnson, T. (1975): *The Professions in the Class Structure*, paper presented to the British Sociological Association's Annual Conference, University of Kent, Canterbury.

Kassarjian, W. (1962): 'A Study of Riesman's Theory of Social Character', *Sociometry*, 25.

Kaysen, C. (1956): 'Anti-Monopoly Policy in Britain and the United States', *Westminster Bank Review*, August.

Kerr, C., Dunlop, J.T., Harbison, F.H. and Meyers, C.A. (1960a): *Industrialism and Industrial Man*. Cambridge, Mass.: Harvard University Press.

Kerr, C., Dunlop, J.T., Harbison, F.H. and Myers, C.A. (1960b): 'Industrialism and World Society', *Harvard Business Review*, 39.

Kerr, C., Dunlop, J.T., Harbison, F.H. and Myers, C.A. (1971): 'Postscript to "Industrialism and Industrial Man" ', *International Labour Review*, 103, 6.

Kindleberger, C.P. (1969): *American Business Abroad*. Yale University Press.

Kingston, N. (1971): *Selecting Managers*. London: British Institute of Management.

Kohn, M.L. (1971) 'Bureaucratic Man, A Portrait and an Interpretation', *American Sociological Review*, 36, 3.

Kroeber, A.L. and Kluckholm, C. (1952): *Culture: A Critical View of Concepts and Definitions*. Cambridge, Mass.: Harvard University Press.

Kroos, H.E. (1970): *Executive Opinion.* New York: Doubleday.

Ladinsky, J. (1967): 'The Geographic Mobility of Professional and Technical Manpower', *Journal of Human Resources*, 2, 4.

Landes, D.S. (1963): 'New - Model Entrepreneurship in France and Problems of Historical Explanation', *Explorations in Entrepreneurial History,* Second Series, 1, 1.

Landes, D.S. (1965): *'French Business and the Businessman: A Social and Cultural Analysis',* in Aitken, H.G.J. (ed.).

Langrish, J., Gibbons, M., Evans, W.G. and Jevons, F.R. (1972): *Wealth from Knowledge.* London: MacMillan.

Lasswell, H.D. et al. (1952): *The Comparative Study of Elites.* Stanford: Stanford University Press.

Lawrence, P.R. and Lorsch, J.W. (1962): *Organization and Environment.* Boston: Harvard Graduate School of Business Administration, Division of Research.

Lee, J.A. (1966): 'Cultural Analysis in Overseas Operations', *Harvard Business Review,* 44, 2.

Leggatt, T.W. (1972): *The Training of British Managers, National Economic Development Office.* London: HMSO.

Leggatt, T. (1978): 'Managers in Industry: Their Background and Education', *Sociological Review,* 26, 4.

Lewin, K., Lippett, R. and White, R.K. (1939): 'Patterns of Aggressive Behaviour in Experimentally Created "Social Climates" ', *Journal of Social Psychology,* 10.

Lewis, R. and Stewart, R. (1958): *The Boss.* Phoenix House.

Lipset, S.M. (1963): *First New Nation.* New York: Heinemann.

Lipset, S.M. and Zetterberg, H.L. (1956): *A Theory of Social Mobility,* Transactions of the Third World Congress of Sociology, 3.

McClelland, D. (1961): *The Achieving Society.* Princeton: Van Nostrand.

McGiffert, M. (ed.) (1970): *The Character of Americans.* (revised edition). Homewood, Illinois: The Dorsey Press.

Maddison, A. (1964): *Economic Growth in the West.* London: Allen and Unwin.

Maddison, A. (1979): 'Long Run Dynamics of Productivity', *Banca Nazionale del Lavoro Quarterly Review,* 128, March.

Management International, The Editors of (1979): 'The Age of Discrimination', *Management International,* 34, 9.

Marriott, R. (1961): *Incentives: A Review of Research and Opinion.* London: Staples Press.

Marris, R. (ed.) (1974): *The Corporate Society.* London: MacMillan.

Marx, K. (1953): *Grundrisse der Kritik der Politischen Okonomie,* Berlin.

Mead, M. and Metraux, R. (eds.) (1953): *The Study of Culture at a Distance.* Chicago.

Merton, R.K. (1938): 'Social Structure and Anomie', *American Sociological Review,* 3, October.

Miller, D.C. (1958): 'Industry and Community Power Structure: A Comparative Study of an American and an English City', *American Sociological Review,* 23.

Miller, P. (1961): *The New English Mind: From Colony to Province.* Boston: Beacon Press.

Miller, S.M. (1960): 'Comparative Social Mobility', *Current Sociology,* 9.

Mills, C.W. (1953): *White Collar.* New York: Oxford University Press.

Mills, C.W. (1956): *The Power Elite,* New York: Oxford University Press.

Nash, M. (1966): *Primitive and Peasant Economic Systems.* University of Chicago: Chandler Publishing Co.

Nath, R. (1968): 'A Methodological Review of Cross-Cultural Management Research', *International Social Science Journal,* 20, 1.

Negandhi, A.R. (1974): 'Cross Cultural Management Studies: Too Many Conclusions not enough conceptualization', *Management International Review,* no.6.

Negandhi, A.R. and Estafen, B.D. (1965): 'A Research Model to Determine the Applicability of American Management Know-How in Differing Cultures and/or Environments', *Academy of Management Journal,* 8, 4.

Nettl, J.P. and Robertson, R. (1966): 'Industrialization: Development or Modernization', *British Journal of Sociology,* 17.

Newcomer, M. (1955): *The Big Business Executive.* New York: Columbia University Press.

Newman, W.H. (1970): 'Is Management Exportable?' *Columbia Journal of World Business,* Jan.-Feb.

Nichols, W.A.T. (1969): *Ownership, Control and Ideology.* London: Allen and Unwin.

Novotny, O. (1964): 'American versus European Management Philosophy', *Harvard Business Review,* 42, 2.

Oberg, W. (1963): 'Cross-Cultural Perspectives on Management Principles', *Journal of the Academy of Management,* 6, 2.

OECD, (1970): *Gaps in Technology between Member Countries: An Analytical Report,* Paris.

Pahl, R. and Pahl, J. (1971): *Managers and their Wives.* London: Allen Lane.

Pahl, R.E. and Winkler, J.T. (1974): *The Economic Elite: Theory and Practice,* in Stanworth, P. and Giddens, A. (eds).

Parsons, T. (1937): *The Structure of Social Action.* New York: McGraw-Hill.

Parsons, T. (1939): 'The Professions and Social Structure', *Social Forces,* 17.

Parsons, T. (1960a): *Structure and Process in Modern Societies.* New York: Free Press.

Parsons, T. (1960b): 'Pattern Variables Revisited: A Response to Robert Dubin', *American Sociological Review,* 25.

Parsons, T. (1966): *Societies: Evolutionary and Comparative Perspectives,* Englewood Cliffs, N.J.: Prentice - Hall.

Parsons, T. (1973): *'Culture and Social System Revisited',* in Schneider, L. and Bonjean, C. (eds.).

Parsons, T. and Shils, E.A. (eds.) (1962): *Towards a General Theory of Action.* Cambridge, Mass.: Harvard University Press.

Payne, P.L. (1967): The Emergence of the Large Scale Company in Great Britain 1870–1914, *Economic History Review,* 20.

Payne, R.L. and Pheysey, D.C. (1971): 'G.C. Stern's Organisational Climate Index: A Reconceptualization and Application to Business Organisations', *Organizational Behaviour and Human Performance,* 6, 1.

Payne, G., Ford, G. and Robertson, C. (1977): 'A Reappraisal of Social Mobility in Britain', *Sociology,* 11.

Pear, R.H. (1968): *'The United States',* in Ridley, F.F, (ed.).

Peaslee, A.L. (1969): 'Education's Role in Development', *Economic Development and Cultural Change,* 17.

Peck, M.J. (1968): *'Science and Technology',* in Caves et al. (eds).

Perkin, H. (1969): *The Origins of Modern English Society 1780–1880.* London: Routledge and Kegan Paul.

Perlmutter, H.V. (1969): 'The Tortuous Evolution of the Multi-National Corporation', *Columbia Journal of World Business,* 4, 1.

Permut, S.E. (1977): 'The European View of Marketing Research', *Columbia Journal of World Business,* XII, 3.

Perrow, C. (1970): *Organizational Analysis.* London: Tavistock.

Perrow, C. (1972a): *The Radical Attack on Business.* New York: Harcourt Brace Jovanovich, Inc.

Perrow, C. (1972b): *Technology, Organisations and Society - Some Mythologies Observed,* paper read to Industrial Sociology Section of the British Sociological Association, 18, October.

Peterson, R. (1964): 'Dimensions of Social Character: An Empirical Exploration of the Riesman Typology', *Sociometry,* 27.

Pheysey, D.C., Payne, R.L. and Pugh, D.S. (1971): 'Influence of Structure at Organizational and Group Levels'. *Administrative Science Quarterly,* 16.

Pierce, F. (1973): *'Crime, Corporations and the American Social Order',* in Taylor, I. and Taylor L. (eds.).

Pierson, F.C. et al. (1959): *The Education of American Businessmen.* New York: McGraw - Hill.

Political and Economic Planning (1966): *Attitudes in British Management.* London: Pelican.

Porter, L.W. (1963): 'Where is the Organisation Man?', *Harvard Business Review*, November.

Potter, D. (1954): *People of Plenty: Economic Abundance and the American Character.* Chicago: University of Chicago Press.

Pugh, D.S. (1964): 'The Structure of Industrial Enterprise in Industrial Society. A Comment', in Halmos, P. (ed.), 'The Development of Industrial Societies', *Sociological Review Monograph No. 8,* University of Keele.

Pugh, D.S., Hickson, D.J., Hinings, C.R. and Turner, C. (1968): 'Dimensions of Organisational Structures', *Administrative Science Quarterly,* 13.

Pugh, D.S., Hickson, D.J., Hinings, C.R. and Turner, C. (1969): 'The Context of Organisational Structures', *Administrative Science Quarterly,* 14.

Quinney, R. (ed.) (1979): *Capitalist Society.* Homewood, Illinois: The Dorsey Press.

Reader, W.J. (1966): *Professional Men: The Rise of the Professional Classes in Nineteenth Century England.* London: Weidenfeld and Nicolson.

Reader, W.J. (1970): *Imperial Chemical Industries. A History 1. The Forerunners 1870–1926.* Oxford: Oxford University Press.

Richardson, S.A. (1956): 'Organizational Contrasts on British and American Ships', *Administrative Science Quarterly,* 1, 2.

Richman, B.M. (1965): 'The Significance of Cultural Variables', *Academy of Management Journal,* 8, 4.

Richman, B.M. and Farmer, R.N. (1965): 'Ownership and Management: The Real Issues', *International Management,* 5.

Rieser, C. (1962): 'The Chief Shows Them How at Indian Head', *Fortune,* May.

Riesman, D. with Glazer, N. and Denney, R. (1961): *The Lonely Crowd.* New Haven: Yale University Press.

Rose, H. (1970): *Management Education in the 1970's,* National Economic Development Office. London: HMSO.

Rothbarth, E. (1946): 'Causes of the Superior Efficiency of USA Industry as Compared with British Industry', *The Economic Journal,* LVI, 223.

Rudd, E. (1969): 'Culture and British Economic Growth, A Comment', *British Journal of Sociology,* 20.

Sampson, A. (1962): *Anatomy of Britain,* London: Hodder and Stoughton.

Sawyer, J.E. (1954): 'The Social Basis of the American System of Manufacturing', *Journal of Economic History,* XIV, 4.

Secretary of State for Employment and Productivity, (1969): *In Place of Strife.* London: HMSO Cmnd 3888.

Servan-Schreiber, J-J. (1969): *The American Challenge.* London: Pelican.

Seyfarth, Shaw, Fairweather and Geraldson (1968): *Labour Relations and the Law in the United Kingdom and the United States,* Program in International Business, Graduate School of Business Administration. Ann Arbor: University of Michigan.

Schecter, A.H. (1968): 'Businessmen as Government Policy-Makers', *Columbia Journal of World Business,* 3, 3.

Schlesinger, A.M. (1970): *'What Then is the American, This New Man?'* in McGiffert, M. (ed.).

Schumpeter, J. (1947): *Capitalism, Socialism, and Democracy.* New York: Harper Bros.

Shils, E.A. (1956): *The Torment of Secrecy.* Glencoe: Free Press.

Shonfield, A. (1965): *Modern Capitalism.* London: Oxford University Press.

Sim, A.B. (1977): 'Decentralised Management of Subsidiaries and their Performance', *Management International Review,* 17, 2.

Simon, H.A. (1947): *Administrative Behaviour.* New York: MacMillan.

Sjoberg, G. (1970): *The Comparative Method in the Social Sciences',* in Etzioni, A. and Dubow, F.L.(eds)

Smith, D.D. (1966): 'Modal Attitude Clusters: A Supplement to the Study of National Character', *Social Forces,* 44.

Solomons, D. with Berridge, T.M. (1974): *Prospects for a Profession. The Report of the Long Range Enquiry into the Education and Training for the Accountancy Profession.* London: Advisory Board of Accounting Education.

Solow, R. (1957): 'Technical Change and the Aggregate Production Function', *Review of Economics and Statistics,* 39.

Sofer, C. (1970): *Men in Mid Career.* Cambridge: Cambridge University Press.

Starbuck, W.H. (1966): 'The Efficiency of British and American Retail Employees', *Administrative Science Quarterly,* December.

Steers, R.M. (1975): 'Problems in the Measurement of Organizational Effectiveness', *Administrative Science Quarterly,* 20, 4.

Steur, M. and Gennard, J. (1971): *'Industrial Relations, Labour Disputes and Labour Utilization in Foreign-Owned Firms in the UK',* in Dunning, J.H. (ed.).

Stewart, R. (1957): 'Management Development: Some American Comparisons'. *The Manager,* January.

Stopford, J.R. (1972): *'Organising the Multinational Firm. Can the Americans Learn from the Europeans?'* in Brooke, M.R. and Remmers, H.L. (eds.).

Stouffer, S.A. et al. (1949): *The American Soldier.* Princeton, New Jersey: Princeton University Press.

Sturmthal, A. (ed.)(1957): *Contemporary Collective Bargaining in Seven Countries.* New York: Cornell University Press.

Sumner, W.G. (1906): *Folkways.* Boston: Ginn.

Sutton, F.X., Harris, S.E., Kaysen, C. and Tobin, J. (1962): *The American Business Creed.* New York: Shocken Books.

Tagiuri, R. and Litwin, G.H. (eds.)(1968): *Organisational Climate.* Boston: Division of Research, Graduate School of Business Administration, Harvard.

Tausky, C. and Dubin, R. (1965): 'Career Anchorage, Managerial Mobility Motivations', *American Sociological Review,* 30, 5.

Theodorson, G.A. (1953): 'Acceptance of Industrialization and its Attendant Consequences for the Social Pattern of Non-Western Societies', *American Sociological Review,* 18, 5.

Thernstrom, S. (1964): *Poverty and Progress: Social Mobility in a Nineteenth Century City.* Cambridge, Mass.:Harvard University Press.

Thistlethwaite, F. (1955): *The Great Experiment.* London: Cambridge University Press.

Thomas, D. (1969): 'The Anglo-American Manager', *Management Today,* February.

Turner, B. (1975): *Industrialism.* London: Longmans.

Turner, F.W. (1920): *The Frontier in American History.* Henry Holt & Co.

Turner, H.A. (1969): *Is Britain Really Strike Prone?* University of Cambridge, Department of Applied Economics, Occasional Papers No. 20, Cambridge University Press.

Turner, H.A., Clack, G. and Roberts, G. (1967): *Labour Relations in the Motor Industry.* London: Allen and Unwin.

Turner, R.H. (1960a): 'Preoccupation with Competitiveness and Social Acceptance among American and English College Students', *Sociometry,* 23.

Turner, R.H. (1960b): 'Sponsored and Contest Mobility and the School System', *American Sociological Review,* XXV, 5.

Tylor, E.B. (1871): *Primitive Culture.* London: John Murray.

United Nations (1977): *Structure and Change in European Industry.* New York: United Nations.

Urwick, L. (1954): 'The American Challenge in Industrial Management', *British Management Review,* XII, 3.

Veblen, T. (1915): *Imperial Germany and the Industrial Revolution.* Michigan: University of Michigan Press (1966 reprint).

Vroom, V.H. (1959): 'Some Personality Determinants of the Effects of Participation', *Journal of Abnormal and Social Psychology,* LIX.

Vroom, V.H. (1964): *Work and Motivation.* New York: Wiley.

Webber, R.A. (ed) (1969): *Culture and Management.* London: Irwin.

Whitely, W. and England, G.W. (1977): 'Managerial Values as a Reflection of Culture and the Process of Industrialisation', *Academy of Management Journal,* 20, 3.

Whyte, W.H. (1963): *The Organization Man.* London: Pelican.

Wilkins, M. (1970): *The Emergence of Multinational Enterprise.* Cambridge, Mass.: Harvard University Press.

Wilkinson, C.C.G. and Mace, J.D. (1973): 'A Shortage or Surplus of Engineers: A Review of Recent UK Evidence', *British Journal of Industrial Relations,* XI, 1.

Wilkinson, R. (1964): *The Prefects.* Oxford: Oxford University Press.

Williams, R. (1973): 'Base and Superstructure in Marxist Cultural Theory', *New Left Review,* no. 82.

Williams, R. and Guest, D. (1973): 'How Home Affects Work', *New Society,* 18 January.

Wilson, C. (1954): *The History of Unilever.* London: Cassell.

Wilson, C. (1965): 'Economy and Society in Late Victorian Britain', *Economic History Review,* 18.

Winkler, J. (1972): *British and Soviety Management: A Sociological Bridge,* unpublished paper delivered to the Industrial Sociology Section of the British Sociological Association. London School of Economics, February.

Winkler, J. (1975): *Corporatism,* paper delivered to the British Sociological Association Annual Conference, Canterbury, Kent.

Woodward, J. (1965): *Industrial Organization: Theory and Practice.* London: Oxford University Press.

Index

Management studies 11–12
Management, style of 64–5, 155, 180
Management training 98, 101–2, 104, 128, 137, 144, 176, 178
Managers, age of 125–6, 134; function in firm 126; hours of work 134–5, 177; inter-firm mobility 129–31, 141; intra-firm mobility 52, 131–2, 177; job security 136; level in firm 126, 134; personality traits 138–42, 159; as professionals 53, 104, 142–6, 178; qualifications of 101–2, 127–9, 176
Marketing function 97–8, 101, 107–115, 126, 128–9, 132, 135, 144, 178, 180
Marriott (1961) 185n
Marris (1974) 85n, 102
Marshall Aid 7
Marx, K. 7–8, 19, 23, 192
Marxist theory 7–8, 23, 161
Mayo, E. 11, 15, 150
Mergers 62–3, 66
Merton (1938) 64, 81n
Miller, D.C. (1958) 41
Miller, S.M. (1960) 44
Mills (1953) 40, 130
Mobility, geographical 36, 42, 141; social 43–5, 165
Monetarism 195n
Monopolies and Restrictive Practices Commission 68
Moore W.E. 14
Multinational companies 13, 171, 192

Nash (1966) 3, 93
Nath (1968) 15–16
National character 9, 14, 138
National Health Service 99, 107, 115, 167
Need achievement 26n

Negandhi (1974) 93
Negandhi and Estafen (1965) 15
Neo-human relations movement 106, 133, 179
New Deal 72
Newman (1970) 26
Northcote-Trevelyan Report 60
Northern states of America 34, 38–9
Nichols (1969) 136, 143
Novotny (1964) 103, 126, 131

Oberg (1963) 26n
Occupational status 45
OECD (1970) 122n, 184n
Organisation man thesis 138–42
Organisational climate 88, 105, 110, 135, 150–9, 179; see also BOCI
Organisational structure 16, 18, 21, 93–119, 133; and autonomy 98, 99, 106, 119; and centralisation/ decentralisation 104–5, 108, 119, 133, 180; and decision making 63, 104–5, 108; and formalisation 94–104, 106, 109, 119, 153–5, 179; and functional specialisation 66, 106, 109, 119, 179; organic 157, 179; mechanistic 179
'Other' direction 138–42
Overseas subsidiary effect xi
Ownership of company 88

Pahl and Pahl (1971) 196n
Pahl and Winkler (1974) 144
Parsons, T. 2, 19–21, 144
Patel (1961) 163
Pattern variables 2, 20–23, 30, 31, 39, 60, 62, 69, 164, 190; affectivity/affective-neutrality 2, 35, 38, 43, 60; ascription/achievement 2, 20, 34, 35, 36, 38, 41, 43, 44, 52, 60, 66, 96, 125, 129, 155, 168; collective orientation/self orientation 35, 43, 57, 58; diffuseness/specificity 20, 35, 38,